Technology Management, Artificial Intelligence, and Machine Learning Strategies to Improve Technology Integration and Usage in the Workplace

Strategies to Increase Leverage Over Competitors and Control Internal and External Risk Factors

RIVER PUBLISHERS SERIES IN COMPUTING AND INFORMATION SCIENCE AND TECHNOLOGY

The "River Publishers Series in Computing and Information Science and Technology" covers research which ushers the 21st Century into an Internet and multimedia era. Networking suggests transportation of such multimedia contents among nodes in communication and/or computer networks, to facilitate the ultimate Internet.

Theory, technologies, protocols and standards, applications/services, practice and implementation of wired/wireless networking are all within the scope of this series. Based on network and communication science, we further extend the scope for 21st Century life through the knowledge in machine learning, embedded systems, cognitive science, pattern recognition, quantum/biological/molecular computation and information processing, user behaviors and interface, and applications across healthcare and society.

Books published in the series include research monographs, edited volumes, handbooks and textbooks. The books provide professionals, researchers, educators, and advanced students in the field with an invaluable insight into the latest research and developments.

Topics included in the series are as follows:-

- Artificial intelligence
- Cognitive Science and Brian Science
- Communication/Computer Networking Technologies and Applications
- Computation and Information Processing
- Computer Architectures
- Computer networks
- Computer Science
- Embedded Systems
- Evolutionary computation
- Information Modelling
- Information Theory
- Machine Intelligence
- Neural computing and machine learning
- Parallel and Distributed Systems
- Programming Languages
- Reconfigurable Computing
- Research Informatics
- Soft computing techniques
- Software Development
- Software Engineering
- Software Maintenance

For a list of other books in this series, visit www.riverpublishers.com

Technology Management, Artificial Intelligence, and Machine Learning Strategies to Improve Technology Integration and Usage in the Workplace

Strategies to Increase Leverage Over Competitors and Control Internal and External Risk Factors

Bradley Fowler

Adjunct Capitol Technology University, Adjunct Avila, University & CTO of DOC Technology Systems, LLC., USA

Bruce G. Chaundy

American Psychological Association Society of Industrial Organizational Psychology, USA

River Publishers

Routledge
Taylor & Francis Group
NEW YORK AND LONDON

Published 2026 by River Publishers
River Publishers
Broagervej 10, 9260 Gistrup, Denmark
www.riverpublishers.com

Distributed exclusively by Routledge
605 Third Avenue, New York, NY 10017, USA
4 Park Square, Milton Park, Abingdon, Oxon OX14 4RN

Technology Management, Artificial Intelligence, and Machine Learning Strategies to Improve Technology Integration and Usage in the Workplace: Strategies to Increase Leverage Over Competitors and Control Internal and External Risk Factors / Bradley Fowler and Bruce G. Chaundy.

Routledge is an imprint of the Taylor & Francis Group, an informa business

ISBN 978-87-438-0970-8 (hardback)
ISBN 978-87-438-0975-3 (paperback)
ISBN 978-87-438-0972-2 (e-Book)
ISBN 978-87-438-0974-6 (e-pub)
ISBN 978-8-743-80971-5 (ebook master)
DOI: 10.1201/9788743809715

This title is dedicated to Judy Chaundy with love and admiration.

Contents

Preface

Dependency on technology in the workplace in both public and private sector is universal. Globally, usage of hardware, software, mobile devices, Wi-Fi, Internet connectivity, data storage, and information assets has become a universal language people of all races, cultures, religions, and beliefs speak and share. So much, many now rely on technology to communicate, share information, store information, develop documents, and secure those documents on some design of technology. Therefore, it is imperative to understand the significance of technology management and the impact artificial intelligence and machine learning has in supporting reliance on technology in the workplace and our individual personal lives. To prepare you for effective technology management through artificial intelligence and machine learning, this knowledge sharing tool delivers a unique approach that can be universally understood and adopted to improve how technology is managed and secured in the workplace. Having this reference as a guide in your day-to-day business and personal operations will enable you to reduce victimization of cyber-attacks, while increasing your knowledge on the value of artificial intelligence and machine learning as assets to support your technology usage needs.

Acknowledgments

GOD, please keep pushing me to be better.

Momma: Thank you for always being there!

Dr. Tracy Irish, Dr. Ian McAndrew, Dr. Matthew Wyandt, Dr. Troy Troublefield, Dr. William Butler, Dr. Bill Kerstetter, Dr. Tahereh Daneshi, Dr. Limon, Dr. Rice, Dr. Boonyapredee, and Allen Exner – Thank you very much for your support and encouragement to be who I have become as a scholar, practitioner, and leader.

A special "Thank You" is extended to Capitol Technology University for being the benchmark educational institution to help mold me into a Doctor of Philosophy and the Cybersecurity Leader I am becoming!

Thank you to the University of Arizona Global Campus for the Master of Technology Management and the curriculum and instruction I endured to earn this degree.

Thank you, Southern New Hampshire University, for providing Bruce with the courage to be an industrial organizational psychologist.

University of Phoenix, it is appreciate being accepted into the Doctor of Management in Information Systems and Technology, an educational experience I relish.

List of Figures

List of Tables and Chart

Tables

Chart

List of Abbreviations

AI	Artificial intelligence
AWS	Amazon Web Services
BCP	Business Continuity Plan
CISA	Cybersecurity and Infrastructure Security Agency
CRM	Customer relationship management
CSF	Cybersecurity Framework
CUI	Controlled unclassified information
CVE	Common Vulnerabilities and Exposure
DRP	Disaster Recovery Plan
ECPA	Electronic Communications Privacy Act
ERP	Enterprise resource planning
ESP	Email service provider
FERPA	Family Educational Rights and Privacy Act
FISMA	Federal Information Security Management Act
FOI	Freedom of information
GDPR	General Data Protection Regulation
GJETA	Global Journal of Engineering Technology Advances
HIPAA	Health Insurance Portability and Accountability Act
IA	Identification authentication
IaaS	Infrastructure as a Service
IoT	Internet of Things
IRP	Incident response plan
ISCM	Information Security Continuous Monitoring
ISP	Internet service provider
ISSP	Issue-specific Security Policy
IT	Information technology
IUP	Information Usage Profile
LAN	Local access network
LMS	Learning management system
ML	Machine learning
NGO	Non-government Organizations
NIST	National Institute of Standards and Technology

OS	Operating systems
OWASP	Open Web Application Security Project
PaaS	Platform as a Service
PCI DSS	Payment Card Industry Data Security Standards
PIPEDA	Personal Information Protection and Electronic Documents Act
SaaS	Software as a Service
SIEM	Security Information and Event Management
SLA	Service Level Agreement
SOC	Security Operations Center
SP	Special publication
SSL	Security Socket Layer
STRIDE	Spoofing, Tampering, Repudiation, Information Disclosure, Denial of Service Attack, and Elevation of Privilege
SWOT	Strength Weaknesses Opportunities Threats
SySP	System-specific Policy
TCP	Transport control protocol
UAC	User Account Controls
WAN	Wide access network
WLAN	Wide land access network

Introduction

The endless efforts deployed by information technology practitioners, information system practitioners, and cloud computing architects, responsible for managing and overseeing information systems, information technology, and cloud applications in the workplace, face tremendous stress trying to understand which technology tools and applications are best capable of managing daily business operations, communication, and support decision-making success. Even more challenging is understanding what methods, strategies, procedures, and policies are required to control risk factors. As a result, weaknesses become vulnerabilities that enable external attack agents to gain entrance and wreak havoc on what are assumed secure systems and applications, relied on to develop information assets commonly developed and created in the workplace. Having systematic control and technology management to effectively support the needs of workplace operations is crucial to controlling costs and ensuring the effective security of information assets. However, to achieve this scale of durability requires knowing what steps and infrastructures are required to ensure the system is working effectively and efficiently, and capable of maintaining the support required to provide the results sought, time and again.

Effective technology management requires understanding the scope of an information system and the components integrated in the system that make the system operate without flaw. This requires technology managers to have current knowledge of trends correlating with each application relied on, and ensuring each application is configured correctly and operating as needed consistently. This can be a daunting task for a technology manager who neglects to remain knowledgeable of all software updates and configurations required to ensure the software co-exists with the hardware and additional applications integrated in the system.

When technology managers lack this clarity and management ability, they place their workplace at risk of being victimized, both internally and externally. Internally, human error plays a role in weakening the workplace's stability. While externally, cyberattackers gain the ability to exploit common weaknesses in software and hardware integrated in today's workplace.

Thus, continued knowledge building and information sharing are required to maintain control over the deployment of efficient technology management. Therefore, integrating artificial intelligence and machine learning has become a vital component to ensure successful management of technology in the workplace.

Thus, a comprehensive technology management process is needed to manage the efficiency of the overall system. After all, research reports that organizations need to increase their speed of adopting new technologies and investing broadly across their organization, as well as increase the utilization of technologies where the control of management is vested in the process owner.[1] This enables organizations to increase cost savings, as process owners are better equipped to resolve problems and improve operational efficiencies, while increasing quality analysis. When determining the risk of adopting new technologies, research reports that one particular risk with adopting new technologies is not meeting the expectations of the organization once the technology is integrated into the system.

Therefore, it is recommended that information technology and information system practitioners have a clear understanding of their need for technology and know the risks associated with the usage of any technology relied on. Maintaining this clarity of knowledge requires due diligence to deploy research that helps identify requirements for new technology to learn what technology can have a significant impact on the decision-making success of the entity. Research also stresses that technology management plays a key role in ushering in new technology. This can be crucial in correlation with how personnel and employees manage their engagement with new technology and how they help the workplace consistently deter human behavior that results in human error, which creates the entrance point for malware, ransomware, or unauthorized intrusion to occur.

In fact, when employees lack the required skills and knowledge to help usher in new technology, department managers and human resource managers must integrate methods of assessing employee performance through training. This requires developing updated declarative training material that can be delivered through PowerPoint presentations, pamphlets, books, articles, journals, white papers, webinars, and digital video files; that is accessible 24/7/365. This also requires developing procedural activities to determine the level of knowledge and skills each employee possesses to conduct their daily tasks in alignment with the needs of the organization, and the new reliance on technology.

Research explains that human resource managers must also be assessed to determine their level of ability to utilize technology in the workplace.

Furthermore, research conveys human resource management consistently evolves, so much so, employees are now relying on e-HR services more than connecting with HR face-to-face. This transformation is forcing HR to modify the way HR professionals look at their positions.[2] Today, human resource professionals need both traditional HR skills and knowledge, as well as the ability to use technology. Technology for HR includes information systems, hardware, software, and business processes that help implement effective services. Almost all workplace environments operate and rely on information systems, hardware, software, and business processes to help implement effective services and provide quality products.

Ideally, the type of information technology structural changes required for effective adoption and adaptation of technology in the workplace include researching the methods of implementing digital transformation and implementing new strategies that improve how new technologies are integrated and relied on. Research conveys that a small percentage of respondents used in a research study on digital transformation in the workplace reported that their organizations' digital transformation helped improve performance, as well as better equipped workplaces to manage the integration of technology changes effectively. In some entities where the adoption of new technology is woven into the fabric of the workplace, research reports that seven percent of those researched shared that workplace performance was improved, but did not have a long-lasting impact on the entity's success.[3]

Additional research explains that one of the reasons teams neglect to comply with requests to adopt new technology systems lies in the implementation process that requires both man-hours and great capital investment.[4] Research reports that creating a win-win for employees and the workplace can be beneficial and increase innovation, because it opens the door for more innovative ideas to be considered.

Thus, unless effectively integrated and managed, technology will cripple the workplace. To be supportive, this book delivers an effective process and comprehensive infrastructure for technology management and provides strategies for effective integration of artificial intelligence and machine learning as components to enhance productivity and decision success. This book provides you with the ability to comprehend technology management and outlines effective steps and measures that should be relied on to maintain leverage over how technology controls information assets and how personnel in your workplace will deploy daily activities in alignment with information security and technology management policy.

Chapter 1 enables you to understand technology and information assurance, information assurance analysis, and distinguish technology and information assurance risk management. This chapter also helps you acknowledge information usage profiles for the workplace and understand technology and information risk factors correlating with your unique workplace needs. A case study is included, and a research article review is provided.

Chapter 2 supports you by distinguishing technology management guidelines that enable you to acknowledge technology management standardizations and understand how to align trends of technology management in your workplace. This chapter also helps you understand the benefits of adhering to technology management guidelines and standards, as well as distinguish guidelines that protect your workplace information assets. Chapter 3 enables you to understand threat modeling and threat modeling diagramming. This chapter also enables you to distinguish technology management threat modeling for your workplace and distinguish commercial threat modeling tools. A case study and research article review are also included.

Chapter 4 enables you to understand three security audit frameworks recommended and, in many industries, required for effective technology management. In alignment with the US National Institute of Standards and Technology and their special publication series, you will learn to distinguish unique modifications to align with your workplace's current policy and deployment of security control, risk management, and cybersecurity framework development, implementation, modification, and policy compliance and penalties. A research article review is provided, validating the significance of effective auditing in the workplace.

Chapter 5 enables you to differentiate the NIST policy recommendations and guidelines that they must adhere to maintain technology management. This includes gaining an understanding of what policies and procedures are enacted, domestically and internationally. This also helps readers improve how they develop and implement information security and technology management policies, as well as explain how to align policy, information storage, and data collection. Readers will learn about domestic and international laws, policies, and regulations, and understand how to define their current information security, information assurance, and cybersecurity policy with global standards in managing technology in the workplace. A case study is provided.

Chapter 6 enables you to distinguish what risk factors currently exist in their usage of technology tools and applications in the workplace. Readers will learn how to distinguish risk factors and mitigate these risks as they learn about NIST security control special publications. This includes reviewing each security control and assessing controls to help improve risk factor security control across all technology tools and applications relied on and utilized for business communication and data and information storage, transmission, and security.

Chapter 7 enables you to understand NIST SP 800-61 Rev. 3, correlating with incident response. Readers will distinguish how to incorporate cybersecurity incident response in alignment with the recommended guidelines outlined in the NIST Cybersecurity Framework. This will enable readers to understand how to prepare for incident response, lower the number of successful cyber-attack incidents internally and externally, and improve their effectiveness and efficiency of incident response detection, mitigation, and recovery activities.

Chapter 8 helps you understand how to prepare and recover from technology usage disasters. You will define a disaster recovery outline that aligns with NIST SP 800-34, Rev. 1, regarding contingency planning for the workplace. This chapter also helps you create a disaster recovery plan, assess the weaknesses and strengths of your plan, and outline mitigation strategies that improve your disaster recovery methods.

Chapter 9 enables you to distinguish which third-party service and product provider best delivers the most effective and secure applications that support automation of artificial intelligence and machine learning. You will distinguish how artificial intelligence and machine learning provide improved security and improve analytic reporting. You also learn how to configure artificial intelligence and machine learning tools offered by Amazon Web Services (AWS) for workplace information systems, and define an infrastructure to assess, design, manage, and secure information systems using AWS partnership services and products.

Chapter 10 provides you with an opportunity to understand the significance of industrial organization and its role in the workplace. It also enables you to understand why the integration of industrial organizational psychology is beneficial to technology management in the workplace. Research and statistics are provided showing the correlation between qualitative and quantitative values of technology management. This includes sharing comparisons of human engagement with technology in the workplace as the key to productivity and business operations, and communication.

References

[1] Young, J. (2021). *Balancing the benefits with the risks of emerging technology*. https://www.techtarget.com/searchsecurity/post/Balancing-the-benefits-with-the-risks-of-emerging-technology

[2] Gowan, M. (2011). *Foreward.* https://www.shrm.org/hr-today/trends-and-forecasting/special-reports-and-expert-views/documents/hr-technology.pdf

[3] McKinsey & Company, (2018). *Unlocking Success in digital transformation.* https://www.mckinsey.com/capabilities/people-and-organizational-performance/our-insights/unlocking-success-in-digital-transformations

[4] Stadler, C., Helfat, E.C. & Verona, G. (2021). *3 Strategies for rolling out New Technologies Within Your Company.* https://hbr.org/2021/08/3-strategies-for-rolling-out-new-tech-within-your-company

1

Technology and Information Assurance

Learning objectives

- Understand technology and information assurance.
- Understand information assurance analysis for the workplace.
- Distinguish between technology and information assurance risk management.
- Acknowledge information usage profiles for the workplace.
- Understand technology and information risk factors in the workplace.

Technology and information assurance are essential components of managing information developed, shared, transmitted, stored, and secured by workplace personnel, regardless of whether that workplace is a corporation, small business, non-profit, or government entity. No two workplaces maintain and manage the same scale and scope of technology and information assurance. Therefore, to effectively implement technology management and information assurance, it is imperative that you, as the information technology manager, personnel, information system manager or personnel, educate your workplace leaders about the value of having an effective team of technology practitioners, who possess the knowledge, experience, skills, and know-how, to define technology and information assurance risk management strategies that can be relied on before, during, and after a cyberattack incident. After all, the growing number of cyberattack incidents targeting corporations, small businesses, non-profits, and government networks worldwide has grown exponentially! This alarming rate of cyberattack incidents forces all workplace entities to improve their method of technology and information assurance and impose stricter policies to govern how technology and information assurance are applied across the entity's business operation infrastructure. Unless cyber incident information and instruction are provided for your workplace

DOI: 10.1201/9788743809715-1

through public sector government regulations, policy, and law, and private sector organizational and industry standards, your workplace will continue experiencing an increased number of cyber incidents. Neglecting to properly assess risk factors will cripple your organization and its ability to thwart successful cyberattacks from impacting the workplace, as well as impacting the ability to work effectively toward 100% information assurance. This chapter provides quality support and recommends guidelines to help you, as a technology practitioner, gain a clear understanding of technology and information assurance. Without clarity of technology and information assurance, and the role these play in supporting your workplace, your ability to control risk factors aligning with the usage of technology and management of information assets remains bleak.

Thus, this chapter helps you understand technology and information assurance analysis that supports you as a workplace technology practitioner in improving how information assets are stored and transmitted across the internet and the intranet commonly relied on. This chapter also helps you distinguish technology and information assurance risk management that enables you as a technology practitioner to acknowledge information usage profiles to effectively understand information risk factors correlating with your unique workplace, and the technology tools, software, hardware, and devices relied on. To help reiterate your learning and comprehension of this chapter, chapter review questions are available at the end of this chapter. Answers to these review questions can be discovered after the listed references.

What is information assurance?

Information assurance is a significant component in the effective management of information assets. In alignment with the CIA triad-confidentiality, integrity, and availability, information assurance clarifies the value of information assets. Many workplaces embody a plethora of information assets, including executive leadership personal information (e.g., name, home address, phone number, email, bank routing numbers, bank account numbers, social security numbers, and date of birth). This vital information has significant value. In fact, executive leadership and personnel information assets are just as valuable as their social media profile information.

Thus, it is imperative to have a reliable information assurance plan and method of management control to reduce risk factors that can impede the ability to decrease the risk of information being stolen or confiscated by both internal and external threat agents, interested in causing reputational, monetary, or both damage to your workplace. Therefore, to be effective in the workplace, technology practitioners must implement quality information assurance. This includes knowing what procedures to deploy to maintain the confidentiality of the information.

Effective management of confidentiality encompassing workplace information assets renders effective privacy of personal and sensitive information, identifying a person, a trademark secret, patent information, or financial asset details. To reduce risk, integrity must be implemented to ensure each workplace defines information assurance, as well as understands how to assess, develop, implement, manage, and secure all technology and information assurance frameworks. When information is valued with integrity, the focus of risk management is on controlling how information is assessed and stored or shared to minimize any risk factors that can increase the opportunity for unauthorized exploitation of such information.

Many workplaces are mismanaged when it comes to their approach to technology management and information assurance. Many workplaces also commonly lack effective information assurance managed with confidentiality, integrity, and availability, in alignment with recommendations and guideline standards suggested by the United States National Security Agency and the US Department of Homeland Security. Each of these government entities has better control over how its information assets are protected and to whom its information assets are shared.

One of the most publicly known methods for cybercriminals to assess weaknesses in any workplace information system and information assurance strategy is deploying research that provides details needed to learn about known vulnerabilities and threats woven in any operating system, software application, or technology device or tool relied on for business communication, information sharing, or information storage needs, which many corporations, small businesses, and non-profits clearly publicize when hiring technology practitioners. Cybercriminals can attain knowledge about any workplace reliance on technology applications and tools by reviewing help-wanted ads. Too often, these ads deliver too much information about the scope of technology utilized in daily business operations.

Take, for example, an Indeed hiring ad for Apple, the ad requests a technology manager with five years' experience in project management and/or IT infrastructure projects. The role required technical experience in Mac, Safari, Google Workspace (G Suite) admin, Slack, Meraki, Jamf, Jira, Splunk, AWS, and other enterprise SaaS applications. It also seeks someone who understands Mac and mobile hardware support for iPhones and iPads. Finally, it seeks someone with a basic understanding of networking principles (DHCP, DNS, and SSID).

Too much information provides adversaries with the ability to learn the type of system applications utilized to understand their weaknesses. Mismanagement of technology in the workplace can lead to a catastrophic event, costing billions to recover from. Ineffective technology management and information assurance can ruin your workplace reputation. The example is a typical disclosure of sensitive information offered by corporations and small businesses trying to remain leverage in a competitive workplace environment.

Usage of payment processing systems, and reliance on third-party software applications offered by Microsoft 365 business, Linux, Mac, Azure, AWS, Oracle, or Adobe, embody risks that can impact the ability of your workplace to be victimized by cyberattack incidents, externally and internally. Internally, cyberattack incidents derive from human error. Human error has become the leading entrance point for successful cyberattack incidents to occur. In fact, on March 4, 2024, it was published by the Cyber Risk Alliance, LLC, that Chief Technology Officers from around the world report that human error is the highest known reason for security breaches, higher than ransomware and phishing attacks.[1]

Thus, publicly known details commonly shared about known vulnerabilities in Microsoft 365 for business include the Microsoft Outlook Remote Code Execution Vulnerability reported July 9, 2024, in the Common Vulnerability and Exposure listing under CVE-2024-38021.[2] Also, included in this publicly available list of risk factors is reliance on Microsoft Office 2016 (64-bit and 32-bit), Microsoft Office LTSC 2021 (64-bit and 32-bit), Microsoft 365 Apps for Enterprise (64-bit and 32-bit), and Microsoft Office 2019 (64-bit and 32-bit).[3] Gaining access to a workplace's information system and technology, known vulnerabilities is step one in knowing how to successfully exploit a weak information system and its technology applications and tools.

Therefore, technology practitioners must stay current in understanding all vulnerabilities woven into the software applications and technology tools and devices utilized, to effectively patch those vulnerabilities prior to them being susceptible to unauthorized intrusion. One way to safeguard your workplace is by implementing information assurance. Doing so correctly requires understanding how to improve information assurance and understanding the role a factor analysis of information risk plays. You also need to understand how to effectively determine asset identification, including hardware assets, subsystems and software assets, cloud-based information assets, virtual assets, information assets, asset classification, and data classification. This requires technology practitioners to define a unique Information Usage

Profile Table that conveys information categorically, such as business records, third-party vendor records, employees' records, trademarks, research patents, software, hardware, information systems, cloud assets, and physical security assets.

The Information Usage Profile Table should include a description of the information assets, scale of sensitivity correlating with each scale of information, as well as report how the information asset is relied on and processed. This should also provide a list of all information systems, technology, and cloud usage or storage capabilities. An example of an effective Information Usage Profile Table is provided in Table 1.1.

Next, it is required to develop and define a risk analysis. To achieve the best scope of clarity when developing a risk analysis, it is recommended to rely on three different analysis formats. The first analysis format requires establishing the needs for information assurance as it co-exists with technology for your workplace and outlines the requirements for effective technology management and information security. Your analysis should convey a list of threats or methods of attack correlating with each type of information technology or business operation your workplace utilizes, and convey the type of information technology and/or business operation that must be protected, including identifying and reporting the type of information relied on, to define a clearly written analysis. The second analysis helps establish a risk profile, which is done using a table format. The third analysis provides a summary of the overall risk analysis, as well as a list of the identified risks and an explanation for any potential impact of risks your workplace might incur if such risk is successfully exploited.

Example of Analysis 1

Each workplace is uniquely different and requires different approaches to technology management and information assurance. One example of the uniqueness of a workplace is focusing on educational institutions. In educational institutions, it is determined by the mass number of personnel working at and managing the institution, that is, executive leaders, administrators, faculty, and staff, who maintain control over the scope of technology management. This can become a daunting task when technology practitioners are stagnating in planning and preparing effective technology management that positions the institution to effectively avoid being victimized by external and internal attack agents, be it adversaries or disgruntled employees.

So, it is important to deploy an analysis to provide a detailed outline of each type of technology utilized for daily business operations and

Table 1.1 Information Usage Profile.

Category of information	**Description of the information asset(s)**	**Scale of information sensitivity**	**Details about how this information is used or processed**	**Type of IT assets reliant on or that store information assets**
Executive leadership and personnel	Name, home address, birthdate, driver's license number, bank routing, and account numbers.	Strict confidentiality	Identify individuals, process payments, direct deposit, send emails, and contact via phone or mailings.	Computer (desktop/laptop, tablet, mobile devices), network servers, Cloud VPN, physical information filing systems, external hard-drive storage, and software.
Trademarks	Brand logos and design.	Confidentiality	Legal ownership/liability suits.	External hard drives, cloud VPN, computer (desktop/laptop/mobile devices/tablets).
Research patents	Research model types, methods, procedures, and storage products.	Confidentiality	Utilized by researchers contracted with the entity. Processed by Word.docx, Excel spreadsheet, and PowerPoint.	External hard drives, software, computers (desktop/laptop/mobile devices/tablet).
Vendor-third party records	Entity registered name, address, contact person, phone number, payment details, and banking information.	Strict confidentiality	Utilized to maintain records of executive leaders and personnel's credit card information, banking information, and medical information.	External hard drives, software, USB drives, computers (desktop/laptop/mobile devices/tablet), network servers, and cloud.

Software assets	Executive leadership and personnel's information, payment processing order numbers, tracking numbers, credit card information, and usernames.	Strict confidentiality	Develop, transmit, and store data files, track information, backup, and archive information in the cloud.	Internal software applications, USB drives, desktop/laptop/ mobile devices/tablets.
Hardware assets	Computer information system back-up and archive, storage files, and RAM (random access memory).	Strict confidentiality	Transmit data files internally and externally.	Desktop/ laptop/mobile devices/tablets, servers, Wi-Fi, and intranet.
Information system assets	Product files, executive leadership and personnel information files, business transaction data files, payroll, and medical health records.	Strict confidentiality	Store, transmit, and secure data files internally and externally.	Telecommunication, Wi-Fi, internet, server, and intranet.
Cloud assets	VPN, instances, IAM, artificial intelligence, machine learning, and natural language processing.	Strict confidentiality	Store and transmit data files securely.	Server, network, and key pair asset details.
Physical security assets	Identification entrance access cards, biometric, printer, fax machine, supplies, and desktop monitors, desktop computers, and laptops.	Strict confidentiality	Workplace security, human resource office, and executive leadership workplace areas.	Primary workplace entrance points into physical offices and computer network storage areas.

communication. This includes listing the type of devices used (e.g., desktop, laptop, mobile hand-held, tablet, printer, fax, USB drive, external hard drives, and telecommunication). And the type of software used (e.g., customer relationship management [CRM], enterprise resource planning [ERP], accounting, calendars, schedulers, timecards, payment systems, Microsoft 365, Active Directory, Google, Wisenet, Workday, Adobe, and Amazon Web Services.

This also includes understanding the type of third-party vendor relationships established and what is expected from these relationships, and knowing how to effectively manage communication with these service providers. After all, many workplace technology practitioners rely on third-party service providers for email accounts. And many of these practitioners never concern themselves with information assurance and security. This approach establishes a risk factor that can become a threat to the security of sensitive information collected, transmitted, and stored on behalf of the entity and its usage of information systems and technology.

Research conveys that internet service providers (ISPs) that provide email accounts often embody risks that can be threatening to end-users' privacy.[4] One leading ISP email service provider commonly integrated in global workplaces is Microsoft 365 Outlook. Unfortunately, many workplace entities neglect to assess known vulnerabilities woven into Microsoft 365 Outlook. Doing so places executive leaders and personnel's sensitive information assets at risk and vulnerable to invasion of privacy.

In fact, the Common Vulnerabilities and Exposure Website reported in 2022 that Microsoft Outlook enables cyberattackers to exploit the HMEF package of poi-scratchpad (Apache POI) that creates an Out of Memory. This is commonly used to read TNEF files with Microsoft Outlook and Microsoft Exchange Server.[5] When the application utilizes poi-scratchpad to parse TNEF files, the application enables users to craft files that can create Out of Memory exceptions. However, there were additional reports made throughout 2022 through 2024, which increased the number of vulnerabilities associated with the usage of this application.[6]

Vulnerabilities include denial of service, elevation of privilege, remote code execution, security feature bypass, MAC spoofing, and information disclosure. Office 2019 and 2021 were both vulnerable. In February 2024, Microsoft shared information that FBX files were disabled in the 3D viewer.[7] So, unless end-users configure their installation files to Link to Files during the installation, they cannot avoid victimization.

Thus, it is essential that technology practitioners stay current in trends of known vulnerabilities, or they risk placing their workplace's usage of

Outlook at risk of victimization. Adhering to this recommendation regarding the usage of this first analysis model should be taken seriously because doing so helps minimize the impact of risk woven in the usage of Microsoft 365 Outlook email application, or any other third-party email service relied on. Neglecting to do so is costly.

Your analysis should assess the risk associated with internet services, Wi-Fi, Bluetooth, wide access network (WAN), wide land access network (WLAN), and local access network (LAN). For instance, when information is transmitted across a wireless local access network (LAN), this establishes an entrance point for an external intruder to attack the wireless client using a peer-to-peer fashion. This method of attack allows an intruder to access the workplace computer network using a legitimate client as their entry point. Furthermore, vulnerabilities integrated in a wide area network (WAN) enable hackers to manipulate traffic and control access to networks. Wireless network attacks encompass several types of attacks, including parking lot attacks, drive-by attacks, wardriving, warchalking, bluesnarfing, bluejacking, bluebugging, and evil twin attacks.

Parking lot attacks involve an attacker parking in a nearby business parking lot and manipulating access to the network, and hacking into vulnerable unsecured networks to deploy malicious actions. These actions can include integrating a botnet attack and retrieving sensitive data files. Unless your workplace network is encrypted using layers of cryptology, your workplace risks victimization. The number of successful parking lot attacks deployed against public sector entities impacted 40% of public Wi-Fi users in 2024.[8] The number of public Wi-Fi users who tap into these applications commonly does so while at restaurants and hotels. The number of Wi-Fi attacks deployed at these entities grows annually because end-users neglect to implement security measures to decrease their chance of victimization. Common errors of usage include paying for meals using a credit card payment service provider while at hotels or a restaurant. Transactions deployed at these locations are often found later when viewing credit card statements. Time has elapsed, and the cybercriminals have escaped without conviction. The victim is left to experience depression and stress trying to recapture the loss of funding stolen during these attacks on their credit card.

Drive-by attacks involve an attacker driving through a community, public or private sector, and connecting to any open network link that is available to obtain access to the network and spy on all electronic communication. This involves an attacker gaining access to a computer network and playing man in the middle to confiscate sensitive documents as they are transmitted across the internet without encryption. These attacks result in documents being modified during transmission and altering content to sabotage or control the delivery of documents in packages.

Wardriving involves utilizing a free open-source software application that can be downloaded offline. Much like drive-by attacks, which enable attackers to identify vulnerabilities in Wi-Fi networks and gain access to the network to deploy and engage in nefarious activities, this type of attack is common. Wardriving can involve attackers downloading software onto a victim's computer, such as a Botnet, to gain control and possibly acquire keystrokes for passwords and other sensitive data. While this type of attack is not new, revised concepts of this type of attack include war cycling, war walking, war biking, and war training.[9]

Warchalking involves locating open access to free networks for wireless internet connectivity. When a hacker is seeking to locate an open-access network and discovers one, they mark that network territory with a symbol or code, often in chalk or some color pen, to signify the location. This enables the hacker to return to the same location repeatedly to gain access without permission.

Bluesnarfing involves confiscating digital asset data from an unsuspecting end-user via insecure Bluetooth. This method requires conducting research to discover open access that is vulnerable through Bluetooth. These are common because many end-users do not disconnect their Bluetooth from their laptop, computers, or mobile devices.

Bluejacking involves a hacker sending unsolicited messages to an open Bluetooth within 30 feet to steal data from a mobile device. This requires end-users to ensure their Bluetooth is disconnected and ensure no one can gain access at all. Too often, end-users neglect to secure these applications, which results in the undiscovery of actual data breach attacks. Smartphone owners are commonly targeted.

Bluebugging involves a similar activity correlating with Bluesnarfing. This enables an attacker to gain control of an insecure device via Bluetooth without the device owner's knowledge. This is commonly deployed to enable attackers to install malware to retrieve data that is commonly stored on a mobile device, including messages, phone call data, and personal data. Mobile device users neglect to delete the cache from each app installed on their mobile device. This data has monetary value to hackers. Too common, attackers can retrieve credit card information that end-users have shared on their mobile devices to make payments. Thus, it is recommended that end-users always, if not every day, every other day, delete the cache from each app installed on their mobile device to prevent victimization.

Evil twin attacks involve hackers establishing a fake Wi-Fi network to capture unsuspecting end-users trying to connect to an open network. This enables the attacker to eavesdrop on activities end-users are deploying while utilizing the assumed insecure network. Hackers utilize this method to steal information and additional sensitive personal information.

Another technological tool commonly used is the fax machine. Fax machines are connected to Wi-Fi. This access connectivity point establishes a vulnerability for cyber attackers to exploit when improperly configured.

In fact, research compiled from the CVE database on August 13, 2024, conveys that Windows Fax Service enables remote code execution.[10] Microsoft Corporation reported this vulnerability on July 9, 2024, and listed this vulnerability as Max Severity: Important.[11] Microsoft Corporation also shared that the confidentiality value is high, the integrity value is high, and the availability value is high. Microsoft Corporation reported that an attacker who possesses normal end-user privileges and who has previously compromised a fax server that a victim is connected to can successfully exploit this system's vulnerability and execute arbitrary code on the victim's fax machine service.[12]

Thus, anyone accessing the fax service with an identifiable fax number can exploit the system and possibly transmit malicious packages to transmit malicious files or messages to their target victim. Office printers are just as vulnerable and embody exploitable entrance points via insecure and misconfigured Wi-Fi connections. Research conveys the list of commonly relied on office printers, including HP Office Jet Pro 9135e, Epson EcoTank ET-2720, Canon PIXMA G1220, Brother MFC-J6955DW, and Canon Pixma G7020 Megatank.[13] Sadly, when reviewing common vulnerabilities correlating with each of these office printers, research compiled from peer-reviewed resources reports the following details conveyed in Table 1.2.

Knowing there are research reports regarding known vulnerabilities integrated in the usage of these office printers and fax machines, and services, invokes a resolution to manage the technology relied on and secure the technology from external attack and victimization. In fact, Neel Punatar reported that vulnerabilities in Wi-Fi systems help external attackers eavesdrop and steal sensitive information transmitted across the internet. Therefore, technology practitioners need to know how to deploy effective measures that ensure security vulnerabilities are being patched as required by manufacturers and software developers. This includes maintaining effective communication with Service Level Agreements and implementing strategies that support recommended guidelines for securing information systems and technology.

Table 1.2 Office printer known vulnerabilities.

HP Office Jet Pro 9135e	No known vulnerabilities have been reported since December 2023. Research shares that some HP Office Jet Pro printers embody vulnerabilities that enable successful denial of service attacks when an end-user sends a SOAP message via the service on a transport control protocol (TCP) port 3911, which embodies a message without a header.[14]
Epson EcoTank ET-2720	CVE reported in 2023 that three primary vulnerabilities associated with Epson printers enable attackers to remotely access a printer and turn it off; this enables attackers to hijack authenticity and deploy operations that force an end-user to view malicious pages and inject arbitrary script.[15]
Canon PIXMA G1220	Canon reported on 9/12/2023 that they discovered that multiple buffer overflow vulnerabilities are in Canon Laser Printers/Inkjet Printers and small office multifunctional printers that can potentially enable a third-party to execute arbitrary code, or the printer could be subjected to a denial-of-service attack.[16]
Brother MFC-J6955DW	In 2024, Brothers Industry, LTD reported to CVE that multiple printers and scanners, correlating with web-based management, enable remote unauthenticated attackers the ability to deploy actions that impact their printers and scanners. This infiltration allows an attacker to impersonate an administrative end-user and unleash malicious software.[17]
Canon Pixma G7020 Megatank	Research reported by Security Week Cybersecurity News explains that Canon printers have known vulnerabilities that enable attackers to execute arbitrary code and deploy successful denial of service attacks.[18]

Example of Analysis 2

The second analysis requires establishing a risk profile outlining the content of threats and the scope of vulnerabilities woven in each type of information and business communication and operation analysis assessed, developed, designed, implemented, deployed, managed, and secured by technology practitioners. This table must convey the scope of risk for each category of technology application and software relied on, describe risk categories, and report the impact of each risk. To effectively implement technology management and information assurance requires the possession of knowledge to patch and mitigate strategies to correct these vulnerabilities, time and again.

Using a SWOT analysis is beneficial in broadening the scale of strengths, weaknesses, opportunities, and threats woven into your technology management and information assurance plans. The level of reliance on the internet and needed security depends on the quality of hardware and software used, and how that software and hardware are configured, managed, updated, backed up, and secured, which can result in system breaches and disruptive system failures. Table 1.3 demonstrates what a risk factor table should contain in correlation with each risk and known vulnerability, and categorizes the risk with the level of impact each risk has on the potential of controlling high cyberattack risk, and the impact level of such risk.

Example of Analysis 3

An entity's technology practitioners lacking knowledge to manage technology tools and assets effectively increases the probability of successful cyberattacks and /or cyber incidents. Therefore, technology practitioners must be required to remain current in trends of technology management and information assurance. Staying current will enable technology practitioners to effectively deploy patches and mitigate vulnerabilities woven into information systems and technology tools, and applications. Maintaining clearly conveyed written reports and logs, and managing clear reports that align with practitioners' names, roles, and responsibilities, establishes the framework that must be adhered to and practiced. This keeps a written record of everything and provides executive leaders and personnel instructions and details regarding what must be deployed and how it should be deployed and managed and secured to stay current in protecting and managing the technology and information system. Knowing how to increase quarterly assessments of technology practitioners also requires establishing who is held accountable for overseeing and managing the workplace information system and technology. This keeps the entity safe, empowers team knowledge, and creates the instruction to perform all related tasks efficiently, while enforcing regulatory implementation of effective assessments and auditing of all technology tools utilized and relied on. This should be done quarterly and/or as needed, to increase security and deterrence, and decrease potential risks embedded in the information system and technology.

When technology management and information assurance are paired, it enables a workplace to improve its ability to understand the value and significance of information assurance and learn why information assurance is important for business development and secure communication. Knowing the impact of information assurance requires knowing how to align actions

Table 1.3 Risk factor table.

Risk ID	Risk title	Description	Risk category	Impact level
001	Data and information extortion at the executive leadership and personnel level.	Ransomware attacks deployed through internal email systems, mismanaged and misconfigured, enable external attackers to retrieve data and information assets without authorization. This results in the demand for monetary payload.	Extremely high	Catastrophic, this can impact the entity's reputation substantially.
002	Human error incidents	Executive leaders and personnel are targeted with phishing scams and emails embedded with malware botnets. These botnets can embody key loggers that track all keystrokes of a computer and provide access to sensitive information stored on the device. This entrance point creates an error.	High	This is major because this can allow malware, ransomware, viruses, Trojans, worms, and spy software downloads that can steal sensitive data and information assets.
003	Infringement of intellectual property	Trademarks, digital signatures, and many workplace documents are valuable assets. Cybercriminals can create mock websites of a workplace web interface to acquire sensitive data from consumers and cause monetary damage.	High-medium	This is moderate because many entities have registered trademarks. However, all documents should be encrypted with notarized watermarks to ensure accuracy, maintain authenticity, and increase document duplication security.

004	Technical hardware failures from misconfiguration of software during installation.	Too often, many workplaces neglect to update software and back up, and archive data and information assets regularly. Doing so results in attackers acquiring access to the computer network, information systems, and technology tools. This is the mismanagement of technology that leads to cyberattacks.	High	This can be catastrophic because entrance points are weakened, and the network is vulnerable to unauthorized intruders. This can enable successful network intrusions that result in large payloads for cyberattackers, while crippling a weak and vulnerable data and information system.
005	Technological obsolescence	Staying current with trends of products or services requires knowing when you can no longer depend on an operating system to store and transmit data and information assets. Microsoft issued a warning to update Windows 10 in June 2024 by October 2025. In August 2024, reports convey that 102 vulnerabilities were discovered and reported via CVE-2024-21302, CVE, 2024-38202, and CVE-2024-38199. Lacking this knowledge leaves an entity vulnerable to unauthorized attack and intrusion.	High	This is major because when systems are outdated, it is easier for external attackers to exploit those vulnerabilities and disrupt systems. This creates major issues that include technicalities and ineffective communication.

(*Continued*)

Table 1.3 *Continued.*

Risk ID	Risk title	Description	Risk category	Impact level
006	Forces of nature	Tornadoes, power outages, hurricanes, and floods.	Medium	The major damage done to paper information systems stored on premises from a force of nature results in an increase in cost to restore and replace assets if damaged.
007	Theft	Executive leaders and personnel engage in theft of workplace property, including theft of computers, USB drives, external hard drive storage, monitors, mobile devices, electronic and physical files, sensitive data, and so much more.	Medium	This is major because data and information assets are the value. These assets are beneficial tools to help establish a unique character for competitors. When theft occurs, it increases additional system vulnerabilities.
008	Hardware and software attacks	Hardware and software applications designed for programming web interfaces often are installed with known vulnerabilities that attackers exploit. This results in system control, system takeovers, SQL injections, denial of service attacks, phishing, spoofing, and malvertising.	High	This is major because it cripples an entity's ability to effectively manage the security of data and information assets. This leads to cyberattacks and increases the cost to upgrade cybersecurity leadership.

009	Vendor and third-party relations	Vendor data and information assets are sensitive assets that should be protected like all data and information assets owned by an entity. When third-party service and product providers neglect to align their security practices and procedures with recommended standardized guidelines, it impacts their security scalability.	High	This is high because third-party vendors are responsible for rendering quality services and products in alignment with federal domestic and international laws, regulations, and policies protecting the sensitivity of data and information assets. GDPR (General Data Protection Regulatory) was enacted by the European Commission to ensure the protection and security of citizens' personal information.
010	Telecommunications	Telecommunications is an essential channel in any workplace. When attackers target telecommunications, they are seizing data and information using covert surveillance.	High	This is major because telecommunication service and product providers make human errors when coding systems and neglect to provide knowledge to end-users regarding default password modification and update requirements. This can lead to unauthorized intrusion.

(*Continued*)

Table 1.3 *Continued.*

Risk ID	Risk title	Description	Risk category	Impact level
011	Physical location	Your workplace security control must align with technology management and cybersecurity leadership. Therefore, entrance access cards with images of the card owner should be required for entrance. Usage of biometric security controls can decrease access to sensitive data and information assets; printers, fax machines, and digitized supplies must be secured. All desktop computers and laptops can be hacked, stolen, or remotely controlled to enable cyberattacks or support other forms of sabotage. This can lead to property damage and an increase in security costs.	High	This is major because the physical location of data and information assets belonging to your workplace and how easy access to such is controlled, can impact the ability to successfully manage technology and deploy cybersecurity leadership.

and activities integrated with technology tools, software, and hardware. Good technology management must align with a clearly conveyed Information Usage Profile (IUP). The IUP is invaluable because it provides details about key business information assets, that is, executive leaders, personnel, third-party vendor records, trademarks, patents, software assets stored and created, hardware assets relied on, information system assets, cloud assets, and physical security assets. The IUP provides a description of each information asset, determines the level of sensitivity for each information asset, and explains how the information asset is utilized and/or processes data and information. This also includes a clear list of all information systems, technology, and cloud usage or storage capabilities. Developing a good and reliable risk analysis establishes the ability to describe the needs and requirements for effective technology management and information assurance. This also provides knowledge empowerment regarding the likelihood of the main source of a threat or cyberattack that could catastrophically impact daily business operations and communication. Reliable and verifiable technology management and information assurance should identify risks and know the potential impact of risks the workplace faces.

Conclusion

Technology management has become intrinsic for many reasons. Ineffective management of technology has resulted in catastrophic events and cyber incidents, leading to reputational damage, monetary loss, and, in some instances, forcing some workplaces to close their doors altogether. Ineffective technology management cripples the ability of an entity to sustain unauthorized intrusion of information systems, information technology, cloud, hardware, software, and networks relied on for business operation and communication. The alarming cyberattack incidents ravaging workplaces globally are enough evidence proving that the threat of victimization is serious, and the need for effective resolutions to thwart and deter successful attacks begins with effective technology management.

Information assurance co-exists with cybersecurity. These two components support effective technology management. Many workplaces lack efficient integration of information assurance and cybersecurity leadership. This is a setup for failure. Even worse, the enactment of federal domestic and international laws, regulations, and policies requiring improved strategies to be developed and implemented to ensure security and safeguard sensitive data and information assets calls for an increase in planning and strategizing to prepare for the worst prior to an actual attack or cyber incident occurring.

Efficient technology management and information assurance must become a normal practice, or issues will remain heightened and impact the overall ability to control risk factors that increase the risk of external intrusion. Utilization of a clearly written Information Usage Profile, as described in Table 1.1, is a logical approach to beginning the implementation of improved information assurance and risk management. When applied correctly, this can be a tool that technology practitioners can define to meet their unique scale of technology usage and begin pinpointing areas of strength, understanding weaknesses, learn more about opportunities, and controlling threats encompassed in the technology and applications relied on. Deploying effective research to gain control of these key areas is essential to winning the war on cyberattacks. To help reiterate what you have learned, try answering the chapter review questions provided.

Case Study

Sharing and acquiring updated information helps continue building communication and knowledge that enriches all workplaces experiencing cyberattack issues and incidents, and who are vulnerable to victimization of such, makes a huge difference in the strategies and methods these entities can deploy and rely on to safeguard data and information assets. Therefore, case studies are useful tools that provide additional leverage and clarity to increase knowledge sharing and empower technology practitioners. I discovered a case study that focuses on a technology management framework for colleges. The author confesses that the purpose of integrating this knowledge is to prove that the global concern of technology management is prevalent and requires resolutions that work. Utilizing this tool of knowledge sharing and contribution, about an educational institution's technology practitioners responsible for managing technology data and information assets, sheds light on a possible remedy.

Title: *Strategic Technology Management Framework for Educational Institutions with Limited: A Case Study of a Local College in the Philippines*

Author: Danilo C. Sabado

Summary:

This case study shares a universal language of technology management for colleges, integrated with current trends in teaching and learning with technology, and administrative processes to integrate into the management of technology. While this framework is intended for local colleges in the Philippines, the language of technology management resonates with any workplace. Author Danilo C. Sabado explains the significance of developing a SWOT analysis to assess strengths, weaknesses, opportunities, and threats that must be examined and understood. Having this knowledge is beneficial because it supports vulnerabilities discovered in additional applications that any workplace relies on, but tends to lack the efficient support of technology management to determine how to assess and manage technology correctly. This broad scope of technology management aligns with workplace contexts and renders a practical model of adoption that can be universally beneficial.

Sabado points out that in the Philippines, the Enhanced Basic Education Act of 2013 is synonymous with K-12 programs and the integration of technology in educational environments to enhance the partnership and propel administrative leadership into the future of educational deliverance and help improve learning experiences and opportunities for students. With the outbreak of COVID-19 and the dependence on asynchronous learning, the risks of increased cyberattack incidents grew. This threat raised a daunting concern of securing technology tools, applications, and systems. Sabado relied strongly on data collection from comprehensive assessments deployed on information and communication technology resources and infrastructures commonly relied on at colleges in the Philippines. The resources encompassed customers, service provider portfolios, curriculum and instruction, robust infrastructure, and security methods.

Reliance on interviews conducted with IT staff, administrators, and faculty helped gain insight into the concerns and problems each college, including in this research, experienced. Observations were deployed on-site to witness the installation and configuration of technology tools, applications, and devices. Internal documentation was assessed and examined relating to information and computer technology resources, correlating with methods of maintenance and procurement. Online resources were utilized to verify services and usage of technology, including social media platforms and official college websites. Of course, an official audit was deployed on hardware and software relied on at these institutions, including the type of devices used and relied on, peripherals, and servers.

Much like the Information Usage Profile discussed in this chapter, Sabado also utilized a similar approach to understand the strengths, weaknesses, opportunities, and threats engulfed in reliance on these applications, systems, tools, and devices, to begin determining the risk factors woven in these components of the overall technology management being infused. Sabado categorized customers to include faculty, students, alumni, staff, administrators, and community partners. These categories are essential to the ongoing lifecycle of any educational institution. The value of data assets these categories possess makes and can often break the strength of any educational institution, particularly when security concerns are neglected. Sabado points out that the service portfolio of educational institutions tends to include teaching and learning, as well as administration. After all, administration is the management of the internal systems of business and communication. The administration of educational institutions is responsible for hiring, training all hire-ins, and developing policy, curriculum, and instruction. When the administration lacks the efficiency to operate effectively, it impacts the overall daily operational success of the institution. This also impacts the ability of technology management to control risk factors that tend to lead to cyberattacks and incidents. Therefore, education institution administrators are essential workers to the growth and ongoing stability of the educational system.

Sabado points out the significance of robust infrastructure, that is, data stored on hardware and software, as well as network components. This includes ports, local access networks, wide access networks, virtual private networks, Wi-Fi, and intranet connectivity. Sabado believes it is imperative to effectively assess these components and determine the scale of risk each embodies to effectively implement strategies to minimize the risks each may or may not possess. He adds that security, disaster recovery, backup, and archiving are key to managing a system and minimizing risks. Sabado also explains that staying knowledgeable of each device, technology tool, and application is crucial to staying ahead of cybercriminals. This includes knowing how to audit these tools, applications, and systems and configuring them as recommended by each manufacturer. Sabado stresses the value of understanding office automation software, operational systems, that is, proprietary operating systems, development platforms, overall educational environment, and the cost of maintenance and updating these systems as required or needed.

However, Sabado neglected to mention the significance of ongoing training of administrators, faculty, and staff, who utilize these technology tools, applications, and systems. Sabado insisted that cross-examining each person interviewed and questioned helps thwart inconsistencies and validates his theories and purpose for his research. The research framework enveloped data gathering regarding organizational background, which includes the mission, goals, and objectives. This also includes evaluating the current state of technology in use and gathering and assessing details about the manpower managing the current state of technology.

The analysis included SWOT analysis, mapping, which encompassed strategies, communication, and governance, as well as operational. Sabado also focused attention on how technology is implemented, such as areas of primary focus, timelines, budget constraints, and risk analysis. His evaluation concluded with updates on risk management practices. Furthermore, the SWOT analysis conveyed some interesting facts.

First, the strengths are common among most educational institutions, that is, willingness to grow and adopt new policy, trust, ethics, and integrity that position any educational institution high ranking, and a collaborative team attitude toward training awareness and preparation, and compliance with policy. However, Sabado noted weaknesses, including online forms, challenges in communication, ineffective staffing, and an absence of reliable information technology strategic planning.[19] In fact, Table 1.4 provides a look at the SWOT analysis, typically aligning with educational institutions.

Sabado defined a technology management framework that resembles the proposed technology management discussed in this chapter. While Sabado focuses on business operations and enterprise resource planning as key components to ensure an improved technology management infrastructure, I find these recommendations to be all too common and often overlooked and ignored by many workplace technology practitioners globally. After all, the discussion of technology management is not new. The threat of cyberattacks has been talked about since the new millennium began 25 years ago. Enough about frameworks that were introduced 10 years ago and are still commonly ignored. It is time to upgrade to a framework that is easily adoptable across all workplace entities. This level of framework must become synonymous as much as technology has become to the internet and information exchange. To learn more from Daniel C. Sabado and his recommendations for improving technology management in a local college, log on to https://ijisae.org/index.php/IJISAE/article/view/6411/5238. Doing so will enable you to grasp a clearer understanding of how to improve technology management for your workplace.

Research Review

Another method of building a strong knowledge defense against cyberattacks and cyber incidents is knowing what cybersecurity leadership is and how this key component cannot be ignored. After all, every workplace information system and technology platform or infrastructure must be integrated with effective cybersecurity, or there will be consequences. The severe consequences are costly. The monetary cost of a cyberattack on an educational institution has climbed to $3.5 million US dollars. Research reports the mean

Table 1.4 SWOT analysis.

Strengths	**Weaknesses**
• Educated administration, faculty, and executive leadership who are willing to support technology reliance and integration. • Educated and skilled IT practitioners who can explain technology and how it is integrated and helpful to the success of business communication and operations. • Trusted infrastructure, that is, email, telecommunication, energy connectivity, and Wi-Fi. • All computer operating systems are updated as needed.	• Website forms are inaccessible. • Transferring customers from person to person, assuming everyone else has the answers. • The absence of quality assurance. • Inadequate hiring of experienced and skilled technology practitioners. • Inadequate hiring of experienced and skilled cybersecurity leaders. • Minimal training for executive leaders, administrators, and faculty. • Limited software applications that students can rely on off-campus to minimize security risks.
Opportunities	**Threats**
• Increasing cybersecurity awareness training. • Increasing technology updates. • Increasing technology audits. • Increasing cybersecurity leadership. • Increasing improvement of policy development and implementation. • Improving consistency in managing technology effectively and efficiently. • Ensuring third-party vendor relationships are managed effectively. • Increasing communication between all executive leaders and technology practitioners.	• Policy non-compliance. • Lack of penetration testing. • Lack of cybersecurity breach drills. • Lack of assessment of risk factors. • Mismanagement of written records and logs. • Inaccuracy of data collection. • Mismanagement of confidentiality, integrity, and availability. • Non-compliance with industry standards, recommendations, and guidelines. • Lack of adherence to federal, domestic, and international laws, policies, and regulations.

cost in 2024 for K-12 educational institutions to recover from a ransomware attack has blown up to $3.76 million US dollars.[20] Research also reports that 60% of educational institutions attacked successfully by ransomware paid their attackers to acquire their data back. And 75% of educational institutions attacked by ransomware were able to utilize their backup systems and restore.[21]

I deployed research using qualitative grounded theory lite research and shared that research study with the Global Journal of Engineering

Technology Advances (GJETA), which published this scholarly article in July 2024. Usage of this scholarly research is beneficial in understanding the role cybersecurity leadership plays in educational institutions. Most importantly, this article outlines recommendations that should be considered, if not completely implemented, to ensure effective technology management is woven into your workplace.

Title: *Cybersecurity Leadership for Institutions of High Education*

Author: Bradley Fowler, Ph.D.

Summary

Qualitative grounded theory lite research helped me validate and answer three research questions. First, I sought to understand why ineffective cybersecurity leadership advocates an attitude of tolerance for ineffective training and non-compliance. Secondly, I desired to understand how to define an improved cybersecurity and information security policy, educational institutions can rely on. I also wanted to know what the best resolution is to decrease human error among executive leadership, administrators, faculty, and staff at educational institutions. As a result, this research not only provided the answers needed to begin cultivating a new resolution for these concerns but this also helped encourage me to continue deploying additional research to encourage and empower you to take charge and become effective cybersecurity leaders for your educational institution.

Research method required the collection of data assets, such as documents compiled from resources such as Holistica Journal of Business and Public Administration, Cybersecurity Infrastructure & Security Agency, FBI, and practitioners working at educational institutions, from which I was fortunate to acquire information relating to 5600 IT professionals, including 410 from higher education, across 31 countries. I was also lucky to acquire details from Freedom of Information (FOI) figures reported by the TIMES, which reported an estimated 1151 cyberattacks were deployed targeting institutions of higher education since 2017.[22] What I discovered to be so enthralling was that ransomware attacks targeting educational institutions are scoring higher than cyberattacks against healthcare organizations, businesses, and financial banking institutions.

I also discovered current theories about educational institutions being easy targets because they are considered weak entities; this is validated across multiple regions, including types of cyber incidents and statistical reports. I also learned that without increased consistency of cybersecurity training at educational institutions for executive leaders, administrators, faculty, and staff, the chance of decreasing these threats remains undefeated. In fact, whenever executive leaders, administrators, faculty, and staff are not made aware of system vulnerabilities and what is required of them to avoid human error, they will consistently practice careless behavior and activities that enable cyber attackers to gain entrance and access to sensitive environments to easily exploit the system weaknesses. Thus, this research helped me validate that human behavior advocates for cyber incidents at educational institutions.

During the discussion of this research, I shared details relating to research conducted on technology experts in Israel. Acquiring this knowledge established new training models and invoked the development of new training material. One thing I learned for sure is the lack of cybersecurity leadership at educational institutions. I also discovered that educational institutions must take note of the Safeguard Rule enacted in October 2022. This rule requires educational institutions to create, impose, and effectively manage their information security programs, which should include administrative, technical, and physical procedures and strategies to ensure the protection of data and information assets the educational institution accesses, collects, processes, protects, stores, utilizes, transmit, dispose of, or how they handle sensitive information of their customers, that is, students, faculty, and staff. This is done to ensure the security and confidentiality of customer information and to protect against potential threats or vulnerabilities that will impact the ability of the institution to safeguard customers' information. I also discovered additional federal laws and policies educational institutions must align with, including:

- Family Educational Rights and Privacy Act (FERPA)
- Federal Information Security Management Act (FISMA)
- Gramm–Leach–Biley Act
- Health Insurance Portability and Accountability Act (HIPAA)
- Higher Education Act
- NIST Risk Assessment and Audit Standards
- Payment Card Industry Data Security Standards

Knowing how to align educational institutions' risk factors with recommended guidelines, such as the National Institute of Standards and Technology

Special Publication Series 800-171, is a prerequisite to securing information systems, information technology, and cloud environments educational institutions store data assets.

The recommended practice of educational institutions to effectively integrate and adopt cybersecurity leadership can be reviewed and understood in this scholarly published work. However, it is recommended that you acknowledge the value of utilizing qualitative grounded theory lite research to discover effective recommendations and guidelines to ensure that implemented security is reliable and valid. As noted, for effective cybersecurity leadership at educational institutions, it is imperative to properly assess, develop, implement, and manage all institutional technology hardware, software, and applications relied on for daily business operations. This may sound like a broken record. However, consistency is validated throughout the world. All technology practitioners and cybersecurity leaders are knowledgeable that threats and vulnerabilities are real. There is without doubt that educational institutions must deploy cybersecurity leadership that thwarts and deters cyberattacks and minimizes cyber incidents. Otherwise, the increase in payout for ransomware attacks will be higher than current rates. This cannot be the way of the future. If this continues, educational institutions are going to need to increase the number of professional experts to manage their technology and cybersecurity infrastructure. But the limited number of efficiently trained practitioners threatens the ability to meet the demands that educational institutions have. To review more about this scholarly article, log on to http://gjeta.com/content/cybersecurity-leadership-institutions-higher-education

Chapter 1 Review Questions

1. What does the CIA triad represent?
2. What does effective management of confidentiality envelope for educational institutions?
3. What method do cybercriminals deploy to assess weaknesses in any educational institution's information assurance strategy?
4. What has become the leading entrance point for successful cyberattack incidents to occur at educational institutions?
5. What CVE listing in July 2024 reported the known vulnerability in Microsoft 365 for business?

6. What are the top three categories of information to include in an Information Usage Profile?
7. What is warchalking?
8. What is bluesnarfing?
9. What is bluejacking?
10. What is an evil twin attack?
11. What does an IUP provide?
12. What does a good and reliable risk analysis establish?
13. What benefit does using a SWOT analysis provide?
14. What are the key components to define a risk factor table?
15. What are the risk categories in a risk factor table?

References

[1] Cyber Alliance, LLC., (2024, March 4). Human Error Cited as leading cybersecurity threat in orgs. https://www.scworld.com/brief/human-error-cited-as-leading-cybersecurity-threat-in-orgs
[2] Microsoft. (2024, July 9). Microsoft Outlook Remote Code Executive Vulnerability. https://msrc.microsoft.com/update-guide/vulnerability/CVE-2024-38021
[3] Ibid
[4] Baggot, A. (2023, May 12). Why ISP email services are terrible, and what to use instead. https://appleinsider.com/articles/23/05/12/why-isp-email-services-are-terrible-and-what-to-use-instead
[5] Common Vulnerabilities and Exposure. (2022). CVE-2022-26336. https://cve.mitre.org/cgi-bin/cvename.cgi?name=CVE-2022-26336
[6] Singhal, S. (2002). Computer World: Top 10 Vulnerabilities in Today's WIFI Networks. https://www.computerworld.com/article/1330253/top-10-vulnerabilities-in-today-s-wi-fi-networks.html
[7] Punatar, N. (2024, May 24). The Overlooked Importance of WI-FI Security in Schools. https://www.splashtop.com/blog/overlooked-importance-of-wi-fi-security-in-schools
[8] Main, K. & Haan, K. (2024, February 9). The Real Risks of Public Wi-Fi: Key Statistics and Usage Data. https://www.forbes.com/advisor/business/public-wifi-risks/

[9] Kaspersky, (2024). What is wardriving? Definition and explanation. https://usa.kaspersky.com/resource-center/definitions/what-is-wardriving
[10] U.S. Department of Homeland Security, (2024, August). CVE-2024-38104, Windows Fax Service remote Code Execution Vulnerability. https://cve.mitre.org/cgi-bin/cvename.cgi?name=CVE-2024-38104
[11] Microsoft Corporation, (2024, July 9). Windows Fax Service Remote Code Execution Vulnerability. https://msrc.microsoft.com/update-guide/vulnerability/CVE-2024-38104
[12] Ibid
[13] Edwards, L. (2024, June 3). Best Printers for Schools. https://www.techlearning.com/buying-guides/best-printers-for-schools
[14] Git Hub Advisory Data, (2023, December 14). Certain HP Office Jet Pro Printers Are Potentially… https://github.com/advisories/GHSA-8xqf-3483-8954
[15] U.S. Department of Homeland Security, (2023). CVE-2023-38556. https://cve.mitre.org/cgi-bin/cvekey.cgi?keyword=Epson+EcoTank+ET-2720
[16] Canon U.S.A., Inc. (2023, September 12). Service Notice: Vulnerabilities Remediation Against Buffer Overflow for Canon Laser Printer/Inkjet Printer and Small Office Multifunctional Printers. https://www.usa.canon.com/support/canon-product-advisories/Service-Notice-Vulnerabilities-Remediation-Against-Buffer-Overflow
[17] U.S. Department of Homeland Security, (2024). CVE-2024-22475. https://cve.mitre.org/cgi-bin/cvekey.cgi?keyword=Brother+MFC-J6955DW
[18] Arghire, I. (2024, February 6). Canon Patches 7 Critical Vulnerabilities in Small Office Printers. https://www.securityweek.com/canon-patches-7-critical-vulnerabilities-in-small-office-printers/
[19] Sabado, C.D. (2024, June 26). Strategic Technology Management Framework for Educational Institutions with Limited Resources: A Case Study of a Local College in the Philippines. https://ijisae.org/index.php/IJISAE/article/view/6411/5238
[20] Ward, M. (2024, July 16). Ransomware recovery costs have more than doubled for K12. https://districtadministration.com/ransomware-recovery-costs-have-more-than-doubled-for-k12/#:~:text=
[21] Ibid
[22] Quorom Cyber. (2021, August 31). Why higher education institutions are a prime target for cyber-attacks? https://www.quorumcyber.com/insights/why-higher-education-institutions-are-a-prime-target-for-cyber-attacks/

Chapter 1 Review Question Answers

1. The CIA triad stands for confidentiality, integrity, and availability.
2. Effective management of confidentiality envelops effective privacy of personal and sensitive information identifying a person.
3. Deploy research that provides the details needed to learn about known vulnerabilities and threats woven into any operating system, software application, or technology device relied on.
4. Human error has become the leading entrance point for successful cyberattack incidents to occur at educational institutions.
5. CVE-2024-38021.
6. Executive leadership, administrator, faculty, and staff; trademarks, and research patents.
7. Warchalking involves locating open access to free networks for wireless internet connectivity.
8. Bluesnarfing involves confiscating digital asset data from an unsuspecting end-user via an unsecure Bluetooth.
9. Bluejacking involves a hacker sending unsolicited messages to an open Bluetooth within 30 feet to steal data from a mobile device.
10. Evil twin attacks involve hackers establishing a fake Wi-Fi network to capture unsuspecting end-users trying to connect to an open network.
11. The IUP provides a description of each information asset, determines the level of sensitivity for each information asset, and explains how the information asset is utilized and/ or processes data and information.
12. The ability to describe the needs and requirements for effective technology management and cybersecurity leadership.
13. Broadening the scale of strengths, weaknesses, opportunities, and threats woven in the technology management and cybersecurity leadership deployed for educational institutions.
14. Risk ID, risk title, description, risk category, and impact level.
15. Extremely high, high, medium, low.

2

Technology Management Guidelines and Standardizations

Learning objectives

- Distinguish technology management responsibilities.
- Acknowledge technology management standardizations.
- Assess how to align trends of technology management in the workplace.
- Assess the benefits of adhering to technology management guidelines and standards.
- Distinguish international guidelines that protect the privacy of information assets.

In Chapter 1, you were introduced to technology management and information assurance as the method of effective risk management for information security and storage, using an Information Usage Profile. You also gained clarity regarding what should be included in this profile and why these categories of tools, applications, software, and hardware are valued, as well as how to score these components using risk categories, that is, Extremely High, High, Medium, and Low. Distinguishing the variance in the scale of risk associated with these components helps you gain knowledge about controlling risk factors, aligning with risks discovered in these applications, and learn how to assess these components in your workplace.

This chapter will increase your knowledge about technology management recommendations, guidelines, policy, law, and standardizations. Some of the policies you will learn about will include controlled nonfederal information systems, risk management framework, artificial intelligence, and generative AI profiling. Furthermore, you will be introduced to the British Columbia Personal Information Protection Act, General Data Protection Regulation (GDPR), Personal Information Protection and

DOI: 10.1201/9788743809715-2

Electronic Documents Act (PIPEDA), and the Australian Privacy Principles/ Privacy Act. While these are some of the most prevalent and well-known policies and laws, new policies and laws are being introduced and enacted globally to increase the measure of security of information assets stored, transmitted, and secured by corporations, small businesses, and non-profits. When applied with technology management, focus should include assessing, developing, implementing, and managing internal policies and methods for your workplace to ensure alignment with effective technology management. However, to help you distinguish the scale of importance of aligning technology management guidelines, policies, and standardizations, this chapter is divided into two parts. The first part focuses on technological management strategies and tactical business methods using cloud applications. The second part focuses on the standardized laws and policies mentioned and explains briefly how to integrate and align these laws and policies in the daily workplace business communication and operations, correlating with technology tools, software, and hardware utilized in your workplace. To help reiterate your learning and comprehension of this chapter's content, chapter review questions are available at the end of this chapter. Answers to these review questions can be discovered after the references listed.

Part 1

In 2024, CrowdStrike published a global threat report, conveying that businesses need to be mindful of the innovative approaches cybercriminals are deploying to gain access to sensitive data assets and information stored on vulnerable networks. CrowdStrike also shared that cybercriminals are gaining leverage over IT and technology practitioners. This means war! But how do we tame a war that we cannot determine how it is being raged. The best way to prepare for cyberwar is cyber defense. As noted in Chapter 1, the usage of an Information Usage Profile can be instrumental. But that is not your only defense. Talk about China and Russia, cyberattacks may sound boring, but these discussions should be taken seriously. Not because it is cybersecurity related, but because it is a way to stay a step ahead of your adversaries.

CrowdStrike reported that the 75% increase in ransomware attacks deployed between 2022 and 2024 guarantees your business, corporation, or non-profit can become a victim.[1] Furthermore, it is reported that cloud infrastructures and platforms have experienced an increase in breaches, resulting in a 75% increase.[2]

What are cybercriminals so interested in acquiring when they launch these attacks? The answer is simple: they want information worth monetary value. This information includes names, addresses, dates of birth, phone numbers, personal email addresses, emergency contact details, tax filing numbers, payroll information, bank account details, and passport details. But these are not the most valued data assets sought. Cybercriminals also seek trademark secrets, patent information, copyright details, and every document that delivers secrets that can be used as barging chips.

IT Governance, a United Kingdom cybersecurity information sharing platform, published a report stating that two public sector IT service providers were victims of a cyberattack that included 5 billion known records to be breached.[3] As a technology manager, it is your responsibility to ensure security breaches do not occur. Understanding the climate of cyberattacks is also a key part of effective technology management. Keeping your business, corporation, or non-profit secure is going to take effort that demands you build a stronger alliance with the third-party service providers you are partnering with to ensure you are knowledgeable of the weaknesses rendered by these partners. This is your only way to safeguard your client. Implementing project management with technology management will be your best alternative to increase effective technology management. In fact, research shared by the Project Management Institute reports that ensuring synchronization of project management and technology management provides increased control of risk factors and assesses weaknesses before external attackers can do it themselves.[4]

Therefore, the significant impact of cyber incidents impacting public and private sectors, invokes the need to increase how technology managers assess current trends of technology management and the vulnerabilities woven in the workplace, and the technology software and services relied on for daily business practices. The most important place to begin assessing vulnerabilities in your workplace technology applications is your operating system.

Commonly relied on operating systems (OS) in the workplace are Windows 7, 10, and 11. Microsoft Corporation issued a warning message to end-users, demanding that everyone update their subscription model of Windows 10 to Windows 11 by October 2025. Neglecting to maintain this update will create a vulnerability for your workplace desktops, laptops, and mobile devices.[5] When manufacturers' recommended updates are ignored, this leads to increased vulnerabilities that enable external attackers to gain access to workplace networks and computer devices to unleash cyberattacks. Research reported on both the Common Vulnerabilities and Exposure website and the Microsoft website, reported on August 7, 2024, shared a report conveying that there is a Windows Secure Kernel Mode Elevation of Privilege

Vulnerability.[6] This report explains that this vulnerability enables an attacker to gain administration privileges and replace existing versions of Windows system files with outdated versions.[7] This enables an attacker to reintroduce previously mitigated vulnerabilities, circumvent some features of VBS, and exfiltrate data protected by VBS.[8]

In August 2023, Microsoft published a report explaining that an authenticated user (e.g., an attacker) could also gain access and enable information disclosure, insisting this vulnerability does not require an administrator or additional increased privileges to deploy this attack.[9] Thus, it is imperative that you increase updates on all desktop computers, laptops, tablets, and additional devices relied on for communication and business practices involving the storage of data and the delivery of such, when relying on Windows OS, particularly, Windows 10. As of October 2025, Windows 10 will no longer be supported.

Another important component to be mindful of when assessing is your servers. Too often, the most common type of server that many businesses, corporations, and technology practitioners utilize is the Apache network server. It is reported that over 1 million corporations or businesses rely on Apache servers.[10] Germany and the United States are two countries that rely on Apache servers more than the Netherlands, Poland, the United Kingdom, France, and India.[11] Some known corporations reported relying on Apache servers, including Costco Travel, Nexstar Media Group, Bank of China, Wayfair, H & M, and Walgreens.[12]

Utilization of the Apache server enables an attacker to deploy malicious or exploitable backend/content generators that can split HTTP responses.[13] This enables an attacker to interject malicious response headers into backend applications, which causes an HTTP desynchronization attack.[14] Although Microsoft introduced a server in 2019 called Microsoft Windows Server 2019, research reported by the National Vulnerability Database cataloged under CVE-2024-6768 shares details explaining that denial of service in Microsoft Windows 10 and 11, and servers 2016, 2019, and 2022, enables malicious authenticated low-privilege users to create a Blue Screen of Death through a forced call to the KeBugCheckEx function.[15]

Furthermore, most businesses and corporations, or non-profits, rely on Microsoft Active Directory and neglect to maintain regular updates. Research reported on the Common Vulnerabilities and Exposure website conveys that CVE-2024-21381 shares details regarding the Microsoft Azure Active Directory B2C software embodies a spoofing vulnerability.[16] A spoofing vulnerability enables an attacker to utilize a variety of techniques to gain trusted IP addresses and modify packet headers, and insert forged addresses.[17]

Thus, mismanagement of technology in the workplace is commonly deployed through human error. This is primarily due to technology managers overlooking ineffective usage of technology in the workplace by personnel and executive leaders. After all, technology managers often neglect to adhere to recommended guidelines and standardizations imposed by technology hardware and software manufacturers. Take, for instance, how often do you deploy research to understand the known vulnerabilities integrated into the operating system you utilize? Human error number one. Human error number two derives from a lack of effective updating of your practices in safeguarding all technology applications, software, and hardware utilized.

One primary way internal human error creates a gateway entrance for external attackers is ineffective multi-factor authentication login credential usage. Multifactor authentication login credentials should always meet the recommended standards published by the National Institute of Standards and Technology (NIST), which published the special publication 800-63 titled *Digital Identity Guidelines*. Aligning practice usage of this special publication enables increased security and privacy controls for digital credential management that meet standardized levels of information assurance, including identity proofing, authentication, and usage of authenticators, as well as credential federation. This also implements risk-level processes to support the assessment of risk factors to improve identity management practice and the selection of the right scale of information assurance and risk factor control.[18]

Another vital scenario that often occurs in the workplace that many technology managers neglect to assess is the sharing of login credentials between employees. A lack of effective multi-factor authentication usage and login credential policy advocates for this scale of violation to happen. This is a leading cause of security breaches. In fact, research reports that studies prove employees often share their login credentials with other employees and tend to leave their passwords out on their desktops.[19]

Thus, an effective proposed technology management resolution must be planned, developed, effectively implemented, assessed, and consistently audited to ensure the current system is secure and that limited vulnerabilities exist. This requires enforcing the workplace policy that governs multi-factor authentication usage, updating, and credential sharing in the workplace. Unless consistency is deployed, employees will neglect to adhere, and you are back at vulnerability status, time and again. This is an issue that requires a firm decision to control this risk factor.

In fact, one proposed technology management resolution you should consider is enhancing existing solutions to improve cybersecurity leadership. This begins with conducting an effective audit of all current daily business communication technologies, digital file exchange transactions, and all engagement activities deployed with technology tools, including software and hardware. The audit process should align with recommended guidelines published in the National Institute of Standards of Technology special publications series 500-153, a *Guide to Auditing for Controls and Security: A Systems Development Life Cycle Approach*; NIST 800-53 for *Security and Privacy Control for Information Systems and Organizations*, NIST 800-181 Workforce Framework for Cybersecurity (NICE), and NIST 800-171 *Protecting Controlled Unclassified Information in Nonfederal Systems and Organizations*. Adopting the recommendations in these special publication guidelines will enable you to implement a standardized approach to governing all technology tools in your workplace and improve how you decrease risks and vulnerabilities associated with the usage of any software and hardware application relied on for business communication and transmission of data and information assets, including data assets at rest.

The next phase of your technology management resolution is assessing all known vulnerabilities enveloped in all software and hardware technology tools and assets. This requires ensuring all devices, that is, desktops, laptops, tablets, and mobile devices owned or leased by your corporation, business, or non-profit for business purposes, are configured and secured correctly to deter unauthorized intrusion of these systems and devices. Furthermore, it is imperative to research all integrated software applications to ensure these applications are configured as recommended by the software developer and product providers. Too often, technology managers will neglect to keep their software updated. However, please be aware that research reports that the utilization of out-of-date software creates major risks for businesses.[20]

It is also important to ensure all technology management practitioners are effectively trained to understand their role and responsibilities and are skilled in communicating with C-suite executive leaders and all employees utilizing technology to develop documents, save documents, transmit, and secure documents. When the technology manager lacks this efficiency, he/she create a work environment that remains silent about the threats and risks enveloped in the office or involved with remote workers.[21] Remote workers have been a cause of network security breaches in some workplaces.[22]

Therefore, it is imperative that policy updates are assessed, planned, developed, implemented, and reassessed biannually to ensure compliance rates are at performance expectancy and to ensure policies align with the needs of the workplace and its usage of technology. The objective is to decrease the number of successful cyberattack incidents and the cost to do so. One way to minimize the number of successful cyberattacks is to increase reliance on cloud computing applications for data and information storage of all on-premises data assets using information assurance security methods. One service and product provider that delivers a reliable supporting system is Amazon Web Services (AWS). AWS delivers dynamic cloud applications. AWS applications provide modernized administrative operations, enterprise resource planning, security applications, and reduce costs.

Utilization of Amazon Web Services (AWS) cloud computing is a recommendation to improve technology management and effective cybersecurity leadership. AWS delivers a reduction of cost per usage, analyzes data, and supports 98 security standards and compliance certifications. AWS renders Software as a Service (SaaS), Platform as a Service (PaaS), and Infrastructure as a Service (IaaS). Usage of AWS enables any workplace technology management practitioner(s) to be more efficient as they focus more attention on procurement of resources, capacity planning, software maintenance, patching, and other undifferentiated heavy moving activities deployed when running workplace applications. Reliance on AWS Platform as a Service (PaaS) provides benefits that can support the IT staff, despite there being small staff to handle the needs of the enterprise technology resources. This means, even though there is a limited technology management staff knowledgeable of the applications rendered by AWS, AWS support is a reliable resource integrated in the leasing of PaaS.

Ideally, implementing technology management with the integration of the AWS cloud platform should also include artificial intelligence and machine learning for automation. This approach can improve the resilience and security of assets. The objective should be to ensure effective technology management through internal personnel training, vendor management, and cloud usage. The resources required to achieve this streamlined reliance of services and products should include establishing an AWS account and leasing AWS EC2 Instances, AWS Cloud Watch Monitoring, AWS AI, and AWS Machine Learning. However, to be effective in adopting and implementing these applications for a smooth transition of service, it is imperative for all C-suite executive leaders and staff to be made knowledgeable of the newly integrated technology and trained to understand their role and responsibilities as such correlate with the technology. Below are outlined recommended personnel roles and responsibilities in correlation with reliance on cloud computing services, platform, or infrastructure:

Senior management roles and responsibilities:

- Human resource managers must take the initiative to increase technology policy development and awareness training in alignment with the needs of the workplace's IT staff. Sergei Golubenko conveys that an organization must rely on both HR and Operations to deploy effective employee training.[23] HR also partners with IT to increase understanding of what is needed in the current IT positioning within the workplace. Additional research explains that Chief Information Officers and Chief Human Resource Officers view digital transformation as a shared responsibility. 45% of high performers and 38% of the digitally mature group agree.[24]
- The IT Director should be responsible for overseeing the management of the IT staff budget and infrastructure to ensure employees are able to access the technology resources effectively, efficiently, and securely. This role is responsible for direct supervision of all IT staff, including coordinating and evaluating technology tools and applications. This also includes overseeing the development, implementation, and management of policies relating to the usage of technology, security of technology, and storage of all information assets, both in transition and at rest. Additionally, this includes interviewing new IT staff and training workers, appraising their performance, addressing issues and complaints, and conducting audits on IT staff and technology tools and applications. In addition, auditing should involve managing vendor relationships, understanding all Service Level Agreements for all external third-party service relationships, and managing effective, well-written reports and discussion logs. Staying knowledgeable of all federal and state policies, regulations, and laws your workplace industry is held accountable to, and updating all policies correlating with information security, information assurance, information technology, and cloud usage is mandatory!

Business and financial service management role and responsibilities:

- Define and deploy strategic plans that align with business office operations, including achieving goals and objectives, implementing strategies to manage financial resources to help maintain budgeting, and controlling expenditures, such as overseeing financial reporting. This role is responsible for upgrading processes that improve efficiency and productivity, managing human resource operations, including recruiting new employees, and overseeing performance management, as well as professional development. This role is supportive in ensuring compliance with workplace regulations and policies, particularly those correlating to finance, procurement, and human resources. This role is also required to collaborate with executive leadership throughout the workplace to provide support and to invoke innovative initiatives, such as fostering a culture of continued development. Responsibilities include securing fiscal support regarding all required training and defining and aligning with procedures that ensure compliance with ethics and integrity, including all applicable laws and regulations.

- In addition, this role is responsible for developing procedures that ensure workplace expenditures are coded effectively and correctly in alignment with funding restrictions, as well as responsible for establishing and monitoring controls to deter an individual from exploiting control regarding standardized methodologies for financial regulatory and identifying any unauthorized transactions. This includes reporting unauthorized transactions discovered to local police and providing efficient safeguards that protect against the loss or unauthorized use of workplace assets, especially data.[25]

Administrative management role and responsibilities:

- Oversee the development and implementation of policies and procedures relating to the management of workplace records, including all employee records. Assessing and auditing the scale of information security as it correlates with the storage of information and data in networks and information systems. Overseeing budget constraints and creating plans for goals and objectives. Furthermore, research explains that this role is responsible for recruiting and training staff, keeping track of projects, maintaining written records of all activities, deploying data analytics, working in alignment with external groups and organizations that can benefit the workplace, and building alliances with local authorities to ensure protection for C-suite executives and employees as needed.[26]

In addition, it is invaluable to consider the financial impact of this proposed technology management resolution. As pointed out previously, the integration of technology management through a shared partnership of services, that is, cloud Platform as a Service (PaaS) rendered by Amazon Web Services, requires assessing the cost and financial investment or burden. Thus, funding should be managed using a fixed rate to cover the cost, which is also considered a metered rate. This approach is pay-per-use and consumption-based pricing. Such a payment structure enables consumers to access unlimited resources and pay only for what they utilize, mirroring daily usage of utilities (e.g., gas, water, and electricity). Usage of cloud computing metered services relates to instances (virtual servers), where businesses need server storage and computing power. In this case, you will be utilizing cloud computing as a pay-as-you-use option. This enables you to acquire a fixed-rate, consistent billing structure. This also provides benefits such as cost savings and predictability, which aid in budgeting and financial planning, and scale usage of this platform. However, it is important to be aware of the disadvantages, including overrun cost, which can result from inconsistent control over cloud usage and over-provisioning. In other words, this can help you avoid wasting money unnecessarily. Therefore, it is imperative to increase the training of technology management staff responsible for managing these applications throughout the software lifecycle. Furthermore, technology management must be required to constantly monitor the usage of these applications to ensure they remain secure and are deployed as needed to ensure enhanced security capabilities are rendered.

One way to understand the costs of usage is to utilize the AWS pricing calculator. The examples provided below in each figure were initially developed for Calvin Technology University, where I estimated their cost of usage to determine their fixed rate. This approach enables Calvin Technology University to select the proposed cloud applications to integrate, including AWS CloudFront, AWS CloudFormation, AWS CloudWatch, and AWS Storage Gateway. Figures 2.1–2.4 display the costs of each service utilized based on the estimated cost of usage per application.

The above estimated total cost of usage for cloud computing with AWS, as configured for 12 months, is $96,661.68 USD. When you add in the cost of hiring two new IT staff members with a salary of $100,000 annually, each, and add the amount needed to train employees about the new cybersecurity leadership and technology management policies and train the IT staff utilizing a pay-as-you-go application, and the cost for usage of telecommunication services and utilities, the total estimated cost investment for Calvin Technology University would be a minimum $700,000 annually.

When referring to the cost of resources identified in alignment with the net present value that best fits this proposed project, it is essential to examine the financial return of this project and calculate the financial metrics by identifying project costs and estimated revenues. Estimated revenues can be

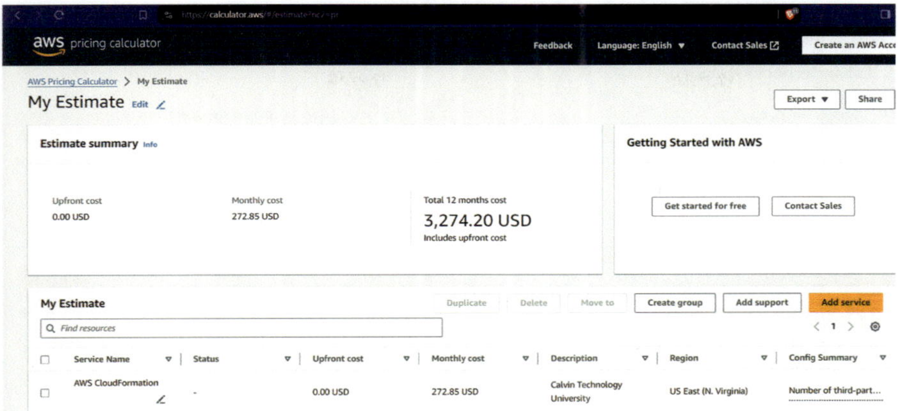

Figure 2.1 AWS CloudFormation.

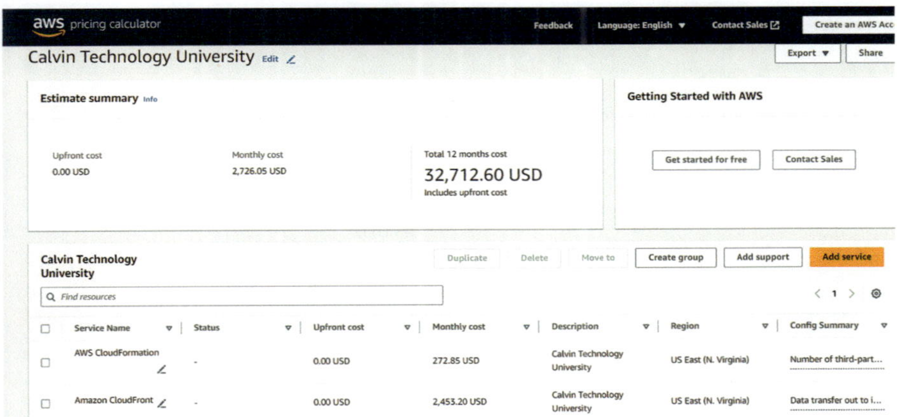

Figure 2.2 AWS CloudFront.

calculated by adding estimated profit and estimated cost. Estimated revenues are a forecasted figure defined by assumptions regarding future sales, costs, and profits.[27] Research explains that net present value requires the definition of the exact value of the cash flow to be discounted for each period considered in the evaluation. This value could be rather difficult, if not impossible, to determine for those innovative projects having great potential in the long run, but for which managers are unable to make a proper evaluation.

While estimated revenue is calculated by the number of new undergrad students that enroll annually, times the average cost of tuition for undergrad

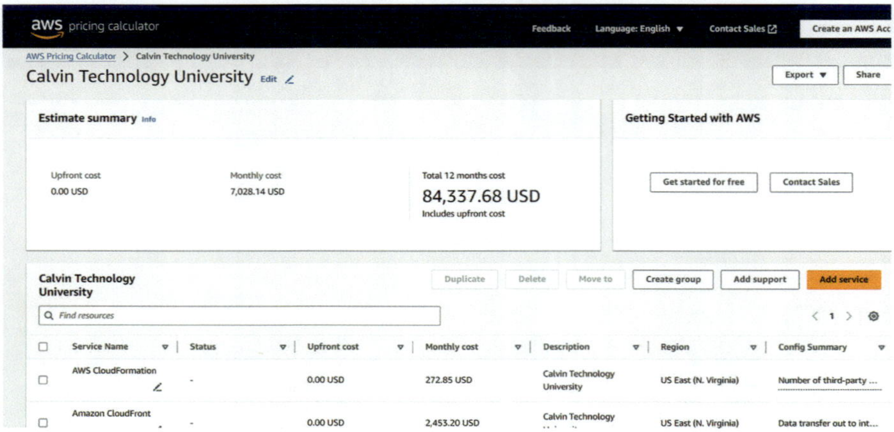

Figure 2.3 AWS CloudWatch.

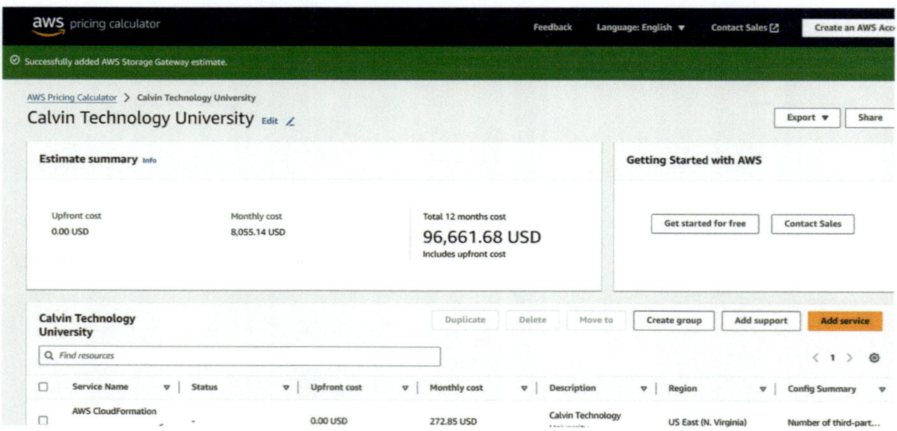

Figure 2.4 AWS Storage Gateway.

tuition per year, that is, $20,000. Tuition costs include $9600 for 24 credits a year, $1500 for books and technology fees, $6000 for room and board, $2400 for transportation, and $600 for miscellaneous. This also includes the cost to hire two new IT staff at $100,000 salary, $5000 for training cost, and the annual cost for flat-rate billing of telecommunication for international to national in-bound/out-bound service and national to international out-bound/in-bound, defined by the chosen gigabytes used for broadband and Wi-Fi usage per month, which can cost an estimated $6000 monthly.

Chart 2.1 Initial investment, estimated revenue, and NPV.

Project	Initial investment	Estimated revenue	NPV
Cloud computing	$97,000	$903,000	**$806,000**
Hire 2 IT staff	$100,000	$703,000	**$603,000**
Staff training (12 months)	$60,000	$643,000	**$583,000**
Telecommunication (12 months)	$48,000	$595,000	**$547,000**

OpenAI (2025). ChatGPT (4-Turbo). https://chatgpt.com/?model=auto

Determining the estimated revenue cost requires calculating the estimated number of undergrads, that is, a minimum of 50 new students, who would earn the institution $1,000,000 annually. When determining the initial investment cost for cloud computing at $97,000, the estimated revenue would be $903,000. Hiring two new IT staff members at $100,000 annually, the estimated revenue would be $703,000. Then the estimated revenue after staff training cost for 12 months at $60,000 would net $643,000. 12 months of telecommunication services at an estimated $4000 is $48,000, bringing the institution's net earnings of $595,000 annually.

Thus, Chart 2.1 provides details regarding the initial investment, estimated revenue, and net profit value.

Despite the net present value outcome for Calvin Technology University's investment in AWS applications, this depiction of net present value also enables you to understand the operational efficiency of integrating this proposed technology management resolution. Migrating to the cloud can support your workplace's ability to maintain daily business operations and communication with technology as a driving force, while decreasing the fears of victimization from cybercrime incidents from external attack agents. Usage of cloud solutions provides sophisticated controls and contributes to an agile and efficient ecosystem. These resolutions offer scalability, allowing your workplace to adapt to changing needs. Moreover, cloud platforms facilitate collaboration and support activities, fostering a dynamic and interactive work environment. The transition to cloud lowers demand for in-house IT resources and leads to improvements in cybersecurity leadership and technology management.

Part 2

Part 2 of this chapter focuses on the standardized policies and laws mentioned in the introduction. One of the most recognized US federal government agencies that publishes recommendations and guidelines for technology management is the National Institute of Standards and Technology (NIST).

Established by the US Department of Commerce, NIST publishes a special publication 800 series to address and render support for the security and privacy needs of US federal government information and information systems, as well as nonfederal information systems. One of the most prevalent laws that technology managers should be aware of is the Federal Information Security Modernization Act (FISMA) of 2014, 44 U.S.C. § 3551 *et seq.*, Public Law (P.L.) 113-283. However, while technology managers need to acknowledge and adhere to FISMA, aligning daily operations with NIST SP 800-series publications is voluntary. However, one specific policy recommendation to consider aligning with is NIST SP 800-171r3, *Protecting Controlled Unclassified Information in Nonfederal Information Systems and Organizations*.[28]

Aligning workplace internal policies with this special publication is important because it renders a clear understanding of the security protocols to consider when effectively securing information assets stored in information systems. Recommendations in this publication have been developed for three reasons. The first reason is considered valuable because both statutory and regulatory statutes are considered for the protection of controlled unclassified information (CUI) in federal and nonfederal information systems.[29] The second reason is also valuable because this policy helps safeguard controlled unclassified information (CUI) in non-federal and federal information systems and organizations. And third, because non-federal organizations can impose a variety of security resolutions to ensure security requirements are met.[30] Keep in mind, it is imperative to research these policies thoroughly to gain a clear understanding of what is required to efficiently protect information assets stored, transmitted, at rest, and secured by your workplace.

Additionally, this publication shares details about 17 parameters of focus that nonfederal organizations should align their security practices in correlation with CUI (controlled unclassified information). These parameters include:

- Access control
- Awareness and training
- Audit and accountability
- Configuration management
- Identification and authentication
- Incident response

- Maintenance
- Media protection
- Personnel security
- Physical protection
- Risk assessment
- Security assessment and monitoring
- Systems and communications protection
- System and information integrity
- Planning
- System and services acquisition
- Supply chain risk management

Understanding how to adopt these parameters into the framework of technology management in your workplace can be a daunting task. One way to achieve this goal is to develop a Key Parameters of Nonfederal Information Systems for the Workplace Table, and integrate each component you learned about in Chapter 1, with the Information Usage Profile.

Table 2.1 provides an example of what the table should resemble and what content should be included in alignment with NIST 800-171r3. Keep in mind, using NIST 800-171r3 as your guide to determine what content to add in your table is key to developing and managing an effective table of organization.

While Table 2.1 provides an outline of each key component, each individual workplace must assess these components to understand how to effectively manage them. It is imperative to understand that this table may not meet the needs of your workplace specifically. So, it is imperative for you to design a table that mirrors this outline and helps you organize your risk factor table with ease. Keep in mind, it is important to update this table as new technology, software, and hardware continue to be integrated. Otherwise, the risk, threats, and vulnerabilities can persist and create entrance points for external attackers to exploit and create increase of cost to rebuild your technology infrastructure. Knowing how to outline this table is why this example was provided. Always use NIST 800-171r3 as your guide. Be sure to read the entire guide to ensure you are adopting recommended procedures that support the needs of your unique workplace.

Table 2.1 Key parameters of non-federal information systems for the workplace.

Access control	Non-authorized and authorized. Non-authorized end-users should be granted access by an authorized end-user with administrative privileges. Credentials rendered by the authorized end-user should be temporary, unless otherwise required, and access codes should be deleted after a certain designated timeline and date to ensure security parameters are consistently met. List types of access controls, that is, active directory, web interface log-in, research databases, networks, computer devices, tablets, mobile apps, and Wi-Fi/internet/intranet.	*Risk levels*: Extremely high to medium, depending on the scale of access and to what level of controlled access is rendered, and for the purposes established. For instance, remote workers, hybrid workers, and temporary workers accessing the network.
Awareness and training	Technology management practitioners are required to develop, implement, and ensure assessment and auditing of any awareness and training they design and provide for executive leadership and employees. Training material should encompass all technological applications utilized to conduct daily business operations and communication, that is, telecommunication, software, hardware, computer devices, tablets, and mobile apps. When updates are implemented to the software, new training must be developed and provided to ensure all end-users are knowledgeable of their role and responsibilities to govern the new technology, if applicable. Assessments must be implemented to test the comprehension of end-users and ensure they are actively complying with their training.	*Risk levels*: Extremely high to medium, depending on the scale of technology training adoption. For instance, when installing a new software application that is universally used by executive leadership or employees, it is imperative that the risk level is extremely high. Neglecting to ensure training can create an entrance point for cyberattack incidents to occur.

Audit and accountability	All technology devices, software, and hardware must be audited to ensure consistency of security is applied and installed accurately. This decreases threats and vulnerabilities. Accountability is enforced to ensure all end-users and technology management practitioners are deploying usage practices as required in alignment with their workplace technology usage policies and procedures.	*Risk level*: Extremely high to medium because the lack of auditing enables human error to become a normal activity of acceptance that creates entrance points of external and internal cyber incidents.
Configuration management	Establishing a baseline of configuration settings on all technology software and hardware enables measures to later discover misconfigured to prove the accuracy of configuration settings, when correction is needed. Otherwise, there is an increased risk of unauthorized intrusion into all technology applications.	*Risk level*: Extremely high to medium. Neglecting to assess and align the configuration with risk factors can lead to vulnerabilities being exploitable.
Identification authentication (IA)	Identification factors embody username/passwords/biometrics utilized to represent who has authorization internally and externally. Lacking governance over these factors creates vulnerabilities that can be easily exploited. Increased IA helps control and minimize these factors. Also included is multi-factor authentication and encryption of identity authentication assets.	*Risk level*: Extremely high to medium. Neglecting to maintain risk control levels enables an ease of exploitability and lowers risk tolerance.
Incident response	Planning, discovering, assessing, containing, reporting, documenting, and recovery.	*Risk levels*: Extremely high to medium. Failing to maintain control over incidents and the outcome results is ineffective in timing response recovery.

(*Continued*)

Table 2.1 *Continued.*

Maintenance	Utilization of package sniffers, penetration testing, software modifiers, and assessing all technology hardware, tools, and devices must be updated as required and recommended to control risk factors and decrease vulnerabilities.	*Risk levels*: Extremely high to medium. This is important; lacking maintenance can enable exploitability. Assessing maintenance is required.
Media protection	External hard drives, USB hard drives, scan disk, magnetic drives, compact discs, and flash drives require the same level of encryption and back-up protection to maintain the security of these devices to maintain the integrity of usage for information storage.	*Risk levels*: Extremely high to low. Risk factors must be considered across each technology tool and device type. Aligning with recommended NIST guidelines to ensure security is effective.
Personnel security	Assessing each personnel's level of authorization to access sensitive databases hosting valuable information should include assessing the level of trust each end-user has and their scale of privilege. Neglecting to do so can result in increased risk and threats becoming extremely high-risk factors that lead to exploits.	*Risk levels*: Extremely high to medium. Personnel are human, errors can and will occur. Training personnel about security, risk, deterrence, and policy compliance reduces the risk of human error.
Physical protection	Entrance points, emergency exits, parking structure, building lighting, CCTV, cameras, entrance cards, and visitor logs.	*Risk levels*: Extremely high to medium. Ensuring all entrances to the building are secure and all assets stored in the building are stored securely. Ensuring limited access to files kept in-house is maintained with a discreet scale of security to protect assets from damage or confiscation.
Risk assessment	Maintain written logs of threats, vulnerabilities, and risks across all physical assets, digital assets, and technology assets, including software and hardware.	*Risk levels*: High to low. Risks are determined by the scale of importance and value of assets and data or information utilized.

Security assessment and monitoring	Effectively assess all technology tools, that is, hardware, software, cloud, multi-factor authentication, passwords, encryption, and back-up files to ensure all applications, software, and hardware are configured correctly and secured. Limited monitoring of security assessments can lead to vulnerabilities being exploited.	*Risk levels*: Extremely high to medium, because the origin of the service is security. Diminishing origin supports attackers' goals and ambitions. Conducting quarterly audits reduces threats. Maintain written records to ensure a comparison and align outcomes with policies.
Systems and communication protection	The information system, telecommunication, and electronic communication systems work in partnership to provide B2B/B2C communication. Ensuring proper cybersecurity leadership and technology management requires securing these applications and implementing effective planning, assessing, developing, and managing all systems securely. Evaluate the system, what software can be integrated? What configuration settings need to be updated? How will you ensure compliance with security policy integration?	*Risk levels*: High to low, because office telecommunications are third-party outsourced; this must ensure services are reliable and can be upgraded as needed. Must ensure all systems and communication tools are secured with recommended guidelines in NIST 800-171 and NIST 800-53. This also must align with domestic and international cyber laws.
System and information integrity	Operating in alignment with the CIA triad provides standardized risk control integrated in the framework and infrastructure of the system, and the responsibilities of the practitioner are outlined to manage the system. Adhering to standards in software and hardware management enables the system to operate efficiently with minor errors. Maintain written records of incidents, set baselines, and measure operability.	*Risk levels*: High. When the system has known vulnerabilities, it creates entrance points for external attackers to gain access and exploit the system. Integrity is a primary objective in securing the system, along with confidentiality and availability. Thus, the usage of standardized NIST guidelines enables rapid reboot.

(*Continued*)

Table 2.1 *Continued.*

Planning	Keeping current in trends of cyber incidents and responses deployed prepares you for incidents and provides a scale of measurement for baselines. Organizing the infrastructure, setting goals, and auditing plans help to minimize incidents. Training of all personnel is a must! Assessments must be made regularly.	*Risk level*: High. Unless planning is repetitive, human error often occurs, resulting in an increase in budget cost to increase security. Planning helps control risks and enforces the implementation of strategies to ensure all plans are achieved with standardized NIST-recommended guidelines.
Systems and services acquisition	Reiterate all actions deployed for planning, systems, and information integrity, system and communication protection, security assessment and monitoring, as well as risk assessments. Neglecting to do so will result in system vulnerabilities being exploited.	*Risk levels*: Extremely high to high. It is imperative that a consistency of security management is implemented, assessed, backed up, and updated as recommended to maintain full-scale security to ensure no component of the system is penetrable.
Supply chain risk management	Service language agreements rendered by third-party service and product providers are key components to ensure all software and hardware relied on is authenticated and ensures the service and product providers are adherent to domestic and international laws and policies relating to risk factors integrated in the usage of technology, software, and hardware. Enforcing awareness training as a method of managing risk factors can be essential to protecting the workplace from external and internal cyber risks and cyberattack incidents.	*Risk levels*: Extremely high to medium. Risk levels can be assessed to determine the scope of the threat to your workplace, which enables improvements to security vulnerabilities. Lacking the ability to stay current with trends of security vulnerabilities woven into software and hardware will result in system breaches. Awareness training is key to reducing threats and mitigating vulnerabilities.

NIST 800-172 focuses on *Enhancing Security Requirements for Protecting Controlled Unclassified Information*. This is a supplement to 800-171r3. However, understanding the purpose of this publication and how it correlates with your unique workplace is key to aligning the recommendations with securing CUI in your workplace. This publication conveys that it was published specifically to enhance security requirements for non-federal storage, usage, transmission, and security of controlled unclassified information in information systems. Enhanced security measures are provided to help thwart successful persistent attacks. However, this publication does not provide controlled regulations regarding what specific information assets should be classified as high, low, at risk, or potentially at risk of theft during a successful cyberattack.[31] To gain a more in-depth understanding of how this publication should be applied to your workplace and its usage of technology applications, be sure to review this publication. It is important to review Chapters 2 and 3. Chapter 2 conveys some assumptions that are utilized to develop enhanced security that should protect CUI, and shares recommendations to apply security across the organization and its technology infrastructure. Chapter 3 conveys 14 families of security enhancements to be considered effective when protecting nonfederal information systems.

NIST 800-137A enables you to assess information security continuous monitoring (ISCM) programs by sharing concepts of developing an ISCM program in your workplace. This publication is useful because it enables you to improve the development of strategies, policies, procedures, operations, and analysis for information security.[32] Specifically, it is imperative to understand that this publication is useful in supporting the control of cyber risk factors and security posture, threats, and vulnerabilities. This publication also aligns with NIST SP 800-37 regarding *Risk Management Framework for Information Systems and Organizations Life Cycle Approach for Security and Privacy* and NIST 800-39, *Managing Information Security Risk: Organization, Mission, and Information System View*.[33] More importantly, this publication can be helpful in developing an ISCM program that aligns specifically with your workplace. Focusing on the proposed outlined process of developing an ISCM program for your workplace is vital. Thus, it is suggested you review every step in the process found on pages 29–48. In doing so, you will ensure you have clarity of what is required of you to meet the recommendations and to decrease potential threats and vulnerabilities that may arise in the future.

NIST SP 800-53A Rev.5 focuses on *Assessing Security and Privacy Controls for Information Systems and Organizations,* and NIST SP 800-53 Rev.5 focuses on *Security and Privacy Controls for Information Systems and Organizations*. The latter was published in January 2022, which is the updated revision from the previous final edition. When assessing these documents, take time to comb through them to find the revisions to ensure you are not missing any vital information that could be useful for your specific workplace. This publication is useful because it provides details about assessing third-party vendor relations and enhancing security control and privacy policy, and regulatory compliance in the workplace. The target audience of this publication includes any person responsible for managing risk, security, privacy, and information systems. Adhering to the requirements of managing information systems can be a daunting task. But knowing how to overcome the obstacles of managing information systems can be eased when you rely on the recommended guidelines rendered in this publication.

NIST 800-60r2 *Guide for Mapping Types of Information and Systems to Security Categories* is an initial draft, but usage of this publication is essential to staying current with updates and recommendations to help support the reliance of information systems and the security required to ensure that such is protected from unauthorized users. Published in January 2024, this publication delivers clarity regarding the classification of sensitive information. This can be considered unique information because each workplace collects its own type of vital and critical information. The type of services and products rendered by each unique workplace forces each entity to define specific categories for its own information and data assets. This publication will help you organize your information and data assets based on the level of security required. From high-level security to low-level security, your workplace may align the details of clients' names with the type of products or services each client receives from your workplace. Furthermore, utilizing this publication will enable you to improve your ability to control risk.

However, unless you take a serious approach to master the recommendations and guidelines in your workplace and align your strategies and methodologies with the recommendations and guidelines of NIST special publications. Results will differ from those anticipated because there are unique barriers that impact the actual outcome of usage results. Therefore, being diligent in updating software and hardware is important. Maintaining lifelong relationships with product and service partners that you purchase software and hardware from helps as well. Keeping clearly conveyed records that outline issues as they occur also plays a role in how effective the usage of this policy and others will be. As you review this policy, be sure to assess other recommended policies. Doing so will enhance your ability to adopt innovative methods of improving the security of your information system.

Take, for instance, on page 7 of this publication, are recommended steps to take to assign levels of security to categorization of data and information system assets. Each of the four steps discussed is outlined for you to adopt and integrate. Adhering to these recommended steps will help improve the outcome of security controls. Step 3.1 helps you assign security methodologies for security levels.[34] Step 3.2 helps you to determine the information type and level of impact. Step 3.3 enables you to assign a system category, and Step 3.4 instructs how to document the security categorization process. Staying aware of the updates published in these policies will enable you to stay current and keep your information system managed effectively and securely.

Take, for instance, the reliance of artificial intelligence on technology management for decision support has become vital to managing information systems. The NIST AI-600-1 is a newly introduced special publication that cannot be ignored. Published in July 2024, this publication titled *Artificial Intelligence Risk Management Framework: Generative Artificial Intelligence Profile* was introduced to support workplace IT practitioners with assessing risk correlating with data privacy, human–AI configuration, information integrity, information security, intellectual property, and value chain integration. Thus, this publication will support your workplace in determining how to integrate AI with your current information system.[35]

Policies are not the only regulatory that technology management managers need to be aware of. The laws enacted by Congress and the President during the Biden Administration, in alignment with National Security matters, are critical components to supporting the workplace to avoid victimization of cyberattacks. Previously enacted laws that technology managers must adhere to and understand include HIPAA. The Health Insurance Portability and Accountability Act sets standards for healthcare organizations and any other organization that collects, stores, transmits, or hosts private data and information about individuals' health and medical information.

The Gramm–Leach–Bliley Act requires financial institutions to report how they share, store, and secure personal information collected from applications for loans, financial and investment advice, or insurance.[36] This law provides details regarding key components of the Safeguard Rule/Section 314.4. This policy will support you in conducting a risk assessment as it correlates with financial information. This will also enable you to improve the training of staff and how they should be aware of security risks associated with the data and information assets compiled relating to the financial details of consumers.

Another important law is the US Department of Homeland Security Act or Federal Information Security Modernization Act, which is a US government-focused law. However, this law should be a component in your research because it helps you improve the coordination and management of federal information in nonfederal information systems. While these laws may have been enacted some years ago, they are still prevalent in securing information and data assets in the workplace.

Additional invaluable laws you should assess to determine if your workplace is held accountable to in correlation with information security and technology management in the workplace, include the British Columbia Personal Information Protection Act, General Data Protection Regulation, the Personal Information Protection and Electronic Documents Act, and the Australian Privacy Principles/Privacy Act.

The British Columbia Personal Information Protection Act was published to impose security measures that must be practiced to govern the collection, use and disclosure of personal information by organizations in a manner that recognizes both the right of individuals to protect their personal information and the need of organizations to collect, use or disclose personal information for purposes that a reasonable person would consider appropriate in the circumstances.[37] If your workplace is collecting, storing, transmitting, or securing information and data assets belonging to Canadian civilians, your workplace is accountable to this law. The same applies to the General Data Protection Regulation.

The European Union enacted the General Data Protection Regulation (GDPR) as a method to control the storage, collection, transmission, and sharing of European Union citizens' personal information. The GDPR will levy harsh fines against those who violate its privacy and security standards, with penalties reaching into the tens of millions of euros.[38] To ensure your workplace is aligning usage of personal information belonging to EU citizens, requires assessing this law and reviewing the actions of service or product delivery rendered by your workplace, as such correlates with this law. Processing data belonging to EU citizens under this law must be done as stated in this law. Specifications include transparency and fairness, purpose with limitation, data minimization, accuracy in data collection and storage, integrity and confidentiality, and accountability. This aligns with the CIA triad.

Next, the Australian Privacy Principles/Privacy Act of 1988, requires effective management and control of individuals' privacy relating to their consumer credit reports, tax filing numbers, and health or medical records.[39]

Like the GDPR, the Australian Privacy Principles/Privacy Act regulates how domestic and international workplaces collect, share, transmit, and secure personal information belonging to Australian citizens. Therefore, knowing what is required and how to organize, categorize, and secure personal information assets and data is invaluable to reducing the risk your workplace is held accountable for and can be liable for, if found in violation of this law.

Conclusion

This chapter is supportive in guiding you toward comprehending what National Institute of Standards and Technology policies you need to be knowledgeable of to prevent your workplace from being held liable or accountable for violation of the privacy protection of consumer data or information. While the usage of these policies is voluntary, knowing how to align these policies with your workplace policies is crucial to reducing risk associated with data or information storage, collection, transmission, and security of data or information assets at rest.

This chapter also prepared you to assess risk factors aligning with key components of your workplace using the Key Parameters of Nonfederal Information Systems for the Workplace table. You also gained knowledge about the AWS pricing calculator to determine the cost of usage. Understanding this information and how to assess the total cost of ownership for integrating AWS cloud applications as components to your information system for information storage and security.

Being a technology manager is challenging when you limit what resources you integrate into your workplace information system. Having a guide and relying on recommendations delivered through industry standardizations enacted by the US Congress and global political and legal agencies is key to reducing the number of targeted cyberattacks against your workplace.

Additionally, you gained knowledge to improve how you align trends of technology management in your office. But most importantly, you learned the significance of how federal laws, policy, and regulations must be applied and adopted to help you protect the information assets of your workplace. Using an Information Usage Profile Table from Chapter 1 is a benefit that helps you outline and detail key parameters of non-federal information systems. Adopting these recommended processes, methods, and strategies outlined in this chapter is not a 100% way to stop cyberattacks. Instead, this enables you to stay current with trends in managing the technology in your workplace, as it aligns with confidentiality, integrity, and accountability. This can also be useful in helping you reduce the cost of expenditure on useless technology software that may not be compatible with the current technology woven into your information system. To reiterate what you learned, below are chapter review questions. Answers to these questions can be found behind the references for this chapter.

Chapter 2 Review Questions

1. In 2024, CrowdStrike published a global threat report conveying what?
2. According to CrowdStrike, what percentage of ransomware attacks were deployed between 2022 and 2024?
3. Mismanagement of technology in the workplace is commonly known to be what?
4. What is one proposed technology management resolution you should consider?
5. What does Amazon Web Services deliver?
6. What is one of the most recognized US federal government agencies that publishes recommendations and guidelines for technology management?
7. Why is it imperative to research all integrated software applications?
8. What NIST special publication recommendation policy protects controlled unclassified information in nonfederal information systems and organizations?
9. What does NIST 800-60r2 represent?
10. What does NIST AI-600-1 represent?
11. What did the European Union enact the GDPR?
12. What does NIST 800-172 represent?

References

[1] Kurtz, G. (2024). Global Threat Report. https://cyberpeople.tech/reports/GlobalThreatReport2024.pdf
[2] Ibid

[3] IT Governance, (2024, May 2). Global Data Breaches and Cyber Attacks in 2024. https://www.itgovernance.co.uk/blog/global-data-breaches-and-cyber-attacks-in-2024
[4] George, J. (2008). Significance of technology management and project management aligned with portfolio management is vital for any project-based organization. https://www.pmi.org/learning/library/technology-project-management-aligned-7144
[5] Doffman, Z. (2025, March 19). Microsoft's Update Decision-New Warning for 800 Million Windows Users. https://www.forbes.com/sites/zakdoffman/2025/03/19/microsofts-update-decision-new-warning-for-800-million-windows-users/
[6] Microsoft (2024, August 13). Windows Secure Kernel Mode Elevation of Privilege Vulnerability. https://msrc.microsoft.com/update-guide/vulnerability/CVE-2024-21302
[7] Ibid
[8] Ibid
[9] Microsoft, (n.d.). KB5028407: How to manage the vulnerability associated with CVE-2023-32019. [Website] https://support.microsoft.com/en-us/topic/kb5028407-how-to-manage-the-vulnerability-associated-with-cve-2023-32019-bd6ed35f-48b1-41f6-bd19-d2d97270f080
[10] Ibid
[11] 6 Sense, (2025). Apache. https://6sense.com/tech/web-and-application-servers/apache-market-share
[12] Ibid
[13] Ibid
[14] Apache, (2024, April 4). Apache HTTP Server 2.4 Vulnerabilities. https://httpd.apache.org/security/vulnerabilities_24.html
[15] Ibid
[16] National Vulnerability Database, (2024, May 29). CVE-2024-6768. https://nvd.nist.gov/vuln/detail/CVE-2024-6768
[17] CVE.mitre.org, (2024). CVE-2024-21381. https://cve.mitre.org/cgi-bin/cvename.cgi?name=CVE-2024-21381
[18] Ibid
[19] National Institute of Standards and Technology, (2023, April 14). NIST Special Publication 800-63 Digital Identity Guidelines. https://www.nist.gov/identity-access-management/nist-special-publication-800-63-digital-identity-guidelines
[20] Sail Point, (2024, March 5). Compromised credentials: How they lead to data breaches. https://www.sailpoint.com/identity-library/how-compromised-credentials-lead-to-data-breaches/

[21] Cybersecurity Infrastructure & Security Agency, (2024). Update Business Software. https://www.cisa.gov/secure-our-world/update-business-software
[22] McNeley, C. (2025). Key Considerations for C-Suite Leaders Involved in Digital Transformation Initiatives. https://uhy-us.com/insights/news/2024/june/key-considerations-for-c-suite-leaders-involved-in-digital-transformation-initiatives#:~:text=It's%20crucial%20that%20C%2Dsuite,is%20responsive%20and%20agile%20by:
[23] POPOV, C. (2024, September 24). How Remote Employees Can Cause a Data Breach of Your Small Business Data (And How to Prevent It). https://www.bitdefender.com/en-us/blog/hotforsecurity/how-remote-employees-can-cause-a-data-breach-of-your-small-business-data-and-how-to-prevent-it
[24] Golunenko, S. (2019, April 5). HR or Operations: Who Should Be Responsible for Employee Training in An Organization? https://elearningindustry.com/hr-or-operations-who-should-be-responsible-for-employee-training-in-an-organization
[25] Nicastro, D. (2019, August 20). Should Your Human Resource Team Be Working More Closely with IT? https://www.reworked.co/digital-workplace/should-your-human-resources-team-be-working-more-closely-with-it/
[26] UC Berkeley, (2024). Financial Management. https://compliance.berkeley.edu/responsibilities-guide/financial-management#:~:text=Financial%20management%20responsibility%20includes%20budgeting,structure%2C%20and%20safeguarding%20University%20assets
[27] Ibid
[28] Calculator Academy Team, (2024, March 28). Expected Revenue Calculator. https://calculator.academy/expected-revenue-calculator/
[29] National Institute of Standards and Technology, (2018, May 21). NIST Special Publication 800-series General Information. [Website] https://www.nist.gov/itl/publications-0/nist-special-publication-800-series-general-information
[30] National Institute of Standards and Technology, (2024, May). Protecting Controlled Unclassified Information in Nonfederal System and Organizations. https://nvlpubs.nist.gov/nistpubs/SpecialPublications/NIST.SP.800-171r3.pdf
[31] Ibid
[32] Ibid
[33] National Institute of Standards and Technology, (2020, May). Assessing Information Security Continuous Monitoring (ISCM)

Programs: Developing an ISCM Assessment. https://csrc.nist.gov/pubs/sp/800/137/a/final
[34] Ibid
[35] National Institute of Standards and Technology, (2024, January). Guide for Mapping Types of Information and Systems to Security Categories. https://nvlpubs.nist.gov/nistpubs/SpecialPublications/NIST.SP.800-60r2.iwd.pdf
[36] National Institute of Standards and Technology, (2024, July). Artificial Intelligence Risk Management Framework: Generative Artificial Intelligence Profile. https://nvlpubs.nist.gov/nistpubs/ai/NIST.AI.600-1.pdf
[37] Sweeney, G. (2025, March 24). Top Cybersecurity Laws and Regulations to Know and About in 2025. https://www.marconet.com/blog/cybersecurity-laws-and-regulations
[38] King's Printer, (2025, April). Personal Information Protection Act [SBC 2003]. https://www.bclaws.gov.bc.ca/civix/document/id/complete/statreg/00_03063_01#section2
[39] European Union, (2025). What is GDPR, the EU's new data protection law? https://gdpr.eu/what-is-gdpr/#:~:text=History%20of%20the%20GDPR,were%20required%20to%20be%20compliant.
[40] Australian Government, (n.d.). The Privacy Act. https://www.oaic.gov.au/privacy/privacy-legislation/the-privacy-act

Chapter 2 Review Question Answers

1. Businesses need to be mindful of the innovative approaches cybercriminals are deploying to gain access to sensitive data assets and information stored on vulnerable networks.
2. 75%.
3. A human error issue.
4. Enhancing existing solutions to improve cybersecurity leadership.
5. A reduction of cost per usage, analyzes data, and supports 98 security standards and compliance certifications.
6. The National Institute of Standards and Technology.
7. To ensure these applications are configured as recommended by the software developer and product providers.

8. NIST SP 800-171r3.
9. Guide for mapping types of information and systems to security categories.
10. Artificial Intelligence Risk Management Framework: Generative Artificial Intelligence Profile.
11. To control the storage, collection, transmission, and sharing of European Union citizens' personal information.
12. Enhancing security requirements for protecting controlled unclassified information.

3

Threat Modeling

Learning objectives

- Assess threat modeling.
- Assess threat modeling diagramming.
- Distinguish between technology management and threat modeling.
- Distinguish commercial threat modeling tools.

Chapter 2 provides information to enable you to understand how to assess and distinguish technology management guidelines and acknowledge technology management standardizations, including policies, laws, and regulations. You also learned how to align trends of technology management with your workplace, and you now understand the benefits of adhering to technology management guidelines and recommendations published by the National Institute of Standards and Technology. More importantly, you learned how to distinguish guidelines that protect information assets and information system databases. This knowledge is a surface scope of how much skills and information you need to know to effectively maintain control threats embodied in the technology hardware, software, and devices your workplace utilizes for daily business communication and operation. However, an additional key component to effective technology management is threat modeling. Adam Shostack introduced his approach to threat modeling in his debut book titled *Threat Modeling: Designing for Security*. Since its introduction in 2014, threat modeling has gained popularity among cybersecurity, information security, and assurance practitioners. Lacking knowledge to effectively develop a threat model infrastructure for your workplace is daunting when threat modeling is your support system in thwarting attacks. Therefore, this chapter is designed to help you meet your goals of threat modeling in three ways. First, you will distinguish what threat modeling is. Second, you will assess how to develop

DOI: 10.1201/9788743809715-3

a threat model diagram. Third, you will architect a technology management threat model for your workplace. More importantly, you will distinguish which threat model meets the needs of your technology management. To help reiterate your learning and comprehension of this chapter, review questions are available at the end. Answers to these review questions can be discovered after the reference list.

Adam Shostack developed a useful way to assess threats integrated in technology through threat modeling. Threat modeling embodies utilizing a diagram to improve how to discover security problems in the technology your workplace relies on for business communication and operation. When using a threat model, you are abstracting details to thoroughly examine all technology tools relied on in the workplace through a broader scope. This is beyond measuring software coding flaws. Threat models are useful because they enable us to discover problems prior to problems occurring.[1]

Microsoft Corporation provides an example of a threat model. You can review this example and align it with your own approach to developing a threat model for your workplace. Microsoft Corporation explains that threat modeling is an element of the Microsoft Security Development Lifecycle.[2] Microsoft Corporation also explains that threat modeling is an engineering technique that enables you to identify vulnerabilities, threats, and attacks, prior to these weaknesses being exploited by cyberattackers. However, no two threat models are identical. What is discovered as a threat or vulnerability in one workplace is not the same threat or vulnerability identified in another.

Thus, it is important to assess the threats, vulnerabilities, and attack weaknesses in the technology applications, software, and hardware integrated in your information system network. To effectively do so, you must define a threat model to thwart and deter successful unauthorized intrusion of your workplace technology hardware, software, cloud services, platform, or infrastructure. Keep in mind that while it is assumed that any third-party cloud provider your workplace partners with, it is not a guarantee that the efforts implemented by your third-party partner will stop an attacker from gaining access to your information system and exploiting weaknesses. So, to assure you of the benefits of threat modeling, assessing Microsoft's threat model as an example should encourage you to take an active role in understanding threat modeling and utilizing this model for your workplace. Microsoft Corporation reports that there are five steps to threat modeling:

- Defining security requirements that align with your workplace technology.
- Developing your threat model diagram.

- Identifying threats.
- Mitigating those threats.
- Acknowledging that all threats have been contained and mitigated effectively.

You can view more about Microsoft Corporation's threat modeling at the following URL: https://www.microsoft.com/en-us/securityengineering/sdl/threatmodeling

When you design your threat model to fit your technological needs, you gain a better understanding of what your security requirements are. The first step to develop this threat model is to develop a threat model flowchart. Usage of shapes is a dynamic approach that helps create a diagram that can be upgraded as needed throughout the lifecycle of the system. The diagram outlined below includes key variables of the STRIDE methodology (e.g., Spoofing, Tampering, Repudiation, Information Disclosure, Denial of Service Attack, and Elevation of Privilege). Figure 3.1 is an example of the diagram you will develop.

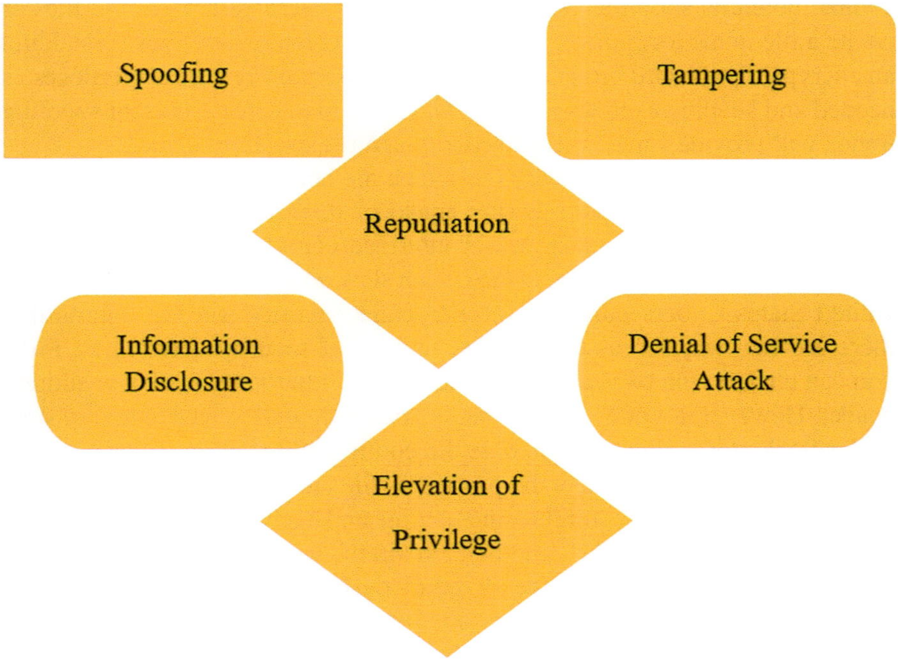

Figure 3.1 Threat model flowchart.

Spoofing occurs when an external intruder gains information about an executive leader or personnel member and successfully exploits that information to gain entrance into the network, information system, and technology tools to unleash malicious activities. Malicious activity can involve installing malware and/or worms, viruses, Trojans, and, in some instances, ransomware. One way to deter the existence of malicious malware requires defining a method to assess ways an external intruder may attempt to use this approach to gain entrance into your system. To successfully outthink the attacker, you need to think like the attacker.

For instance, what information is readily available on the organization's web interface. Often, companies and organizations list the names of personnel on their website interface. This provides sensitive details for website viewers to learn more about each person with a virtual employee bio page. Commonly posted are employee names, their role, and their work email address.

Thus, it is recommended to avoid adding these vital information resources on the web interface so an external site visitor cannot collect data and information that provides them the opportunity to use this information maliciously. Only authorized internal personnel should have access to this information. Furthermore, account control on the organization's computer system will help combat potential spoofing. After all, an attacker could gain access to files or create a file in the local directory. This includes creating new files and adding an encrypted password protection to each one. Rendering access privileges as needed and keeping executive leaders and staff up to date on current spoofing trends will provide some layer of security against spoofing incidents.

Knowing the layer of malicious attack methods cybercriminals use will provide the leverage needed to stay ahead of their sophisticated, nefarious efforts. To increase security on the web interface, encryption should be applied. Usage of Security Socket Layers (SSL) can slow down external attackers. The United States Cybersecurity & Infrastructure Security Agency reports that there are two ways to assess the authenticity of security certificates. First, you can click on the padlock icon positioned next to the https://www address header. However, if your web browser is not configured to enable you to view the padlock, you will need to update the configuration settings to access this lock. Secondly, you can view the properties file and security options.[3] Doing so will enable you to configure the setting and view this icon. Figure 3.2 shows an example of an SSL padlock icon in the web address.

The next flowchart of the diagram design is tampering. Tampering involves extracting data files as they are transmitted across the internet, internally and externally. For instance, when emails are sent across the intranet and internet, the content can be viewed, extracted, manipulated, and distorted

Figure 3.2 Example of SSL padlock icon.

to present the receiver with a different scope of data or information than the sender sent. To deter this, it is recommended to implement encryption on all email messages. Utilizing encryption provides a layer of security. Another benefit is the use of public and private key systems. This key system enables the key sender to maintain control of both private and public key encryption/decryption, authentication, and to send the receiver a private key to decrypt the encrypted information. This key enables the email receiver to unlock the data files and review the data content without concerns of message tampering.

Each email message is assigned a unique time stamp and date. An example of an email time stamp is Sun, Sep 1, 4:32 PM (5 days ago). However, this example was collected from a Google email account. Microsoft Outlook email time stamps are displayed differently, that is, Thu 9/5/2024 2:00 PM. So, when investigating potential cyberattack incidents captured through email, knowing when an email was sent enables you to assess the length of time it took for that email to arrive.

Microsoft Corporation conveys that when assessing what time an email was sent versus when it was delivered, collect the message header, and in the Outlook desktop recipient inbox, click the email, File<properties, and copy all the internet headers>; paste the copied message in the header analyzer. You can access that analyzer at the following URL: https://mha.azurewebsites.net/pages/mha.html

Click on the analyzer button to acquire the results.[4] You should see the time the email message was sent and the time it was delivered. Often, if there is a long delay in delivery, there is evidence of tampering.

Research reported by Hacker News in 2024 under the header, A deep dive into email deliverability in 2024, it is conveyed by an anonymous poster that considering the weight of trust consumers invest in "Gmail," "Outlook," and "Yahoo" email, what if someone deployed a different type of attack on business entities and classify it as "targeted failed deliverability." This attack model involves a victim (particularly a business or mailing list, or NGO) that sends out bulk emails to which the attacker has access. Even sourcing this out to shady offshore click farms would work too. An attacker marks a victim's email as Spam in a Gmail/Yahoo/Outlook account. The artificial intelligence Spam filter attaches this email as a new Spam activity and marks all future emails as Spam prior to such emails reaching real customers. This can impact an organization's email marketing and advertising budget because it impedes their ability to effectively manage how many of their emails are being delivered and read, or classified as Spam and deleted. This leads to ditching email marketing altogether.[5]

Additional research reports that the usage of email deliverability testing is becoming a beneficial way to ensure emails are delivered as intended. Glock Apps reports quarterly email deliverability testing results on some popular email service providers, including Google, Mailgun, Outlook, Amazon SES, and SendGrid. In 2023, Google rated 41% and Outlook rated 13%.[6] In 2024, Google rated 37% and Outlook rated 12%. Both email service providers rate high in deliverability, but Google outranks Outlook. However, according to Glock Apps research, the top 10 email service providers (ESP) with the highest inbox deliverability includes Mimecast with 76%, AWeber with 58%, Hubspot with 57%, Klaviyo with 56%, Amazon SES with 54%, GoDaddy with 54%, Mailgun with 53%, Mailchimp with 51%, Mailjet with 51%, and Dotmailer with 50%.[7] This shows an increase in consumer trust in ESP brands often ignored, and certainly shows that Google and Outlook are falling behind these brands in providing email deliverability with minimal tampering.

Microsoft Outlook has become a "go-to" for many business email accounts. Research reports in 2024 there were eight reported known vulnerabilities associated with the usage of Outlook email accounts, including remote execution vulnerability, spoofing vulnerability, and elevation of privilege.[8] In 2023, the US Department of Defense Common Vulnerability and Exposure (CVE) library reported these vulnerabilities existed 10 times. In 2022, the CVE reported these vulnerabilities five times, as well as three times in 2021. Seemingly, Outlook continues experiencing vulnerabilities that place consumers at risk of victimization.

Usage of encryption on email services should be introduced as a primary option regardless of the email service provider chosen. Making sure the email service provider renders reliable encryption on email should be a priority to ensure all email content is secured and delivered as needed. Not only will this reduce tampering. This will protect confidentiality.

The next flowchart figure is repudiation. Repudiation requires reassessing all previously deployed steps to ensure effective deployment of security and technology management is applied and that nothing is overlooked or ignored in protecting information assets from email tampering. This reduces the risks of spoofing. When applied to technology management, it is crucial to be aware of system failures, which could result in entrance points being exploited. Thus, it cannot be stressed enough the value of maintaining updates on all technology tools, hardware, and software. Making sure back-ups are done as required by the proposed plan implemented during the installation of new and current utilized technology hardware, software, and devices is necessary.

Research explains that a repudiation attack occurs when any application or system is not effectively controlling and properly tracking end-users' actions via log reports. This can enable malicious manipulation or forging new attack actions. Such an attack can be deployed to modify the authoring information of methods executed by a malicious end-user to log incorrect data to log files. This can also be extended to general data manipulation using the names of others, like spoofing email messages.[9] When this attack method is successful, it invalidates and renders misleading log report data. Since repudiation encompasses gaining clarity on what has occurred and how the issue was discovered, securing enough evidence to decipher what has occurred helps comprehend the problem. Therefore, it is imperative to maintain effective written logs and reports that include records for research. Adding protective layers of security to make sure logs are secure and non-rewritable will enable better security and decrease the chance of any technology hardware, software, or device from being breached.

In fact, due to Information Disclosure, you must strive to maintain control over network accessibility. This can be achieved by implementing User Access Accounts, that is, administrators. This also includes technology access control, including Group Policy, which can effectively control users' scripts for logging on and off the system, folder redirection, and browser settings, as well as account restrictions. Additional steps should include installing and maintaining updates on the Firewall and servers, as well as any embedded operating systems. Because the network could face flooding in a denial-of-service attack, you should evaluate exhaustible resources and work to ensure that resource consumption is greater. This will make any attempt at a brute-force attack impossible.

Consistently deploying penetration testing provides a clear approach to managing and controlling potential threats and vulnerabilities that could harm the workplace website interface. However, technology management must include investigating the web interface for potential malware, spyware, or rootkits.

Spyware is deployed through software downloaded on a computer or network without evidence of its presence. Research reports that this software is relied on to gather information from a device and end-user to send to a third-party without written consent. Not knowing if spyware is installed on the network or a computer can impact the success of effective technology management.

Rootkits are also malicious software installed without being easily identified. Rootkits enable attackers to remotely access the device and control it. Research reports this software can be on a device without the device owner knowing he/she is being surveillance. This software can track your keystrokes, enabling spies to collect your passwords as you input them to access emails.

Therefore, you must effectively install secure components that can prevent unauthorized access and prevent interruptions from occurring. This also provides leverage in protecting the operating system. This is why Elevation of Privilege is included in the flowchart. Ensuring all executive leaders and personnel members are trained and aware of their authorized access to network resources they need to meet their job responsibilities can prevent unauthorized access to sensitive data. This is why information assurance technology risk management control is necessary to protect from internal and external threats and/or unauthorized intrusion.

As discussed previously, defining policies that stipulate authority levels and setting perimeters as to what authorized access should be granted and to whom, when necessary, must be considered. Defining a STRIDE Threat Model and maintaining effective, clearly written logs and reports will be an ongoing process to control potential threats and vulnerabilities that may affect daily operations. When updating the flowchart diagram, it must include the following security infrastructures:

- Focus on the flow of data.
- Add more details and/or construction to the flowchart process as necessary.
- Demonstrate any changes, instead of pre-writing instruction. Provide clear step-by-step processes of what happened, who helped it happen, what time they did the change, and the date of such changes.
- Make sure the diagram conveys a clear storyline of what has been going on and how it's been defined.

Table 3.1 provides an example of a STRIDE Threat Model that can be adopted and defined to meet the needs of any workplace. Keep in mind that technology hardware, software, and types of devices differ. Thus, it is important to define your STRIDE Threat Model efficiently with your specific needs.

Staying up to date with trends in cyberattack incidents and human error incidents will help you maintain a STRIDE Threat Model; you can modify it as needed with the upgrading of new technology, as well as with the omission of any technology that becomes obsolete. The description for each category of this

Table 3.1 STRIDE Threat Model.

STRIDE	Threat	Vulnerabilities	Risks and controls
Spoofing	Someone accesses the Windows OS without authorization, impersonating an executive leader or personnel member, and utilizes a default password or deploys a human error incident.	Malicious software is downloaded and unleashes malware on the intranet system.	*Risk*: This can cause a monetary impact and reputational damage. *Control*: To deter this, you should secure data by updating passwords monthly. And ensure everyone is trained as needed to know how to recognize these types of attacks and how to respond to such attacks.
Tampering	An external hacker gains access and confiscates usernames/passwords, accessing secure files on peripherals, and as files are transmitted across the Internet.	Unauthorized intrusion of data files. Network flooded with malware, viruses, worms, or Trojans.	*Risk*: Data files are misconfigured and lack authenticity, which corrupts the organization's reputation. *Control*: Keep passwords updated and implement multi-factor authentication and encryption on all email services.
Repudiation	Misconfiguration of software and hardware creates an entrance point for a cyberattack or cyber incident.	Employee downloads or accesses malicious software that embodies ransomware or malware. Website experiences a distributed denial of service attack.	*Risk*: Sensitive data and files become compromised. *Control*: This requires the implementation of encryption and password protection, which must be deployed on all data files.

(*Continued*)

Table 3.1 *Continued.*

STRIDE	Threat	Vulnerabilities	Risks and controls
Information disclosure	The fax or printer is hacked, causing data to be compromised. Lack of updates deployed on Windows OS enables attackers to gain access to sensitive data files.	Missed updates and lacking effective back-up archives create an entrance point that can be exploited by external attackers when he/she/they/them discover vulnerabilities exposed.	*Risk*: Unauthorized intrusion caused by configuring system security. *Control*: Utilization of a Firewall and ensuring all updates are deployed as required can control this risk. Also, manage back-ups effectively and correctly.
Denial of service	Website interface sabotage, blocking end-users' usage of the Web applications.	Firewall is not kept up to date; default passwords are not updated as needed, and required to ensure effective security is deployed to thwart attacks.	*Risk*: Non-accessibility. *Control*: Requires updating and managing authenticated Security Socket Layers (SSL) on all web pages and upgrading and configuring the system regularly.
Elevation of privilege	User access control policies and penalties for non-compliance.	Internal and external human error create weaknesses in securing Windows 11. This can impact other technology devices, including fax/printer machines and the telecommunication, that is, VOIP phone system.	*Risk*: Can cause unauthorized intrusion and cause monetary impact. *Control*: Risk management control, which should include policies and non-compliance penalties. This requires all personnel to be trained consistently to ensure compliance.

sample table differs greatly from the table you will design. However, this is a useful way to define a strategy that enables you to stay ahead of your adversaries and maintain control of risk factors woven into threats and vulnerabilities.

In addition, defining a clearly conveyed threat and vulnerability mitigation resolution table is another way to understand and categorize each asset, and provides an opportunity for you to outline the threats and vulnerabilities with each asset and determine your possible mitigation resolution when a threat or vulnerability exploits the system. This table can be updated as necessary and should describe each unique asset your organization owns or leases. Therefore, it is important to make sure you keep this table updated; doing so is crucial to effectively manage all technology tools, software, hardware, and devices you are using.

In fact, I suggest maintaining a written action plan. The overall objective of your action plan is to define mitigation strategies you will implement to deter illegal or unethical activity. Your plan should include the integration of state and federal laws that apply to the usage and security of technology, information systems, and cloud for storage. It should also include all industry policies that are essential to helping control risk factors, as well as outline all technical controls. The action plan will also help you implement effective methods to deter and thwart unwanted system intrusion and maintain multiple layers of security that will prohibit the destruction of the network. This also ensures an increase in security across the network.

Additionally, it is important to maintain updates on all computer security configurations. This should be deployed using reliable and manageable patches and installing antivirus software updates, configuring Firewalls, using User Account Control, protecting against theft, creating data backups, and preparing for unauthorized attacks, threats, and vulnerabilities. Furthermore, the network Firewall must be located on the edge of the network and configured to protect all technology devices correlating and connected to the network. This Firewall must be a separate hardware device, providing a sophisticated range of filtering mechanisms. An effective external Firewall device should be one of the following:

- Netgate 2100
- Ubiquiti Unifi Security Gateway (USG)
- Cisco Meraki MX64
- Watchguard Firebox T25
- Fortinet FortiGate 30E[10]

In addition, User Account Controls (UAC) is invaluable. UAC levels range from always notify users, who must be informed prior to programs making changes to the computer or to Windows settings, which requires administrator permission on a secure desktop. Although this can be pre-configured, I recommend maintaining a written record of when updates are scheduled to ensure updates are deployed on schedule and to ensure no one downloads or installs unauthorized software on any device. Data back-up also must be done regularly to protect against system failures and data loss. This will help protect against attacks, hardware malfunctions, user error, software corruption, and natural disasters. Back-up devices should include portable USB hard drives (e.g., external hard drives) and individual computer device hard drives. It is recommended to consider a cloud-based backup system. Antivirus and malware protection must be installed and updated regularly. System configurations must be conducted as needed, and written reports must be maintained with timeline stamps that include dates, usernames, and details regarding when updates and configurations were done and when they are scheduled to be done.

Security policies must be included, such as the Issue-specific Security Policy (ISSP), which sets rules that define acceptable behavior within a specific organizational resource, that is, email or internet usage. And a System-specific Policy (SySP), which merges with technical and managerial intent. This includes managerial guidance for the usage and implementation of technology and technical specifications for all configurations. Keep in mind that consistent security education, training, and awareness programs must be developed and utilized. This helps keep your organization on its toes and prepares executive leadership and personnel members for potential risk factors.

Table 3.2 is an example of what your threat and vulnerability mitigation resolution table should mirror. Notice that security scales are distinguished by their designated risk color paired in the risk color grid. The listed assets, threats, and vulnerabilities presented will differ. However, this is a dynamic way for you to understand the significance of utilizing this Table. Keep in mind to review the risk security levels to ensure you remain knowledgeable of the scale and level of risk each listed tool or asset embodies.

Security levels:

High Risk level

Medium Risk level

Low Risk level

Table 3.2 Threat and vulnerability mitigation resolution.

Assets	Threats	Vulnerabilities	Mitigation resolution
Windows 10	As of October 2025, Windows 10 will no longer receive regular security updates. This means you need to stay aware of the configuration of the Windows 11 OS. Keeping the software updated is recommended by Microsoft Corporation.	There are commonly known vulnerabilities to be aware of when using the Windows 10 OS. Because there are different types of systems for this OS, that is, 23H2 for ×64-based systems, 21H2 for ARM64-based systems. You need to conduct research to determine what known vulnerabilities are integrated into the OS you are using.	Upgrading to Windows 11 OS delivers services with minimal vulnerabilities. You need to ensure you integrate Windows Defender and configure it correctly. I also recommend installing malware prevention software, that is, Malwarebytes, and conducting penetration testing as needed. Also, maintain regular system updates with automatic system configurations.
Network intrusion detection system	Unprotected systems are susceptible to remote code execution and unauthorized access.	Reported insecure deserialization with specific workflows aligning with the IPS Manager. Attackers can manipulate the IP address parameter with a request, enabling attackers to redirect communication to a server managed by the attacker's control.	Continually monitor this problem using the CVE.mitre.org site for updates.

(*Continued*)

Table 3.2 *Continued.*

Assets	Threats	Vulnerabilities	Mitigation resolution
10 Lenovo Laptop computers	This laptop server embodies a default database that end-users can configure with a single password.	Reports find that attackers can gain access to escalate privileges and deploy arbitrary code. Also, a buffer overflow can allow an attacker to execute arbitrary code.[11]	Maintain the manufacturer's update on the firmware, making sure to disable any antivirus or security suite during the updating of the BIOS.
10 WD-easy store 4TB External USB 3.0 Hard Drives-Black	Security holes	Enables anyone with physical access to decrypt data files even when locked down with passwords.[12]	Partition and Format a WD Drive on Windows 11.
1 HP-Laser Jet Pro Black and White Laser Printer	Enables remote attackers to cause a denial-of-service attack via unknown vectors.	Enables remote attackers to cause a denial-of-service attack via unknown vectors.	Configure the device for Windows 11 64-bit; research embedded OS and configure the system to increase security. Maintain regular system updates via the manufacturer and keep a record of all modifications and installations.
1 Epson-Workforce Pro WF-R4640 Eco Tank Wireless All-in-one Printer	Wi-Fi enabled	Unauthorized external access	This device is compatible with Windows 11, as well as Server systems, Windows Server 2012. Install Cloud security application; configure password protection.

1 Brother-Fax-2840 Laser Fax/ Printer/ Copier	Ransomware can be deployed successfully through the fax.	Default passwords for Wi-Fi or internet connectivity.	Upgrade from default passwords. Also, drivers and utilities are not compatible with Windows 11; therefore, relying on a new system should be proposed.
VoIP Business Phone System	This system enables remote authenticated users to deploy arbitrary commands by commanding the system method in the body of a request, which is demonstrated via deploying unauthorized services, modifying the directory permissions, and changing files.	Default passwords	Rely on a cloud-based phone system. Ensure consistent user password protection and implement regular system updates. This should also include keeping regular system reports, that is, name, date and time, and assessing these reports to ensure accuracy of all information content.

Defining a secure information system and maintaining risk control factors associated with each asset relied on is vital to ensure the system remains impenetrable. To reiterate what was conveyed previously, it is imperative to utilize a Client-server network, which includes a file server. Doing so will enable each computer in the network to connect. One advantage of utilizing this approach is that security envelops the resources centralized on the server. Using this directory server establishes a group security association. Therefore, any time an employee is integrated into the group, he/she will have two user accounts, that is, a local account on their computer and a domain account. The domain controller is a server operating in response to security authentication requests within a Windows Server domain that will be responsible for validating the credentials of all users.

Thus, enabling an access token, which is an object conveying security content of a thread or process that will list resources each user is allowed access to within the network, regardless of where the resource is located. This also provides a centralized administration and a single sign-on, which reduces broadcast traffic and enables scalability.

Remember, it is imperative that you conduct updates on all computer defenses, that is, managing patches, installing antivirus software updates, configuring firewalls, using User Account Control, protecting against theft, creating data backups, and preparing for unwanted attacks, threats, and vulnerabilities. Also, remember to utilize a network Firewall. A Firewall should be a separate hardware device that renders a sophisticated scope of filtering mechanisms.

Next is User Account Controls (UAC), which should be deployed on standard accounts and administrator accounts. UAC levels should range from always notifying users who are informed prior to programs making changes to the computer or to Windows settings that require administrator permissions, with a secure desktop. Data back-ups must be conducted regularly to protect against computer attacks, hardware malfunctions, user error, software corruption, and natural disasters. Backup devices should include portable USB hard drives (e.g., external hard drives) and individual laptop device hard drives. Usage of a cloud-based backup system should be considered. However, be aware that the system must be updated with an antivirus and malware protection regularly. It is also important that system configurations are deployed as needed and reports are managed and utilized as updates and back-ups are configured. These reports should include the name of the author who authored the report, the timeline the report was conducted, the date, month, and year, and provide details regarding each specific update and configuration.

Furthermore, as previously explained, it is also important to maintain a security policy. Two types of policy include the Issue-specific Security Policy (ISSP). This policy sets rules that define acceptable behavior within your organization and the type of resources utilized daily, including email servers or service providers, that is, Microsoft 365 Outlook. The Issue-specific Policy embodies three characteristics:

- Focuses on specific technology tools relied on.
- Requires consistent updating.
- Embody an issue statement conveying the organization's position regarding specific issues.

The outline of this policy includes key components, such as:

(a) Statement of purpose
  - Focus and applicability
  - Meaning of all technology addressed
  - Responsibilities

(b) List of authorized users
  - User access
  - Fair and required responsibilities usage
  - Scale of protection and privacy for users

(c) Prohibited uses
  - Interference use or noncompliance
  - Criminal usage
  - Offensive or harassing documents, videos, or images
  - Copyrighted, licensed, or additional intellectual property
  - Additional restrictions

(d) Systems management
  - Managing all stored documents, images, files, and videos
  - Monitoring of employees
  - Virus protection

  - Physical security
  - Encryption

(e) Policy Non-compliance

  - Methods to report violations
  - Penalties for non-compliance

(f) Policy assessment and updates

  - Timeline for policy review
  - Methods for updating policy

(g) Standardization of liability

  - Statement for each liability
  - Disclaimers

Table 3.3 conveys the advantages and disadvantages of policy types. Keep in mind, although this is a modern approach to policy development types, this framework is an example of what your organization should consider creating to depict its own policy administrative groups.

Table 3.3 Advantages and disadvantages of policy types.

Policy type	Advantages	Disadvantages
Email usage	• Controls password protection. • Minimize vulnerabilities. • Decreases the number of cyberattack incidents.	• Often lacks control of password protection, which results in cyber incidents. • Impediment of poor policy dissemination and enforcement.
Social media usage	• Controls the type of content employees can share and post on social media. • Helps control misuse of social engineering incidents.	• Can skip focus on all threats. • Can create misinformation that leads to non-compliance.
Data and information storage policy	• Establishes the balance between each policy type and the comprehensive approach for each policy type. • Creates an outline that must be adhered to by all.	• Can be costly if ignored. • Challenges arise during implementation.

With any framework, there is always a need to modify and update as necessary. Doing so will enable effective management of the resources and help control how policies are developed, implemented, and adhered to. However, policy is not effective when just implemented. All face-to-face, hybrid, and remote workers must be trained to understand each policy, know how they are to respond and adapt to each policy, and know the penalties for not adhering to each policy. Neglecting to align this approach results in a decrease in adherence and can threaten the culture of cybersecurity leadership and technology management.

The second type of policy is the System-specific Security Policy. This policy can be divided into two groups: (a) managerial guidance and (b) technical specifications. Managerial guidance policy is developed by management to control the implementation and ensure effective configuration of all technology tools and applications utilized, and to address the human behavior that employees should demonstrate in alignment with the usage of all technology tools and applications. Typically, many organizations create their ISSP and SSSP at the same time to align these two sets of policies.

Technical specifications are typically developed by technology administrators, system administrators, and/or information systems/information technology managers. Generally, the system administrator architects technical specifications, which are established using the local security policy settings. This setting includes audit policy, user rights assignment, and security options. Technical controls include access control lists and configuration rules. Access control lists include user access lists and capability tables, which establish rights and privileges for each user. This includes asking: Who, What, When, Where, and How. Also important to consider are configuration rules. These should include instructional codes that help guide the deployment of the system, specifically when information is transmitted through it.

Threat modeling benefits any organization striving to define an effective management framework that supports the use of technology. With the growing number of cyberattack incidents, it is imperative to have a reliable technology management system that enables the organization to avoid victimization and decrease the threat of reputational damage. To help decrease victimization, relying on useful attack libraries and databases can be a key asset to enable improved defense against such threats. This should include combing through each software application manufacturer's information blogs to determine any "known" threats that have been discovered during the last 12 months. This can help improve your ability to mitigate and patch such threats effectively. Two commonly known database libraries for threats and vulnerabilities include OWASP and CVE.

OWASP is an acronym for Open Web Application Security Project. This open-source database has been rendering quality support since December 1, 2001, but gained 501 (c) status in April 2024.[13] This organization strives to educate and empower the world about insecure software. This organization has worldwide events and chapter meetings and provides educational resources and publications on its website.

CVE is an acronym for Common Vulnerabilities and Exposure. Developed from concepts shared in a white paper authored and published by David E. Mann and Steven M. Christey in January 1999. Originally defined by 321 CVE Records, this library of vulnerabilities and exposures has evolved into an attack library that renders vulnerability reports on all software published domestically, under the enforcement of the US Department of Defense and authority invested in the National Institute of Standards and Technology. In fact, countless operating system service providers domestically and internationally integrate CVE IDs in their alerts to ensure they are managing vulnerabilities and exposures. End-users can benefit from knowing what issues are encompassed by each CVE ID. This helps decrease the lack of effective risk management.[14]

Keep in mind that the OWASP and CVE database libraries embody details and information regarding threats, exposures, and vulnerabilities integrated in each software application. Diving deeper into researching these issues will also require asking questions of the developers to determine what other problems may have existed prior to discovering current vulnerabilities. Neglecting to do so can result in ineffective technology management of technology assets, software, hardware, and computer devices, including cloud applications, services, infrastructure, and platforms. As a result, it is important to be able to distinguish the best commercial threat model tools to use that can meet the needs of your workplace.

Research reports there are currently 18 threat modeling tools considered top tier in 2024. Examining four of these listed, that is, OWASP Threat Dragon, Threat Modeler, Irius Risk, and Varonis Data Security Platform, you can gain a better understanding of which of these tools can serve the needs of your organization. However, optimizing two or three threat modeling tools can ensure improved implementation and effective usage, and results every time threat modeling is deployed, upgraded, and relied on.

OWASP Threat Dragon

This model supports the creation of diagrams. This is a free, open-source model that is easily adaptable to every organization when assessed and implemented correctly. It is available in 13 languages, and this tool can be deployed in a Web application or desktop mode. You can utilize this model with STRIDE and configure a rule engine for auto-generating threats and their mitigation methods.[15]

Threat Modeler

Threat Modeler is a one-click approach to deploying effective threat modeling that can be relied on to ensure compliant applications are integrated within your information system. This approach helps you reduce costs in incident response, remediation costs, and regulatory fines.[16] Utilizing this tool also renders support to DevOps to ensure effective security of all IT tools and applications via automation for both mobile and Internet of Things. You can use this tool to help improve your ability to effectively deploy mitigation across any security flaw. You can also improve your visibility of attack surfaces and reduce threats that can envelop the software development life cycle. This tool enables you to develop and implement compliance within your framework. This is a great asset to align with the usage of cloud enterprise migration and deployment.

Irius Risk

Deployed via artificial intelligence under the code name Jeff. This threat modeling tool is known for reducing the cost of threat discovery to eight hours or less.[17] Funded by the European Union and European Cybersecurity Competence Center, this tool enables you to import your infrastructure as code to automatically generate a unique threat model to fit the needs of your organization. You can also import additional threat intelligence tools that enable you to view a single assessment of the overall security posture encompassing your information system, technology, and cloud applications, if necessary. Furthermore, this tool can be understood by non-security end-users, which helps improve adoptability and integration with other threat model tools. You can gain hands-on training in partnership with this service provider, and you can copy and paste blocks of code, which Jeff will take charge of defining a model that can be uniquely configured to support your threat modeling requirements. Jeff is a humble AI tool that works in partnership with end-users and renders quality support you can depend on.

Varonis Data Security Platform

Considered a "go-to" approach to ensure data security, this platform is relied on by many Fortune 500 corporations. This platform utilizes machine learning to assess permissions and to highlight end-users to determine who has authorization to access what type of data assets.[18] This tool is considered an effective asset in decreasing data breaches and removing threats and exposures. This tool enables automation and can be supportive in setting baselines regarding abnormal activities. This tool also renders user and entity behavior analytics, which is useful in generating alerts for all end-users. A great way to determine what behaviors are commonly deployed by each end-user authorized to utilize and access the network, information system, and technology tools and applications.

You can rely on some of the traditional commercial threat modeling tools, such as SecurlTree and Little-JIL. SecurlTree is a software application that supports risk-based security decisions about information system threats. This is a tree-based model that can assess hundreds of potential attack methods commonly deployed against a defender's system.[19] All attacks are effectively assessed by comparing an attack vector's capabilities in alignment with the resources needed to effectively execute an attack. Attacks are also assessed to determine what scale of satisfaction can be discovered in an attacker's approach. This helps understand the attacker's motivation. Probability is useful in estimating the scope of an adversary's feasibility and desirability. Published in 2007, so it is important to acquire as much knowledge about this tool to ensure effective usage as well as to ensure that limited risks exist. You can review the library of threat trees to help you discover which variables of your threat model are beneficial and operating as needed.[20]

Little-JIL is also known to be useful and supportive for threat modeling. Research reports that Little-JIL embodies two hypotheses: the first hypothesis conveys that coordination structure can be divided from additional process language concerns. And secondly, the methodology is deployed by agents who are considered knowledgeable on what is required to effectively perform their strategies, while also benefiting from collaborative support.[21] Little-JIL is a graphical language that enables you to define processes that align activities of autonomous agents and these agents' resources deployed during their performance of tasks.[22]

As conveyed, there are more than 18 threat models reported as "best" approaches to threat modeling. However, it is imperative to invest time in understanding which threat model approach is suitable for your organization. While usage of a third-party software application may be an easy route to implement automation, it is essential to determine how effective that third-party service and product provider is in rendering quality products that can be relied on and that reduce the impact of potential risks, threats, or vulnerabilities woven into software. The OWASP and CVE database libraries can be useful in helping you gain clarity regarding the vulnerabilities known within a software.

However, utilizing software that embodies minimal to no known threats or vulnerabilities is your best alternative to achieving an improved methodology to avoid victimization that can impact your organization's reputation.

Conclusion

Utilization of the STRIDE methodology cannot be effectively implemented without implementing your desirable properties. The components of the STRIDE model have opposites. For instance, spoofing is a threat the countermeasure is authentication. With authentication, you are responsible for deploying verifiable credentials that increase security, while also protecting the organization's information assets. Authentication requires the use of multi-factor login credentials and a username that should be updated every 30 days to ensure consistency in protection. Usage of two-factor authentication is considered best. Tampering is the threat; the desirable property is integrity. This aligns with the CIA triad, where the "I" represents integrity. Enforcing integrity will help you protect your organization's assets from arbitrary tampering.

Furthermore, all email messages must be sent across the intranet and internet with encryption effectively and securely. This ensures that the organization's files are unwritable, and files will be subject to modification by the enumerated authorized personnel. Repudiation is the threat. The desirable property is non-repudiation. This requires maintaining logs and ensuring these logs are secure and protected, and the logs will resist unauthorized tampering from unauthorized users.

Information disclosure is the threat; the desirable property is confidentiality. This includes data files, and all communication exchange is enveloped in secure applications (i.e., encrypted and cryptology). Denial of service is the threat; the desirable property is availability. This ensures all publicly utilized services and products offered by the organization are available as they are supposed to be. This requires the system to be up and running 99% of the time with a 100% accessibility rate. Only those with authorized credentials can have access. The system should be impenetrable and resist a customized DoS by a 50,000-host botnet. While elevation of privilege is the threat, desirable property is authorization. Thus, the system must embody a centralized authorization engine, and that centralized authorization engine must have a configurable policy, and any authorization control relied on should be stored with access control (ACL).

As stated previously, usage of a threat model for your workplace is invaluable to effective cybersecurity leadership and control of information systems, information technology, and cloud management, maintenance, and upgrades. Knowing how to align the STRIDE model to your threat model is crucial to assuring you are defining an effective security model that decreases the chance of your organization being victimized by external attack agents or internal human error actions and behaviors. Threat modeling is a method of outlining threats and known vulnerabilities, distinguishing threats and vulnerabilities, and defining methods of mitigation and implementing a process of recording details encompassing each threat or vulnerability. Lacking the knowledge to effectively deploy this model can be hazardous to your ability to control external and internal threats and vulnerabilities.

To reiterate the significance of implementing threat modeling, a case study is discussed along with an article. Conducting a review of a scholarly published article on the topic of threat modeling is instrumental in gaining additional information about the value of threat modeling in the workplace. Additionally, there are Chapter review questions, and the answers to these chapter review questions are discoverable behind Chapter 3's list of references.

Case Study

New York City is a huge concrete landscape operating on an annual income beyond billions in monetary spending, stock market trading, ecommerce and retail purchases, import and export shipping, and conglomerates in financial institutions. Each of these entities target for high-risk cyberattacks. However, with the usage of threat modeling, researchers compiled results that help support threat modeling as a method to decrease the volume of cyberattack incidents. Reliance on case studies can be instrumental in helping you gain a stride in understanding how threat modeling impacts risk management strategies and lowers the threats and vulnerabilities surfacing in today's technology-innovative workplaces.

Title: *The Battle for New York: A Case Study of Applied Digital Threat Modeling at the Enterprise Level*

Authors: Rock Stevens, Daniel Votipka, Elissa M. Redmiles, Michelle L. Mazurek, Colin Ahern, and Patrick Sweeney

Summary

During a 120-day period, research was deployed on 25 participants. However, only 20 research participants regularly reported evidence that could be used in this research study. Researchers reported that the usage of threat modeling helped deter 541 unique intrusion attempts, prevented hijacking of privileged user accounts, and improved self-efficacy.[23] Researchers also reported that prior to this study being conducted, New York never implemented threat modeling as a method of deterrence. Researchers also explain that after 30 days of implementation, it was reported and proven that threat modeling is invaluable to supporting New York enterprise settings in decreasing cyber-incidents.

147 mitigation strategies were deployed by the research participants. Even though this case study reports that 64% of these strategies were uniquely different and were never implemented before. Research explains that during a 120-day timeline, the number of cyber incidents reduced, and this correlates with countless US enterprises. Of course, reliance on the STRIDE framework was instrumental and provided the scale of clarity needed to decipher what threats and vulnerabilities existed, as well as the Center of Gravity framework, which was coined in the early 19th century as a military strategy. Researchers conveyed that this approach was selected because it embodies key characteristics deriving from additional pervasive frameworks, as well as enabling practitioners to find a top-down method to assess and discover internal components of vulnerabilities. This method is like the STRIDE framework shared in this chapter. You can review this case study in-depth by logging on to https://obj.umiacs.umd.edu/usenix_papers/Mazurek_Paper_USENIX.pdf

Research Review

The STRIDE model has been relied on since its introduction in 2014 by Adam Shostack. Researchers at Carnegie Mellon University Software Engineering Institute reported that one effective method to prevent threats from gaining leverage of system flaws is threat modeling.[24] It is reported that several threat modeling types have been introduced, some focus is also on abstraction, while others are people-centric. There are also some threat models that focus on defining a robust perspective of potential threats. In fact, this article conveys that STRIDE was introduced by Loren Kohnfelder and Praerit Garg in 1999 and adopted by Microsoft in 2002. This article recommends aligning the usage of STRIDE threat modeling with NIST policy guidelines and recommendations, instead of using Microsoft's security mediation methodologies.

Title: *Threat Modeling: A Summary of Available Methods*

Author: Natalie Shevchenko, Timothy A. Chick, Paige O'Riordan, Thomas Patrick Scanlon, PhD & Carol Woody, PhD

Summary

Consistent threats and vulnerabilities integrated in software applications and information systems create a daunting task for information systems and information technology practitioners. The introduction of STRIDE threat modeling has become a "savior" for many practitioners hoping to define a strategy that effectively thwarts and deters cyberattacks. But STRIDE threat modeling is just the tip of the iceberg in the deployment of threat models. Additional threat models include PASTA, LINDDUN, CVSS, attack trees, Persona non Grata, Security Cards, Trike, OCTAVE, and others. Each of these models provides a different scope of clarity on threat modeling and impacts the ability to deter and decrease vulnerabilities. Having knowledge about attack trees and data flow diagrams with system boundaries is important to determining what scope of the threat model that is beneficial to your organization.

This article was selected because it delivers in-depth knowledge regarding the potential threat modeling embodied and explains each threat model to help you determine which threat model you should rely on and how. Taking these recommendations to define a strategy for your organization must include additional research to gain a broader scope of understanding these models. To learn more about each threat model, log onto https://insights.sei.cmu.edu/documents/569/2018_019_001_524597.pdf

Chapter 3 Review Questions

1. Who developed a useful way to assess threats integrated in technology?
2. Why are threat models useful?
3. What corporation explains that threat modeling is an engineering technique that enables you to identify vulnerabilities, threats, and attacks?
4. When does spoofing occur?
5. What year did the US Department of Defense Common Vulnerability and Exposure (CVE) library report that known vulnerabilities existed 10 times?
6. How many ways are there to assess the authenticity of security certificates?
7. What is one way to understand your institution's assets and provide an opportunity to outline the threats and vulnerabilities with each asset?

8. What security policy can be divided into two groups?
9. What does the acronym OWASP mean?
10. How many characteristics does the Issue-specific Policy embody?
11. What software application supports risk-based security decisions about an educational institution's information system threats?
12. What two authors' "white paper" helped establish the CVE database?
13. What should you rely on to improve defense against threats?
14. What is useful and supportive for threat modeling relied on by research universities?
15. What threat model tool is deployed via artificial intelligence under the code name Jeff?

References

[1] Shostack, A. (2014). Threat Modeling: Designing for Security, 1st edition. John Wiley & Sons, Inc. Indianapolis, IN.

[2] Microsoft, (2024). Threat Modeling. https://www.microsoft.com/en-us/securityengineering/sdl/threatmodeling

[3] Cybersecurity Infrastructure & Security Agency, (2021, February 1). Understanding Website Certificates. https://www.cisa.gov/news-events/news/understanding-website-certificates

[4] Microsoft, (2023, September 29). How can I see what time an email was actually sent versus when it was delivered? https://answers.microsoft.com/en-us/outlook_com/forum/all/how-can-i-see-what-time-an-email-was-actually-sent/bda44ec9-db6e-4dc2-834a-53aab097a510

[5] Hacker News, (2024, May). A deep dive into email deliverability 2024. https://news.ycombinator.com/item?id=39888383

[6] Glock App, (2024). Email Deliverability Statistics 1Q 2024: What Percentage of Emails When to Inbox? https://glockapps.com/blog/email-deliverability-statistics-2024-did-the-average-email-deliverability-rate-change/

[7] Ibid

[8] Common Vulnerability and Exposure, (2024). Microsoft Outlook. https://cve.mitre.org/cgi-bin/cvekey.cgi?keyword=Microsoft+Outlook

[9] OWASP, (2024). Repudiation Attack. https://owasp.org/www-community/attacks/Repudiation_Attack#:~:text
[10] Netgate, (2024). 5 Popular Work-from-Home Network Firewalls for 2024. https://www.netgate.com/resources/articles-5-popular-work-from-home-network-firewalls-for-2024
[11] Lenovo, (2024, March). Multi-vendor BIOS Security Vulnerabilities. https://support.lenovo.com/us/en/product_security/ps500610-multi-vendor-bios-security-vulnerabilities-march-2024
[12] Perez, R. (2015). SC Media. Retrieved from: https://www.scmagazineuk.com/self-encrypting-western-digital-hard-drives-found-to-be-littered-with-security-holes/article/534513/
[13] The OWASP Foundation, Inc. (2024, October 1). About the OWASP Foundation. https://owasp.org/about/
[14] The MITRE Corporation (2024, October 2). CVE History. https://www.cve.org/About/History
[15] The OWASP Foundation, Inc. (2024, October 2). OWASP Threat Dragon. https://owasp.org/www-project-threat-dragon/
[16] Threat Modeler, (2024, October 2). Threat Modeler Security Everywhere. https://threatmodeler.com/
[17] Irius Risk, (2024, October 2). Secure by design with AI-generated and automated threat modeling. https://www.iriusrisk.com/
[18] Varonis, (2024, October 2). Data Security Platform. Powered by AI. https://www.varonis.com/products/data-security-platform
[19] Amenaza, (2024, October 2). An Attack Tree Based Threat Modeling Approach to Risks and Predictive Analytics. https://www.amenaza.com/securitree-what-is.php
[20] Shostack, A. (2014). Threat Modeling Designing for Security. John Wiley & Sons, Inc. Indianapolis, Indiana, p. 209
[21] Cass, G.A., Lerner, S. B., Sutton, M.S., McCall, K.E., Wise, A., & Osterweil, J.L., (2000, June 1). Little-JIL/Juliette: a process definition language and interpreter. https://dl.acm.org/doi/10.1145/337180.337623
[22] Shostack, A. (2014). Threat Modeling: Designing for Security. John Wiley & Sons, Inc. Indianapolis, Indiana.
[23] Stevens, R., Votipka, D., Redmiles, M.E., Mazurek, L.M. Adhern, C. & Sweeney, P. (n.d.) The Battle for New York: A Case Study of Applied Digital Threat Modeling at the Enterprise Level. https://obj.umiacs.umd.edu/usenix_papers/Mazurek_Paper_USENIX.pdf
[24] Shevchenko, N., Chick, A.T., O'Riordan, P., Scanlon, P.T. & Woody, C., (2018, July). Threat Modeling: A Summary of Available Methods. https://insights.sei.cmu.edu/documents/569/2018_019_001_524597.pdf

Chapter 3 Review Questions Answers

1. Adam Shostack.
2. Because they enable you to discover problems prior to problems occurring.
3. Microsoft Corporation.
4. When an external intruder gains information about an executive leader, administrator, faculty, staff, or student and attempts to successfully exploit that information to gain entrance into the network.
5. 2023.
6. Two ways.
7. Defining a clearly conveyed threat and vulnerability mitigation resolution table.
8. System-specific Security Policy.
9. Open Web Application Security Project.
10. Three characteristics.
11. SecurITree.
12. David E. Mann and Steven M. Christey.
13. Attack libraries and databases.
14. Little-JIL.
15. Irius Risk.

4

Auditing and Accountability for Effective Technology Management

Learning objectives

- Understand auditing for technology management.
- Interpret three audit frameworks.
- Distinguish how to align your workplace audit policy with NIST recommendations and guidelines.
- Apply risk management and cybersecurity frameworks.
- Understand why penalties for noncompliance are significant.

One critical method of effective technology management is implementing auditing. Auditing information systems, information technology, cloud computing applications, artificial intelligence, and machine learning is important when considering integrating these software and hardware components in a workplace system. Lacking effective auditing procedures can impose on your ability to assess potential threats and vulnerabilities in the system, the software, or hardware utilized to support business operations and communication. The National Institute of Standards and Technology (NIST) has become instrumental in defining what effective auditing processes and procedures should include. The key to aligning your workplace usage of auditing is understanding what steps you should take and how you should assess those steps to ensure compliance in the workplace. To help you increase your knowledge of auditing using NIST recommendations and guidelines, this chapter will support your interest. First, you will assess auditing for technology management as it is currently introduced in the IT industry. You will understand three security audit frameworks you need to be familiar with. You will also distinguish how to align the current audit policy with NIST

DOI: 10.1201/9788743809715-4

recommendations and guidelines. You will distinguish how to apply risk management and cybersecurity frameworks. And understand why penalties for noncompliance with workplace policy are significant. To reiterate your learning and comprehension of this chapter, chapter review questions are available at the end of this chapter; answers for these review questions can be found after the list of references.

Auditing for Technology Management

Technology management in the workplace differs greatly from the public and private sectors. Government agencies align technology management with policies and laws enacted by the government, domestically and internationally, to ensure consistency of technology management practice and procedures that are standard. However, while the private sector is held accountable under federal law, the policies the government aligns with do not necessarily require the public sector to agree or implement. In the IT sector, subject matter experts in the industry establish the guidelines private sector follows. The federal policies enacted are recommended guidelines and not required by law to be adhered to. Only federal laws, domestic and international, are private sector entities required to align business practice, communication, and operation with.

Since the establishment of the National Institute of Standards and Technology was birthed through the US Department of Commerce, and since its introduction, a consistent development and revision of auditing practices and procedures have been introduced. Some of the standard actions deployed in government auditing of technology management derive from three NIST special publications, including NIST 800-53 *Security and Control Framework*, NIST 800-37 *Risk Management Framework*, and the NICE Cybersecurity Framework. Each of these publications outlines methods of assessing and auditing technology applications and software relied on for business and communication. These methodologies are key components in helping IT practitioners, domestically and internationally, understand what, when, where, and how. What needs to be assessed? When does it need to be assessed? Where to locate the components you are assessing? And how to effectively assess the technology applications to ensure efficient and consistent deployment of each application securely?

When a technology manager in the private sector is faced with configuring software, updating software with recommended updates suggested by the manufacturer, he/she/they/them, are alone in determining what steps and procedures they/them/he/she must deploy. Lacking knowledge of the weaknesses or vulnerabilities integrated in the hardware, software, or information system utilized leads to misconfiguration of settings, and can be a cause of a security breach. Effective technology management is crucial to minimizing these concerns. IT practitioners are leaders in their workplace, and when these leaders neglect to lead efficiently, it hinders the growth of the workplace with current trends in technology adoption and usage, as well as impacts the ability to decrease risk factors that lead to security breaches.

One effective approach to leadership among IT practitioners is developing, implementing, and managing policy. Although this has been considered a technical matter. Ideally, technical problems can be solved with existing knowledge and effective technology management skills. Also useful is implementing cohesive teamwork. Staying current with NIST policies that align with the needs of your workplace and the technology applications relied on requires teamwork. Therefore, technology management must develop a team that can exhibit critical thinking and who are comfortable with ambiguity and have a willingness to accept prudent risk, as well as possess the ability to make rapid adjustments based on a continuous assessment of the circumstances.[1]

To achieve a strong teamwork approach requires building a mechanism to enforce team processes and assess team performance. Teamwork mental models should be collective knowledge structures to support team members in understanding and forming expectations about other members' responsibilities, needs, and behaviors.[2] This is achieved by establishing time to create a team that works together and points out what issues need policy improvement and how to effectively modify current NIST policy to meet the demands of the workplace. Doing so will encourage team members to become adept at processes, including communication, decision-making, taking effective actions, and having contextual awareness.[3] Additionally, it is important that policy teams understand that to become more adaptive requires developing personal skills that help enhance performance. This requires having an attitude that can adapt easily to adaptive performance. Having a well-developed team of policy leaders within the workplace can reduce the level of stress commonly associated with assessing, developing, implementing, and managing workplace policy. So, this can be the next step in developing an increased technology management and security awareness model that helps decrease the number of successful cyberattacks that impact your workplace's economic stability and productivity.

Selecting employees to be a part of a team that assesses, develops, and implements policy that governs the technology applications in the workplace requires determining which employees have leadership traits and can emulate professional behavior that can be beneficial with the integration of a policy team. When considering leader traits, you should focus on gender, intelligence, and the Big Five personality traits. Collectively, these leader traits span the demographic, task competence, and interpersonal dimensions.[4] When focusing on leader behaviors, it is important to focus on transformational leadership, as well as specific components of transactional leadership. But if department management lacks effective leadership skills, establishing a policy team within the workplace that can effectively assess the NIST series publications may not necessarily work out as planned.

Therefore, leadership must begin at the top of the organization. Unless there is effective leadership deployed at the executive level, it will impact how department-level managers and team leaders implement and manage their own leadership approach. Thus, it is invaluable that improved leadership training becomes a normal way of operating and continues to be assessed as needed to improve the overall performance of the organization and the usage of NIST policies for technology management. Furthermore, executive leaders and department managers need to assess the self-efficacy of those elected to be policy team members. However, leadership must embody ethics.

Leadership ethics is important to build trust, integrating effective diversity, as well as inclusion. When leaders operate with ethics, they are most effective at helping the organization establish a non-biased relationship of communication with all followers that helps foster trust. When followers respect leaders and feel that they are respected and valued, this helps create better idea sharing and decreases mistrust. When leaders lack ethics, this opens the door for corruption to become the norm and accepted as a key variable in business practice.

Leadership ethics define the culture of any organization. When attention is given to integrating relationships, functions, and introspection within an organization, this creates workplace environments that support ethical behavior.[5] When leaders lack ethics, they introduce a modification of business operations, functions, and relationship-building efforts that can easily deteriorate relationships that have been previously built. When leaders embody the need to balance continuity and flexibility, it fosters healthy cultures that respect everyone, despite their unique skills and attributes. This shows respect for individuals' rights and moral autonomy.[6] This healthy culture strengthens connections in empathy, increases relationship building, and makes it capable of improving collaborations.

Leadership ethics is important because it impacts the ability to respect diversity and inclusion within the workplace. Diversity and inclusion are complementary and essential to the ongoing cultural health of the workplace.[7]

When diversity is applied to fostering stronger trust in followers, it helps create a climate of inclusivity, which takes followers' ideas into account and is respected, as well as given consideration in how the organization conducts business, innovates, and grows.

When leaders lack ethics, they modify the culture climate of the workplace, impacting how followers feel about their role in the workplace, which incites discomfort. Leaders are generally perceived to allocate their efforts and differentiate their levels of engagement across multiple teams, a fact that exerts significant influence on structural team empowerment and effectiveness.[8] Thus, leaders who lack ethics poison the ability of the organization to empower followers effectively. Leadership ethics is invaluable to mitigating the expected negative relationship shared between relational diversity and outcome variables, that is, performance. This requires leaders to consider how they are perceived, as well as how followers will respect them. One of the most interesting methods of introducing change to an organization is implementing an age-old approach introduced through the Burke–Litwin change model.

Burke and Litwin emphasize the significance of understanding the effect that variation in the external environment requires to change one or more factors within the throughput elements of the organization.[9] Burke–Litwin approach to the placement of each element in the model helps align an organizational hierarchy that can be easily followed and implemented to enable any workplace to achieve goals and align its general focus. Using this approach will help you improve how you define teams for policy development, implementation, and modification throughout the lifecycle of the workplace.

These dimensions are utilized to diagnose workplace performance in several ways. First, leadership in the workplace must be able to effectively assess, develop, implement, manage, and secure a model of structuring processes and procedures to achieve any goal enacted for continued success. When examining how management practices are used to diagnose workplace performance, it is important to understand the significance of each management practice and what is required for such a practice to be instrumental in helping the company succeed.

In fact, the type of research that might be required for each element of the Burkin–Litwin change model includes assessing other managers' feedback that can be acquired through practitioner organizations and associations, as well as professional journals. A good, reliable source is the Journal for Management. This informative publication offers information about business strategies and policies, organizational behavior, human resource management, organizational theory, and research methods.[10] Additionally, research regarding work climate can be attained by combing through the Quarterly Journal of Economics. Furthermore, research regarding organizational structure can be discovered by combing through various mediums of information sharing and knowledge gathering.

However, keep in mind that limitations may arise when using these knowledge-based resources to address performance in non-compliance from team members. After all, there could also be a lack of resources to meet the needs of the workplace that may impede the ability of the workplace to achieve both short-term and long-term goals. There may also be limitations that impact the workflow and operations at the leadership level. But management practices may also face challenges that impact the ability to achieve goals on time.

For example, there could be miscommunication issues between team members. There could also be issues regarding scope creep during the progression of a project. These are issues that commonly impact the ability of organizations to reach their respective goal of defining clearly conveyed policy. This is why organizational structure, systems, and policies are essential.

Thus, leadership is essential because it encompasses strategies and plans to define the goals and missions of the workplace when considering what policies need to be developed and implemented, as well as updated and modified. Leadership creates a climate where actions are consistent with stated directions.[11] Unlike management, leadership takes on the role of empowering managers. Research explains that leaders and managers differ in fundamental ways.[12]

Leaders are loners, risk takers, and visionaries.[13] Management practices are important because these procedures are what managers do to support their organization's activities to achieve the organization's mission. The work climate is defined as a physical and mental presence that people have a feeling for and may be best explained in terms of workers' ideology of how they perceive they are managed, as well as how they believe their workplace is established and maintained. This also includes how workers feel about their purpose and performance. A valued work climate enhances performance. When workers can focus and relax to achieve their daily goals and complete their tasks, they stay motivated, and the work climate remains calm and empowering for all.

Organizational structure encompasses achieving the maximum performance of each member of a team. The structure embodies how the organization succeeds in deploying and implementing the strategies to achieve objectives.[14] However, there are different types of organizational structure.

First, there is vertical structure, which embodies functional and divisional. Functional structure separates employees by their function and specialization. Divisional structure is defined by region or market.[15] There is also a matrix organizational structure, which embodies both functional and divisional structure to establish a dual command.[16] The matrix structure shares key people, which minimizes cost and establishes a better balance overview of a product that is manufactured in several areas or sold by various subsidiaries in different markets.[17] Systems and policies are both invaluable because systems also include procedures, as well as workplace practices, which include people and the business operations. Systems also analyze both quantitative and qualitative assessments of performance, perceptions, and experiences. Since workplace systems are dynamic and nonlinear, systems function within a designated framework. However, systems are not random nor are they defined by a specific behavior; systems are unpredictable.

Each one of these elements reflects a system thinking approach to addressing challenges because system thinking is the ability to see the consequences of our own actions.[18] System thinking in alignment with leadership equates to how leaders respond to situations that serve the needs of the organization and its goals and mission. System thinking in correlation with management practices focuses on understanding a system by examining the linkages and interactions between the components that comprise the entirety of that defined system.[19] This enables managers to assess effective methods to implement strategies to increase productivity and decrease lack of motivation among employees.

The significance of the placement of each element in the model is to examine how change enables leaders to improve how they define methods of empowering their teams, and what is required to improve their teams' lack of motivation. Instead of focusing on new concepts of technologies and how these technologies can be integrated within the workplace, it is beneficial to improve the work processes that improve efficiency.

So, when analyzing your workplace, consider using the Burke–Litwin change model. After all, it is the leadership that is instrumental in guiding the workplace through daily operations and helps maintain the infrastructure of business processes. Technology management practices have been key in aligning with the structure implemented by the leaders. So, it is important to understand that these two hierarchy roles support one another and enable each other to exist and work in partnership to decrease miscommunication, empower employees, set tasks, create deadlines, and assess workers' performance.

While leaders play a role in making sure managers are doing their job effectively and efficiently. Managers are making sure teams align performance with the goal of each project and meet the demands as requested by their leaders. Technology managers must become good leaders. Being a good leader and technology manager, you acknowledge that auditing for technology management is essential to governing how technology is integrated, relied on, modified, secured, backed up, and archived.

Let us examine an effective technology management outline, you can adopt and integrate as a guide to help support your unique need to audit technology and the culture of your workplace. Relying on this audit template will become a “go-to” you will become familiar with throughout the lifecycle of technology usage and integration. Remember, you can modify this template to meet the unique needs of your workplace. Having clarity of what should be audited and how to audit assets is key to maintaining a thorough understanding of effective technology management.

However, it is important to keep in mind that innovation audit processing enables you to consider what types of innovation, that is, technological, market, human resource, finance, information, and organizational innovation, are valued and necessary for the continued growth of products and services. Therefore, planning and preparation are the first phase of defining a technology management audit. This phase includes defining the audit objectives, determining the audit scope, developing your audit plan, collecting background information, and identifying key stakeholders.

Phase 1

When defining the audit objectives, you need to assess the unique cybersecurity requirements for your workplace. This should include software assets and governance of IT operations. Depending on the size of the organization determines the cybersecurity required across the organization and its technology applications relied on. An organization that has an employee base of 10-100 will differ from an organization with 100 or more employees. Therefore, aligning cybersecurity needs should be assessed effectively as it is applied to technology management.

To achieve this, you will need to know what scope of cybersecurity aligns with each department and the level of business operation and communication that is deployed daily to conduct business. What type of technology is relied on? Telecommunication systems, Wi-Fi, internet, computer systems, operating systems, software, log-in credentials, peripherals, and access codes. What are the responsibilities of this department, and how valuable are the operations in this department that can impact the outcome of the workplace if a successful security breach occurred? These are some of the things to consider.

Next, it is imperative to consider the scope of the audit. This means you need to identify systems, departments, processes, and procedures, as well as timeframes. This can be overbearing. However, it is important to consider the network, information system, information technology, cloud, if applicable, artificial intelligence, if applicable, and machine learning, if applicable. Neglecting to consider each component of the system can cost you in the long run. Therefore, make sure you remember to rely on the Information Usage Profile, you developed in Chapter 1. Doing so will enable you to stay aligned with the outline you have already created for your workplace.

Now, you need to develop an audit plan. This audit plan should include the tasks needed.[20] The timeline to complete each task. And how you will be held accountable throughout the auditing process. As the technology manager, you may be working alone in your leadership role. You may be fortunate to have several team members to work with and assign key responsibilities that can ensure you are being assessed as you complete each phase of the auditing process and plan.

Once you do this, you need to begin collecting background details and information to help organize your plan effectively and efficiently. This should include reviewing current policies being applied to ensure compliance and enforce back-ups and archiving data assets and information in the information system database. Regardless of whether this is on-premises or in the cloud, you must have a process of determining how these steps are assessed, implemented, managed, secured, and backed up and archived. You also need to assess previous audits, if such were deployed. Knowing how long ago an audit was conducted gives you some idea of how outdated the system and its software may be. This can also be an alarming point if auditing has not been deployed in some time.

You will also need to consider utilizing organizational charts. Gantt charts are useful for project management. Utilization of the Gnatt chart software could be the tool to support these efforts. Trello is another innovative tool that can be helpful. Deploying research to help you determine what tools and software are beneficial is your alternative when you lack sufficient tools needed to effectively implement the usage of such. Another key component to consider is network diagrams.

When identifying key stakeholders, consider each IT personnel and team member. Personnel also include any on-site security, as well as department leaders and managers. Neglecting to consider these variables will impact the outcome of a good audit. The focus should be on who has authorization to access sensitive data and information files. What type of access is given to each personnel member and why? It is also important to consider the scale of trust that is invested in each personnel member and their security level in correlation with the scope of accessibility to sensitive information relating to external clients, product trade secrets, copyrighted documents, personnel personal information, including birthdates, social security numbers, home addresses, zip codes, phone numbers, names of children, and medical information that may be stored in personnel members files, and additional sensitive information that can be valued.

Phase II

The second phase is risk assessment. In this phase, focus must be invested in establishing an objective for conducting a risk assessment. This includes determining what areas in the workplace are potentially high-risk or mid-to-low risk and assessing the scale and scope of this risk and the impact of this risk on business operations, reputation, and financially. Relying on the Information Usage Profile from Chapter 1 enables you to collect data utilized to help you establish the objective of your risk assessment. Because no two workplaces operate with the same level of technology, operating systems, software, hardware, artificial intelligence, or machine learning, it can be challenging to determine the approach that meets the needs of your specific workplace.

Thus, to achieve this goal, you need to identify the critical systems and sensitive data that can lead to each scale of risk. This can include the network and all open ports that may be vulnerable to external and internal attacks. This includes operating systems relied on, that is, Windows, Unix, Linux, Mac, or databases. What are the known risk factors encompassing the usage of these operating systems and information systems, and how can you reduce these risk factors? What is the impact of risk if the operating system is breached? How will you bounce back?

Research reports that private sector entities that experience a security breach do not acknowledge the breach immediately. The average timeline for discovery is 277 days.[21] More importantly, you need to be aware of the laws enacted domestically and internationally that your workplace is held accountable to regarding the reporting of an actual security breach occurring. After all, the timeline to report a breach in the United States is 72 hours after discovery.[22] However, globally, timelines to report a security breach differ.

For instance, in India, there is a 6-hour reporting timeframe after discovering the security breach.[23]

You also must assess risks. This assessment should include security threats that could occur. Normal threat behavior includes human error and unauthorized access. Intrusion detection systems and prevention systems can be helpful in supporting the need to automate some of these concerns. But knowing how to assess risk and what needs to be classified as risk is your responsibility.

One way to help you overcome this obstacle is to rely on NIST special publications, as mentioned previously. NIST 800-30 is your recommended support. This publication outlines how to plan and deploy an effective risk assessment.[24]

Also, you need to focus on compliance violations. This must align with federal laws, domestically and internationally, as well as state laws and policy. Understanding the policies and laws your workplace is held accountable to is essential to avoiding liabilities and the cost of those liabilities.

Furthermore, you must assess all software in the information system. What software is current with recommended updates? What software is outdated and needs to be updated? How often does this software need to be updated? Do you have a Service Level Agreement (SLA) with the software manufacturer, you can review and assess to help you maintain updates as needed? Can these updates be configured for automation?

What about authorization? Who is accessing systems and technology applications storing sensitive data and information assets that should not have access? Does the CEO need access to personnel's human resource files? Why? Does the IT manager need access to trademark secrets? Why? These are questions you need to assess and answer. Maintaining a written log report regarding these questions and the depth of the assessment to enable you to stay ahead of your responsibilities in controlling the scope and scale of authorization to specifics.

Please do not forget to evaluate controls. This includes reviewing technical and administrative controls that are currently enacted. As pointed out before, workplace policies and regulations are key variables to support the control of risk factors. These components help reduce risk and threats. However, these tools must be clear. Everyone in the office must have knowledge of the regulations and policies, and know their role and responsibilities they are held accountable to. Furthermore, administrative control needs to be developed and correlated with human resources. In fact, research reports that IT policies are integral to human resource management.[25]

Phase III

In this phase, you must detail the extent of the examination you will conduct during the audit. Your examination should include reviewing the current information system, information technology, cloud, if applicable, artificial intelligence, if applicable, and assessing the measure of support these applications play in supporting the workplace toward achieving all business goals. Much like the Information Usage Profile outlined in Chapter 1, it is recommended that you consider defining a profile panel that can be utilized to outline each variable and assess such variables as they scale in risk factors. In doing so, you can deploy research that supports your need to configure settings to enhance security and decrease known vulnerabilities and threats that have been reported through the US Department of Defense and its Common Vulnerability and Exposure website (www.cve.org).

When assessing the hardware, compile a written report of each hardware tool, including peripherals, that is, computers, laptops, desktops, computer keyboards, monitors, scanners, flash drives, headsets, compact disk, mouse, speakers, joysticks, modem, composite devices, hard disk drives, webcams, projectors, input devices, card readers, output devices, 3D printers, and tablets. Each one of these hardware tools embodies software. Each one of these tools must be assessed for its role in storing and transmitting sensitive data and information vital to the ongoing success of daily business communication and operation.

For example, you might consider mapping out a table that mirrors the example provided in Table 4.1. Adopting this table as an example enables you to modify this to meet the needs of your workplace and the hardware relied on for workplace usage. Updating this tool can also include software, cloud, if applicable, and artificial intelligence, if applicable. Doing so is essential to staying ahead of potential risks that can become pathways of entrance to access the workplace network.

The next step is assessing software applications utilized for daily business communication and operation. This includes operating systems (e.g., Windows 10/11, MAC, Unix, or Linux). Staying current with recommended updates of these systems is critical to minimizing risk, which attackers target to exploit. Internally, human error continues to play a leading role in exploitation, so it is imperative to consistently train personnel about their usage of these systems to minimize human error incidents.

Software is in the peripherals. So, it is imperative to assess each peripheral utilized for business and determine the type of updates needed to support your audit of these tools. Building alliances with software manufacturers is

Table 4.1 Hardware auditing assessment.

Type of hardware	Purpose of hardware in the workplace	Known risk factors	Mitigation of risk factors	Date of risk discovery	Date of risk assessment	Auditor's name/ID#
Computers (e.g., Dell, Asus, Lenovo, HP, Samsung)	To develop documents, store documents, and transmit documents internally and externally.	Depending on the brand and model of the computer used will determine the known risk factors. For example, Dell's XPS 14 laptop was reported in 2024 to enable exploitation vulnerabilities woven in the BIOS, which was reported as weak authentication.[26]	Utilize Openai.com to support your lack of knowledge when considering your best steps in mitigating issues that can result in potential threats and vulnerabilities to your system. Doing so can help you improve your leverage in controlling the risk associated with any hardware you are relying on. Contact the support services of the computer you are mitigating to learn about the recommendations they offer to support your ability to decrease risk factors discovered with the hardware you are reliant on.	00/00/2025	00/00/2025	Mark Sullivan/914

(Continued)

Table 4.1 *Continued.*

Type of hardware	**Purpose of hardware in the workplace**	**Known risk factors**	**Mitigation of risk factors**	**Date of risk discovery**	**Date of risk assessment**	**Auditor's name/ID#**
Computer keyboards	To enable activities for business communication and operations that support daily workflow.	Enables keylogger installations and encryption misconfiguration to lead toward malware integration and eavesdropping of data in transit.[27]	Using openai.com with direct requests for examples is a good way to determine your strategies in supporting your need for methodologies to resolve these issues. But like computer hardware, you need to contact the developing manufacturer and configure settings as suggested, as well as apply those suggestions outlined by openai.com. In doing so, you can effectively meet the needs of your request with minimal setback.			
Flash drives	Used to store information assets, documents, image files, etc.	Malware attack, keystroke injection, and malicious firmware reprogramming. [28]	Always mitigate your flash drive by researching the brand name. The manufacturer is required to provide details about the mitigation of these tools under US Department of Defense requirements for contractors.[29]			

Webcams	Webcams are used for video conferencing and virtual meetings.	Password recovery exploitation.[30]	It is suggested to always update the firmware; check the manufacturer's website for information about system updates. Use a firewall. Keep this camera covered when not in use and adhere to recommendations that help decrease the risk associated with the usage of webcams on computers, laptops, and desktops.

a best-fit approach to minimizing stress when determining what risk factors there are and how to resolve the issue before it becomes a larger problem.

One of the most important components to assess, both prior to partnering with a third-party service provider and during the lifecycle of third-party software usage, is the Service Level Agreement (SLA). This document will differ from one third-party partnership to another, so it is imperative to invest time to research the document thoroughly to determine what the service/product provider renders, covers under warranty, as well as supports in maintenance and technical support services. Technical support for software is what you must pay attention to. Research reports that key components of the SLA include the agreement overview, which outlines what you can expect the service provider to do to aid in your usage of the software. This can also include a description of services and how services are delivered.[31]

There are three types of SLA. The first SLA is a customer SLA, which is shared between the provider and consumer.[32] The second type is internal and focuses primarily on an IT department. And the third type is multilevel, which embodies several layers of agreements. Research conveys that SLAs for data centers often encompass details regarding the timeline, services, or network availability. This might be 90% service availability or 50%, determined by the level of service provided by the service provider. This will also outline the meanings of environmental conditions, which include standards for air conditioning, heat, and ventilation services required to align with the usage of the services rendered. Thus, staying aware of the SLA is crucial to knowing what your workplace is getting for the investment. This also enables you to grasp clarity on the role the service provider will play in supporting your usage of the services acquired.

Furthermore, auditing must include data management and cybersecurity controls. What type of data management is currently installed? How is this data management implemented? What current system oversees the applications' hosting data, and who is responsible for ensuring this data is secure? What policies are currently governing data management throughout the workplace? How is the management of data currently evaluated? Who is held accountable for this evaluation? How is the evaluation weighed to ensure the accuracy of audits?

Research suggests that when conducting a data audit, you should deploy the following steps. Define the objective of this specific audit. This can include assessing compliance with personnel who are accountable to standards in the usage of technology tools and software. This also aligns workplace implementation with manufacturers' recommendations for integrating technology into the workplace, and as mentioned previously, updating and backing up technology to ensure effective configuration.[33]

Furthermore, it is imperative to map data flow. This enables you to acknowledge the current orchestration of data throughout daily business transactions and implement upgrades where necessary. Neglecting to do so will impact the consistency of data exchange, including how data is sourced, stored, transmitted, and secured. Research suggests that documenting how long data is stored, where it is stored, how it is stored, and who has access to that stored data should be included in your data audit procedures.[34]

Another step is evaluating the quality of data. This includes determining the value of data assets and classifying the data on a scale of risk measured by the value. For instance, clients' or consumers' demographic details have a high value because this data is identifiable data that enables someone to profit from selling it. Data value can be placed on copyright files of programming charts, images, etc. Placing value on the data enables you to determine the scale of risk that must be placed on that data and to determine the level of security needed to protect high-risk data from data that is considered low-value risk. Low-value risk data can be emails that are absent sensitive information that normally identifies a person, a product identity design, or authentication identifiers, that is, log-in credentials, usernames, and passwords.

Next, you need to assess security measures across all data assets. How is data identified, and how is data secured? What file organization is implemented to ensure data assets are being safeguarded from the threat of exploitation? Knowing how data is secured enables you to determine if additional layers of security are needed and how to apply such. One way to ensure data assets are secure is by placing data in encrypted files, zipping those files, and placing password protection on each file or enclosed document files. Maintaining a private key control system on data assets increases the level of security.

Also important are federal and state compliance regulations that your workplace must align with daily business communication and operations. Federal laws domestically and internationally are of essential importance to know. When technology is a key factor in securing data, you need to be aware of all NIST regulations and policy recommendations, and guidelines. This has been mentioned previously. Therefore, it is imperative to understand each specific NIST special publication that each technology application, hardware, and software aligns with. This includes information systems, information technology, cloud computing, artificial intelligence, machine learning, natural language processing, and IoT. Neglecting to adhere to these regulations, policies, and laws will haunt your workplace with reputational damage, civil liabilities, and loss of contracts and consumers.

Maintaining an audit report for data assets is essential to any other resource of audit reporting outlined in the workplace. Having a template to adopt and utilize will be the best approach to ensure consistency that can be updated as needed. Neglecting to do so will impact the outcome of data audits and affect your ability to effectively deploy this scope of an overall audit. Thus, learning how to interpret three auditing frameworks is essential to deploying an effective audit.

Three auditing frameworks you need to consider aligning your workplace audit with include NIST SP-800-171 *Protecting Controlled Unclassified Information in Nonfederal Systems and Organizations*. This framework supports your ability to develop information security standards and guidelines to protect data and information from unauthorized users. This publication enables you to determine the security control for access management, awareness and training, configuration management, identification management, incident response reporting, maintenance of technology, personnel security, physical security, risk assessment, security assessment and monitoring, system protection, communication protection, system and service acquisition, and scale of security needed for supply chain management.[35]

On page 21, you can discover the Audit and Accountability section. Use this as a template as well. Doing so will enable you to define a unique audit across the entire workplace. Keep in mind that auditing differs by workplace design, industry, type of technology, and software utilized and relied on. Thus, reviewing the listed guide number 03.03.01 – *Event Logging*, you will be able to grasp a framework that enables you to specify the event type. Review the Discussion section to determine how this supports your audit plan.

Section 03.03.02 – *Audit Record Content* provides an outline of what must be included (e.g., type of event, when the event occurred, where the event occurred, source of the event, outcome of the event, and who was associated with the event).[36] As you continue reading to understand how each section of this publication aligns with your auditing needs, be sure to be specific in details and record your responses. Maintaining this approach will be helpful throughout the lifecycle of your auditing process.

Section 03.03.03 – *Audit Record Generation* is beneficial because it will enable you to generate audit records and retain them effectively. However, be sure to read the Discussion in this section. It is key to understanding how each audit record you generate is developed, as well as enabling you to comprehend methods of retaining your audit records.

Section 03.03.04 – *Response to Audit Logging Process Failures* helps you determine your alert method and helps you determine the actions to take when such alerts are sounded. This should focus on both hardware and software alerts. This also should include details regarding steps to reduce risk and determining when to omit prior audit methods to improve current methods. This helps you stay on top of security matters that can be exploited by external attackers if neglected.

Section 03.03.05 – *Audit Record Review, Analysis, and Reporting* is the next step to assess personnel's roles in alignment with their accessibility to technology tools, data assets that are hosted in technology, as well as security logging. This can include multi-factor authentication, as well as remote accessibility, wireless connectivity, and how to deploy maintenance across technology. Staying up to date with this review analysis is key to supporting the outcome of the overall audit and enables you to maintain clearly written records.

Section 03.03.06 – *Audit Record Reduction and Report Generation* will be needed after an audit record is generated. This aligns with Section 03.03.07 regarding *Time Stamps*. This is essential in helping avoid unauthorized modification of audit records once they are generated. Both sections correlate with Section 03.03.08 – *Protection of Audit Information*. As previously mentioned, who has access to data determines the scale of security that must be applied to ensure data remains protected.

Another framework you need to become familiar with is NIST SP 1800-5 *IT Asset Management*. Introduced in 2018, this framework is essential in supporting your ability to effectively plan security across your workplace for determining improved security alert systems, increasing cybersecurity, rendering quality auditing, reducing help desk response time, and reducing the attack surface of each device relied on and integrated in your information system.[37] Much like the previous NIST SP publication, this publication aligns with the cybersecurity phase of auditing. This includes all IT components, that is, servers, desktops, laptops, and network appliances. While this publication is small in page count, you will benefit from following this publication and its recommendations as key components in your audit framework. Ignoring the benefits of this publication will impact the outcome of a consistent audit of your information system, information technology, cloud computing, artificial intelligence, machine learning, natural language processing, and IoT, if applicable to your workplace.

The third publication you need to have in your infrastructure is NIST SP 800-53 rev. 5 *Security and Privacy Controls for Information Systems and Organization*. Published in 2020 and updated in 2025, this publication supports your ability to control systems and acquisition and supply chain risk management for information systems, system components, and system service development.[38] To effectively utilize this publication requires assessing the security controls and safeguards of your information system. This includes the selection, design, and implementation of security and privacy controls essential for operation and implication of operation across the workplace.[39]

During the next phase of auditing, it is important to define your reporting methods. Reporting methods can be done through digital transcription and stored in hard-drive files on a computer or external hard drive, such as a USB flash drive. Doing so is a traditional approach. However, it is imperative to implement security to control access to these files. Implementing password protection on files is crucial to controlling who has access and can update or modify these reports. Remember, reports should include dates and time stamps. This helps control the potential risk of modification of documents. Reports should also have the name of the report writer, including their employee ID number, if applicable. Reports should be designed with clear written statements and provide definitions of technical terminology. Using Excel and PowerPoint can be useful tools when developing reports. Having a flexible mapping system will be instrumental in how these tools are created and defined.

Finally, it is imperative to always follow up and reassess what has been reported. Making modifications as needed when necessary is key. When you lack the diligence to keep your records up-to-date, major changes to the system can be a setback that impacts the ability of the records and reports to be valid and consistent. Thus, be sure to maintain copies of every written or digitally transcribed report developed.

Furthermore, it is imperative to align risk management and cybersecurity frameworks. Technology management, risk management, and cybersecurity go hand in hand; one cannot exist effectively without the other. The National Institute of Standards and Technology has prepared frameworks under the special publication series that support your required risk management and cybersecurity integration. Relying on these publications is crucial to staying current with recommendations and guidelines to decrease the growth of cyber-attacks deployed against your workplace.

Two noted risk management frameworks that you should include in your risk management assessment are NIST 800-30 Rev.1 *Guide to Conducting Risk Assessments* and NIST 800-37 Rev. 2 *Risk Management Framework for Information Systems and Organizations*: *A System Life Cycle Approach for Security and Privacy*. Both publications are instrumental in supporting how you prepare and plan your risk management strategy. While the latter publication, NIST 800-30 Rev. 1 *Guide to Conducting Risk Assessments*, is considered outdated because it was published in 2012. You can utilize the framework to create a template and update it to meet your specific workplace needs. That is why using the NIST 800-37 Rev. 2 publication, published in

2018, is the companion publication. Using both is the best approach to enable you to achieve a thorough grasp of controlling risk factors in your workplace.

In addition, this publication is beneficial because it supports your need to effectively integrate information security. This publication is consistent with the security requirements for Office of Management and Budget Circular A-130: Security Agency Information Systems.[40] This document will help you complete each step in the risk assessment process, that is, prepare for the assessment, conduct the assessment, communicate the results, and maintain the assessment.[41]

This publication is useful because it enables you to understand the risk management process and how to conduct an actual risk assessment. You will also learn how to understand key risk concepts and communicate the risk assessment, as well as share your assessment with others. Thus, it is imperative to review this publication thoroughly and align your steps and actions with the recommendations. Doing so will enable you to maintain leverage over your risk factors, aligning with each technology tool, application, hardware, and software integrated in your information system.

NIST 800-37 Rev. 2 was published in 2018, but this publication is still a crucial component to managing risk factors. While this publication was developed for federal information systems. This publication can be utilized by information security managers, senior leaders, senior agency information security officers, auditors, system security and privacy engineers, as well as business owners.[42]

This publication, in concert with NIST 800-30 Rev 1, will help you correlate linkage with effective communication with C-suite executive leaders, enabling you to convey your ideas clearly and in a way that is understood. Because of technical terms, it can be challenging to present risk management strategies and methodologies to C-suite executive leadership. This publication will enable you to promote the development of secure software and systems that align with the lifecycle of your workplace.[43] This publication is also a great tool to help you integrate the NICE cybersecurity framework.

The NICE Cybersecurity Framework has been updated under the 2.0 title. This updated version is designed specifically for all organization types. This updated version was released on February 26, 2024. This publication was developed for executives, boards of directors, technology professionals, risk managers, lawyers, human resource specialists, and cybersecurity and risk management auditors.[44]

Utilizing this publication will enable you to improve your cybersecurity risk management organization and communication. This publication will also support your ability to understand the core functions of cybersecurity and deploy steps to create and utilize a cybersecurity framework for your workplace profile. Most importantly, this publication will enable you to improve risk management communication.[45] Adopting the procedures and recommendations offered in this publication in alignment with the risk management guidelines is an asset to your workplace's ability to meet the demands of cybersecurity, as it correlates with technology management.

Integrating these frameworks is essential to understanding why penalties for non-compliance with workplace information security and cybersecurity policy are invaluable. Penalties are important because they enforce regulations and hold personnel accountable. When penalties are absent, it impacts the ability to control risks. When you cannot control risk, there is an increase in security incidents that lead to cyberattacks and security breaches.

Research conveys that well-written security policies play a pivotal role in fostering a security-conscious organizational culture.[46] Research also suggests the value of non-compliance extends beyond regulatory fines.[47] Non-compliance impacts your workplace's bottom line, disrupts operations, and impedes customer trust. Most importantly, penalties for non-compliance help reduce liabilities that can cause the workplace to be fined by federal security agencies or criminalized. How you impose penalties determines how personnel comply with the policies implemented.

Conclusion

Having clarity of the Service Level Agreement (SLA) when partnering with third-party service providers is vital to understanding what this partnership provides during the lifecycle of services. When you are not knowledgeable of what is required to manage the services rendered, you risk placing your workplace technology tools and applications becoming vulnerable. As suggested, effective technology management auditing should align with recommendations and guidelines published by the National Institute of Standards and Technology mentioned in the three primary special publications reviewed in this chapter. Doing so enables you to safeguard your workplace efficiently and increase the security control needed to reduce risk.

Risk management is crucial! Knowing how to assess risk and adopt strategies and methodologies to lower risk is one reason why relying on NIST special publications is important. Not only do these publications guide you, they are instrumental in helping you create templates that can be updated as needed and modified as new technologies are integrated and old technologies omitted.

Knowing how to make necessary upgrades in each phase of the audit process outlined in this chapter, in your workplace when needed, is important. Furthermore, having guidance to meet the demands of your workplace and the unique technology utilized daily is vital to controlling the outcome of the audit process. Neglecting to manage effective written reports and securing those reports can also be costly.

Thus, it cannot be said enough, but research is your best friend. Neglecting to research current trends in auditing procedures. Adopting those trends and aligning them with your current technology tools and applications enables you to define a foolproof infrastructure that is specific to the lifecycle for your workplace. Using industry journals and association or organization databases is the best alternative to improving your research efforts. Keeping a portal of information that helps you understand each component of technology in your workplace will help you avoid setbacks when you are absent clarity on what is required to avoid technology security breach victimization.

To help reiterate your reading and enable you to apply these practical methods to your workplace, I have embedded a research article review. This article was selected because it outlines some concepts of workplace technology auditing currently being implemented in the accounting and business workplace setting. Reviewing this practical concept of technology management auditing will give you an increased understanding of the significance of auditing and technology management.

Research Article Review

Title: *Embrace Technology in Audit*

Author: Liz Fischer, Journalist

Summary

The accounting and business industries are two global industries that continue experiencing challenges in integrating technology in the workplace. Over the years, IT practitioners working in accounting firms or the business industry sought effective strategies to redefine their approach to integrating technology tools and applications to reduce the stress of effective auditing. Journalist Liz Fischer shared details in her article reporting that usage of artificial intelligence has become a "go-to" in supporting these two industries toward reaching the goal of effective technology auditing. She conveys that a new playbook titled *Audit and Technology Playbook*: *a practitioner's guide*, produced by the ACCA and Chartered Accounts of Australia and New Zealand, is beneficial in supporting any firm, large or small, in managing risk aligned with technology.[48]

Liz explains that seven technology tools and applications, including cybersecurity, artificial intelligence, machine learning, blockchain, Internet of Things, automation, and big data and analytics, are useful components in significant auditing.[49] According to Liz, the managing director of the National Audits Group Australia, small businesses are utilizing off-the-shelf software that is impacting their ability to deploy effective technology auditing. This impacts the ability to avoid victimization due to risks not discovered through the use of ineffective software applications.

Thus, this new playbook provides guidance on some new software to support the needs of small businesses' auditing endeavors. However, there are risk factors often overlooked when using any software. For instance, the usage of generative artificial intelligence ushers in additional risks.[50] While it is believed that the usage of generative AI can be helpful, Liz explains that the quality output of the response can be poor. Furthermore, Liz explains that IT auditors must use skepticism when relying on generative AI for auditing. She reports that it is necessary to research the outcome of reports provided by generative AI to ensure accurate reporting and analytics.

Liz also shares that the International Auditing and Assurance Standards Board must be researched to learn about current trends in updating auditing methods for technology in the workplace.[51] Liz explains that reviewing the new playbook on technology auditing is essential to understanding what you need to know to avoid ineffectively auditing your workplace technology tools and applications. She shares five recommended tips you should consider when using advanced technology tools to help you audit your technology, including:

- Implement a team to determine the goals of the audit and to set milestones.
- Rely on a change management strategy.
- Insist on consistency of skill development and training.
- Revise your talent for efficient in-house development.
- Establish guidelines, regulations, and policy.

Liz's suggestion of utilizing the new playbook aligns with the recommendations I have suggested in this chapter. You can review this article more in-depth at the following URL: https://abmagazine.accaglobal.com/global/articles/2024/oct/practice/embrace-technology-in-audit.html

Chapter 4 Review Questions

1. The private sector does not have to align technology usage practices with NIST special publications. (True or False)
2. The National Institute of Standards and Technology provides current recommendations and guidelines that should be considered valuable in supporting technology auditing in the workplace. (True or False)
3. The first step in defining your audit is reviewing the type of technology relied on in the workplace. (True or False)
4. In what phase should you consider the scope of your audit?
5. In what year was NIST 800-37 Rev. 2 published?
6. What is the average timeline before a security breach is discovered?
7. What is the most important component relied on to assess, both prior to partnering with a third-party service provider and during the lifecycle of third-party software usage?
8. What NIST special publication supports your ability to develop information security standards and guidelines to effectively protect data and information from unauthorized users?
9. What NIST special publication is essential in supporting your ability to effectively plan security across your workplace and for rendering quality auditing?
10. What NIST special publication supports your ability to control systems and system components?
11. What two NIST special publications are instrumental in supporting how you prepare and plan your risk management strategy?
12. Why is NIST 800-37 Rev.2 beneficial?
13. Who is the new updated NICE Cybersecurity framework developed for?

References

[1] Dunn, R. (2020). Adaptive Leadership: Leading Through Complexity. International Studies in Educational Administration (Commonwealth Council for Educational Administration & Management (CCEAM), 48(1), 31-38, p. 34

[2] Ibid
[3] Ibid
[4] Derue, D.S., Nahrgang, J.D., Wellman, N., & Humphrey, S.E. (2011). Trait and Behavioral Theories of Leadership: An Integration and Meta-Analytic Test of Their Relative Validity. Personal Psychology, 64(1), 7-52. https://doi.org/10.111/j.1744-6570.2010.01201
[5] Skeet, G.A. (2019). Culture Self-Assessment Practice: Defining Healthy Organizational Culture. Markkula Center of Applied Ethics. Santa Clara University. https://www.scu.edu/ethics/culture-assessment-practice/defining-healthy-organizational-culture/
[6] Ibid
[7] Smith, A. & Angood, B.P. (2020). Diversity & Inclusion: Tough Decisions, Rich Rewards. American Association for Physician Leadership Journal, p. 21
[8] Gortis, G. & Grimani, K. (2016). Diversity as an aspect of effective leadership: integrating and moving forward. Leadership and Organizational Development Journal. Volume 37. No. 2, p. 241
[9] Pershing, P.S. & Austin, K.E. (2015). Organizational Theory and Governance for the 21st Century, SAGE Publications, Inc. Thousand Oaks, CA., p. 185
[10] Southern Management Association, (2023). Journal Description. [Website] https://journals.sagepub.com/description/JOM
[11] Pershing, P.S. & Austin, K.E. (2015). Organizational Theory and Governance for the 21st Century, SAGE Publications, Inc. Thousand Oaks, CA., p. 185
[12] Burke, W.W. (n.d.). "Leadership as Empowering Others" [PDF] https://www.researchgate.net/profile/W-Burke/publication/246661498_Leadership_as_Empowering_Others/links/56aa400608aeaeb4cefaf595/Leadership-as-Empowering-Others.pdf
[13] Ibid
[14] Ibid
[15] Ibid
[16] Ibid
[17] Society of Human Resource Management, (2023). Understanding Organizational Structures. [Website] https://www.shrm.org/resourcesandtools/tools-and-samples/toolkits/pages/understanding-organizational-structures.aspx#:~:text=an%20organizational%20structure%3F-,Organizational%20structure%20is%20the%20method%20by%20which%20work%20flows%20through,individual%20functions%20to%20manage%20tasks.

[18] Ibid
[19] Senge, P. (2015). What is System Thinking? [Video] https://www.youtube.com/watch?v=V38HrPnYkHI&t=68s
[20] Chryssou, C. (2023, November 5). Innovative Audit. Retrieved from: https://www.tamegon.com/innovation-audit
[21] Mitnick Security, (2024, February 12). How Long It Will Take to Recoup From a Data Breach? https://www.mitnicksecurity.com/blog/data-breach-recovery
[22] PwC, (2025). Cyber breach reporting to be required by law for better cyber defense. https://www.pwc.com/us/en/services/consulting/cybersecurity-risk-regulatory/library/cyber-breach-reporting-legislation.html
[23] Sukianto, A. (2025, January 7). India's 6-Hour Data Breach Reporting Rule (Clearly Explained). https://www.upguard.com/blog/indias-6-hour-data-breach-reporting-rule
[24] Cynet, (2024, November 7). NIST Risk Assessment: Process, Tiers, and Implementation. https://www.cynet.com/nist-cybersecurity-framework/nist-risk-assessment/
[25] Denut-Samuels, C. (2024, October 30). How To Implement IT Policies & Procedures: A HR Perspective. https://www.thepolyglotgroup.com/blog/how-to-implement-it-policies-procedures-a-hr-perspective/#:~:text=What%20Are%20IT%20Policies?%20IT%20policies%20are,clear%20understanding%20of%20acceptable%20and%20unacceptable%20behaviours.
[26] CVE.org, (2024). CVE-2024-52541. https://www.cve.org/CVERecord/SearchResults?query=Dell+XPS+14+Laptop
[27] Muraleedhara, P. & Bhangepatil, A. (2024, February 29). Wireless Peripheral Devices-Security, Risk, Exploits and Remediation. https://www.cyberdefensemagazine.com/wireless-peripheral-devices-security-risk-exploits-and-remediation/
[28] Nason, A. (2024, March 18). Why USB Attacks Are Back and How to Prevent Them. https://www.coro.net/blog/why-usb-attacks-are-back-and-how-to-prevent-them
[29] Coker, J. (2024, October 14). US DoD Tightens Cybersecurity Standards for Defense Contractors. https://www.infosecurity-magazine.com/news/dod-cybersecurity-standards/
[30] Kirvan, P., Rosencrance, L., & Louissaint, S. (2025). Service level agreement (SLA). https://www.techtarget.com/searchitchannel/definition/service-level-agreement#:~:text=A%20service%2Dlevel%20agreement%20(SLA)%20is%20a%20contract%20between,generalized%20form%20of%20an%20SLA.

[31] Ibid
[32] Ibid
[33] Brook, C. (2024, March 11). What is Data Auditing? Why You Need It & How To Conduct It. https://www.digitalguardian.com/blog/what-data-auditing-why-you-need-it-how-conduct-it
[34] Ibid
[35] Ross, R. & Pillitteri, V. (2024, May). Protecting Controlled Unclassified Information in Nonfederal Systems and Organizations. https://nvlpubs.nist.gov/nistpubs/SpecialPublications/NIST.SP.800-171r3.pdf
[36] Ibid
[37] Stone, M., Kauffman, L., Irrechukwu, C., Perper, H. & Wynne, D. (2018, September). NIST SP 1800-5 IT Asset Management. https://nvlpubs.nist.gov/nistpubs/SpecialPublications/NIST.SP.1800-5.pdf
[38] Joint Task Force, (2020, September). Security and Privacy Controls for Information Systems and Organizations. https://nvlpubs.nist.gov/nistpubs/SpecialPublications/NIST.SP.800-53r5.pdf
[39] Ibid
[40] Joint Task Force Transformation Initiative (2012, September). Information Security. NIST-800-30 Rev. 1. https://nvlpubs.nist.gov/nistpubs/Legacy/SP/nistspecialpublication800-30r1.pdf
[41] Ibid
[42] Joint Task Force, (2018, December). Risk Management Framework for Information Systems and Organizations: A System Life Cycle Approach for Security and Privacy. https://nvlpubs.nist.gov/nistpubs/SpecialPublications/NIST.SP.800-37r2.pdf
[43] Ibid
[44] National Institute of Standards and Technology, (2024, February 26). The NIST Cybersecurity Framework (CSF) 2.0. https://nvlpubs.nist.gov/nistpubs/CSWP/NIST.CSWP.29.pdf
[45] Ibid
[46] Scale Computing, (2023, August 10). Why You Need an Information Security Policy. https://www.scalecomputing.com/resources/why-you-need-an-information-security-policy
[47] Mohan, V. (2024, December 16). Information Security and the Cost of Non-Compliance. https://www.datacore.com/blog/information-security-and-cost-of-non-compliance/
[48] Fisher, L. (2024, October). Embrace technology in audit. https://abmagazine.accaglobal.com/global/articles/2024/oct/practice/embrace-technology-in-audit.html
[49] Ibid

[50] Ibid
[51] Ibid

Chapter 4 Review Question Answers

1. True
2. False
3. False
4. Phase 1
5. 2018
6. 277 days
7. Service Level Agreement
8. NIST SP 800-171 Protecting Controlled Unclassified Information in Nonfederal Systems and Organizations.
9. NIST SP 1800-5 IT Asset Management
10. NIST SP 800-53 rev.5 Security and Privacy Controls for Information Systems and Organization.
11. NIST 800-30 Rev.1 and NIST 800-37 Rev.2
12. Because it supports your need to effectively integrate information security.
13. All organizational types.

5

Public Policies and Implementation Procedure

Learning objectives

- Evaluate domestic and international artificial intelligence and technology management public policy.
- Understand NIST policy recommendations and guidelines for technology management.
- Demonstrate how to align domestic and international technology management public policy in the workplace.
- Identify global standards of cybersecurity, information security, and technology management for workplace partnerships.

In Chapter 4, you gained clarity regarding the National Institute of Standards and Technology (NIST) special publication public policies that align with technology management and auditing. You were introduced to three specific frameworks that have become standard models for workplace management of technology tools and applications. However, those three frameworks are not the only frameworks you must consider aligning your workplace policies with when integrating information systems, information technology, cloud computing, artificial intelligence, machine learning, natural language processing, Internet of Things (IoT), or quantum computing. You also need to become familiar with other domestic and international public policies. Neglecting to adhere to many countries' public policies implemented to control how data and information assets are stored, transmitted, and secured is not acceptable. After all, these policies are essential to your workplace conducting business and/or communicating with consumers in other countries. One country that has enacted laws and public policies regarding technology

DOI: 10.1201/9788743809715-5

communication and business operation is Canada. In 2022, the Canadian Government enacted the Digital Charter Implementation Act, ensuring protection for all Canadians' personal information. Under the Act, Canadians can demand their personal information be deleted from files when that information is not being utilized.[1] Furthermore, Canadians can be assured that violators of this Act will be fined 5% of their revenue or $25 million dollars.[2] Additionally, businesses seeking to conduct business in Canada and communicate with Canadians are held accountable for the usage of artificial intelligence when storing sensitive information assets. This strong Democratic country insists Canadians' privacy is protected and secured with integrity of elections and against online threats and disinformation.[3]

Canada is not alone in the fight to control the privacy of citizens' personal information. Research conveys that 120 countries have taken steps to safeguard their citizens' privacy by passing laws and enacting public policies. One of the most widely recognized public policies is the General Data Protection Regulation (GDPR) enacted by the European Commission. This public policy was enacted to control how citizens in the European Union personal information is stored and transmitted across the Internet. China has also enacted the Personal Information Protection Law. Australia enacted the Privacy Act. Brazil enacted the *Lei Geral de Proteçao de Dados* (LGPD). And Chile amended its Constitution to include protection for its citizens' personal data. In addition, Egypt considered Law 151 in 2020, which was also to ensure the protection of privacy information for its citizens. India also passed its Personal Data Protection Bill in 2019, and Israel passed its privacy protection law in 1981 and updated that law in 2017.

While additional countries are taking an active lead in protecting the personal identifiable information of their citizens, not all countries are doing the same. For instance, Bolivia has not enacted a proposed bill or law as of May 2025. Neither has Iran, Iraq, Pakistan, or Bangladesh.[4] Thus, it is crucial to have knowledge of how those countries that have passed and enacted laws and public policy align with the business practices and communication of your workplace engagement globally. Knowing these laws, regulations, and public policies enables you to prevent liabilities and avoid fines for violations. Therefore, this chapter will be your gateway to interpret some of these regulations and understand how to modify current workplace policy to integrate requirements to meet these demands. This chapter will also help you understand additional NIST policy recommendations and guidelines for technology management, which you have not learned about in previous chapters. You will also learn how to align domestic and international technology management policy in your workplace for each type of technology tool and application utilized. And identify global standards of cybersecurity, information security, and technology management for workplace partnerships. To reiterate your learning comprehension, this chapter ends with chapter review questions; you can discover answers to those questions after the listed chapter references. Furthermore, this chapter shares a case study to help you understand how others are applying some of these regulations in their workplace.

Domestic and International Artificial Intelligence and Technology Management Public Policies

While Canada is noted for its implementation of effective privacy control legislation, as shared previously, 120 countries have each taken the liberty to define public policy and laws that seek to reduce the violation of privacy for the sensitive data and information assets owned by their citizens. Table 5.1 provides an outline of each country that has enacted public policies and laws protecting the privacy and sensitive information of citizens. Using this table should enable you to gain clarity of the domestic and international technology management public policies you need to be knowledgeable about, to help reduce liabilities, your workplace is held accountable for. Staying knowledgeable of these regulations is essential to aligning your current workplace information security policy and information system and technology management policy. These regulations will also enable you to define your workplace policies, aligning with the usage of artificial intelligence, machine learning, Internet of Things (IoT), and cloud computing.

While this table has provided some clarity regarding the scope of public policy encompassing these countries listed, this does not conclude the broad scope of public policies being introduced annually. Staying knowledgeable of these policies will enable you to maintain the leverage over competitors and adversaries desiring to deploy attacks against your workplace technology infrastructures. It is essential to always use keywords to help you achieve the best path to learning about public policies in every country your workplace partners with to achieve short and long-term goals.

Keywords to use when searching for artificial intelligence and technology management policies should include keywords such as public policy for artificial intelligence worldwide, public policy for technology management globally, laws for technology management worldwide, what are the new public policies for information technology usage worldwide, and how can I apply artificial intelligence in the workplace worldwide. Asking questions in a search query is important. It enables the search algorithm to understand your need for responses and improves the outcome of your response populated.

Table 5.1 Domestic and international technology management law and public policy.

Country	Law/public policy	Information systems	Information technology	Cloud computing	Artificial intelligence/ machine learning
Australia	The Online Safety Act of 2021. Privacy Act Review Report. Australia Human Rights Final Report: Human Rights and Technology.[7]	Not applicable	Not applicable	Not applicable	Australia: No federal regulation; however, New South Wales implemented a regulation intended for project teams using AI, operational teams using AI, Senior Officers managing the usage of AI in the workplace, and internal workplace auditors.[5] If your workplace is using a third-party AI service/product manufacturer, you are not required to comply. The Online Safety Act of 2021 is crucial to assessing what additional legislation is required. The Artificial Intelligence Ethical Framework of 2019.[6]

Brazil	A Bill of Law 2338/2023 was passed for approval. If approved by the Government, this law will establish protection for Brazilian citizens' right to all information regarding their personal data and information being used, stored, transmitted, and secured.[9]	Not applicable	Not applicable	Not applicable	Bill of Law 2338/2023 in the House for approval.[8] If passed into law, citizens will be protected against discrimination based on their personal and private information assets.
Canada	Artificial Intelligence and Data Act & Digital Charter Implementation Act. The Canadian Human Rights Act.	Not applicable	Not applicable	Not applicable	In 2025, modifications to the Artificial Intelligence and Data Act will align with the Companion document Bill C-27.[10] Additional legislative policies include the Bank Act and the Consumer Product Safety Act. Canada requires AI end-users to be transparent, provide meaningful reasons for AI usage, and deploy ethics and integrity when using AI for the storage, transmission, and security of Canadian citizens' personal information.

(Continued)

Table 5.1 *Continued.*

Country	Law/public policy	Information systems	Information technology	Cloud computing	Artificial intelligence/ machine learning
China	Regulations on the management of in-depth synthesis of Internet information services.[11] Administrative Provisions on Deep Synthesis of Internet Information Services (APDSIIS).[15] Cybersecurity Law of the People's Republic of China (CLPRC). Data Security Law of the PRC (DSLP). Personal Information Protection Law of the PRC (PIPLP). National Internet Information Office Order No.16.[22] China Cross-border Data Transfer.[24]	Regulations on the management of in-depth synthesis of internet information services: Chapter 2 – General Provisions: Article 6 – protect the interests of society. Article 7 – service providers must implement information security, including registration, algorithm mechanisms,	Regulations on the management of in-depth synthesis of internet information services: Chapter 3 – Data and Technology Management Standards. Article 14 – must contain the consent of Biometric data (i.e., human face).[13] Article 15 – verify the mechanism generating synthetic algorithms.[14]	Applicable to the following: APDSIIS CLPRC DSLP PIPLP	Data Security Law of the PRC. The Personal Information Protection Law of the PRC regarding the protection of citizens' sensitive information, including names, biometric information, as well as verifying data collected using AI, and avoiding fraud and the dissemination of misleading information.[16] Shanghai AI Regulation applies to municipalities and government controls.[17]

increase data security, and protect personal information. Article 9 – deploy an assessment of real identity information to avoid violating laws.[12]	National Internet Information Office Order No.16 – Promote and standardize data cross-border flow regulations: Article 2 – identify and declare important information.
The Personal Information Protection Law – accuracy of information, purpose for usage of personal information, openness and transparency, data minimization, and imposes accountability.[18]	Article 3 – data collection must be protected under a cross-border personal information protection certification. Article 4 – only personal information of international.

(Continued)

Table 5.1 *Continued.*

Country	Law/public policy	Information systems	Information technology	Cloud computing	Artificial intelligence/ machine learning
		This applies to anyone rendering services or products to Chinese citizens. Service providers must have the consent of citizens to use their personal information.[19] This requires gaining consent prior to handling personal information of any Chinese citizen. Review Chapter V of this regulation.[20] There is a 24-hour notification for security	Article 5 –cross border payment systems are required to be exempt from being accountable under the Personal Information Protection Certification. Note: Review the regulations under National Internet Information Office No. 13.[23]		

		breaches; this applies to all citizens who have been impacted.[21]			
European Union	Artificial Intelligence Act 2024. General Data Protection Regulation (GDPR).	Developers and deployers must convey to end-users that the usage of ChatGPT is applicable.[25] GDPR regulates all forms of data protection, regulating personal data.[28]	GDPR applicable.	GDPR applicable.	The AI Act demands unacceptable risk associated with AI systems and enforces risk factors to be managed effectively.[26] Adherence to the June 2023 AI and Personal Data Guide for DPOs should be your companion in managing how you integrate and utilize AI and machine learning for business operations relating to security and transmission of personal data assets.[27] GDPR applies to both AI and machine learning. Adherence to the EU regulations and laws is fundamental under the EU's

(Continued)

Table 5.1 *Continued.*

Country	Law/public policy	Information systems	Information technology	Cloud computing	Artificial intelligence/ machine learning
					jurisdiction, and all private and public sector entities are required to respect and deploy business transactions encompassing the usage and storage of individuals' personal data and information in technology applications. Violators face steep penalties ranging from 6% of the preceding financial year's annual revenue.[29]
Israel	Israel Policy on Artificial Intelligence Regulations and Ethics 2023.[30]	Not applicable	Not applicable	Not applicable	Public sector entities are held accountable to international laws and policy in alignment with the proposed new AI policy regulating control of risk factors associated with the usage of technology and artificial intelligence for securing and transmitting personal identifiable information and data assets. While there is no current

					enacted legal power regulating the enforcement of AI in business transactions, the private sector is held accountable under Israel's laws governing privacy, ethics, discrimination, and disclosure of AI interactions.[31]
Japan	Transparency and Fairness of Specified Digital Platforms of April 2020.[32]	Violators include individuals and business entities such as service or product providers. These are held accounts under the Transparency and Fairness of Specified Digital Platforms. Violators can be fined up to 1,000,000 million Yen and as low as 500,000 Japanese Yen.[33]	Not applicable	Not applicable	Not applicable

(Continued)

Table 5.1 *Continued.*

Country	Law/public policy	Information systems	Information technology	Cloud computing	Artificial intelligence/ machine learning
New Zealand	Algorithm Charter. AI Cornerstones.	Not applicable	Not applicable	Not applicable	Māori Data Sovereignty Principles. Requires anyone utilizing AI for data storage or transmission to align with the principles and ethics required to secure the private data of citizens. Data belonging to citizens of Maori is requested to be hosted in Maori when possible.[34]
Saudi Arabia	Personal Data Protection Law. Open Data Policy.	Anyone hosting data externally or internally is held accountable to this policy and approach. Under the PDPL, you are held accountable to specific standards requiring permission or consent to	Not applicable	Not applicable	Under the PDPL, you are held accountable to specific standards requiring permission or consent to collect and store consumer data when AI is relied on.[36]

		collect and store consumer data when AI is relied on.[35]			
Singapore	National Artificial Intelligence Strategy. The Cybersecurity Act of 2018. Protection from Online Falsehoods and Manipulation Act 2019.	Requires all information systems to be effectively secured and to monitor risk factors that can increase cybersecurity attacks.[37] Laws under the Cybersecurity Act of 2018 apply to anyone hosting data wholly or partly in Singapore.	Not applicable	Not applicable	Not applicable
South Korea	The AI Act is expected to be enacted.	Not applicable	Not applicable	Not applicable	Not applicable

(*Continued*)

Table 5.1 *Continued.*

Country	Law/public policy	Information systems	Information technology	Cloud computing	Artificial intelligence/ machine learning
United Kingdom	The Data Protection and Digital Information Bill was introduced in 2022 and is in its final stages to receive a Royal Assent.[38] The Data Ethics framework.[39] Intelligence Security Tools.[40] The Roadmap.[41]	Public sector entities must deploy transparency, fairness, and accountability in protecting sensitive data assets when utilizing such internationally. Under the Roadmap, data assets must be secured and protected from unauthorized users.	Public sector entities must deploy transparency, fairness, and accountability in protecting sensitive data assets when utilizing such internationally.	Public sector entities must deploy transparency, fairness, and accountability in protecting sensitive data assets when utilizing such internationally.	It is recommended that private sector entities deploy compliance when working with and on data using artificial intelligence.[40] The Roadmap requires due diligence in securing data correlating with the use of medical devices. Regulatory requirements outline five principles to adhere to, including: Safety, security, and robustness; transparency and explainability; fairness; accountability and governance; contestability and redress[42]

United States	States have enacted laws that must be adhered to, correlating with AI usage for data storage and transmission. States with such regulations include: Connecticut Data Privacy Act Connecticut Artificial Intelligence Law Illinois Artificial Intelligence Video Interview Act Colorado Privacy Act Gramm–Leach–Bliley Act Fair Credit Reporting Act Health Insurance Portability and Accountability Act California Children's Online Privacy Protection Rule	Connecticut law requires data protection controllers to deploy a data protection impact assessment to ensure data is secured and risk management is implemented effectively to reduce unauthorized access and usage of such data.[44]	Not applicable	Not applicable	When operating a business in Connecticut through AI, you must avoid discrimination against consumers and conduct internal and external auditing to ensure AI does not violate these regulations.[43]

It is also recommended that you search every search engine. Google is a popular choice when searching for many information resources, but it does not necessarily meet the demands of a global search. Top search engines to query include:

- Lukol.com
- Perplexity.ai
- Duckduckgo.com
- Dogpile.com
- Swisscows.com
- Baidu.com
- Yandex.com
- Naver.com (translate into English)
- Ecosia.org
- Qwant.com
- iask.ai

While this list is commonly known, there are countless other search engines you should become familiar with. Staying ahead of adversaries is key to winning the war raging against your workplace, and it helps you control access to your workplace data assets and information resources.

NIST Policy Recommendations and Guidelines for Technology Management

As conveyed in previous chapters, the National Institute of Standards and Technology (NIST) is a key partner in the war on technology management and artificial intelligence. Understanding the role this entity plays in supporting your workplace's reliance on artificial intelligence and technology management is vital. To increase knowledge sharing, below are a few recently published guidelines encompassing the usage of artificial intelligence as it aligns with technology management in the public sector. While these publications may be outdated in their initial publication date, they are essential guidelines you must respect and adhere to for your workplace to maintain leverage in controlling external attackers and internal policy violators.

- NIST AI 600-1 *Artificial Intelligence Risk Management Framework:* Generative Artificial Intelligence Profile was released in July 2024, with the purpose of providing recommendations and guidelines relating to the usage of artificial intelligence for information security, intellectual property, information integrity, human–AI configuration, data privacy, and risk assessment correlating with AI.[45] Reliance on this publication is important because it will support your ability to effectively manage AI as a tool for securing and storing data assets. On page 7, you learn that generative artificial intelligence poses a threat to the privacy of data. It is important to review how this aligns with your workplace and its reliance on AI for information and data storage. It is also suggested that the usage of AI places sensitive information at risk. This can be costly if exposed to your consumer base. Although this publication is guidance, it is your responsibility to assess data security effectively to avoid misconfiguration. This publication will enlighten you on the significance of human–AI misconfiguration. I sincerely recommend researching this publication thoroughly as your partner in determining what scale of AI is reliable and what should be trusted by the output of AI.
- NIST 800-218A *Secure Software Development Practices for Generative AI and Dual-Use Foundation Models*: An SSDF Community Profile was published and released in July 2024, with the purpose of educating AI model producers, AI system producers, and AI system acquirers. While this is limited to this audience of readers, it is important to acknowledge the recommendations and guidelines as tools to support your workplace's reliance on AI. This publication stresses that the outdated recommended guidelines offered in previously published NIST special publications need to be aligned with newly released published documents to ensure consistency of accuracy.[46] This publication also enables the reading audience to understand how to secure software during the development lifecycle to ensure that AI producers, system producers, and system acquirers are aware of the outdated cybersecurity recommendations in previous publications. Thus, it is essential to do your own research and determine what level of guideline recommendation best meets the needs of your workplace and its reliance on artificial intelligence applications.
- NIST AI 100-4 *Reducing Risk Posed by Synthetic Content*: An Overview of Technical Approaches to Digital Content Transparency was introduced in November 2024, with the purpose of introducing innovative concepts

of reducing risk factors aligning with the usage of AI for generative AI child sexual abuse material and non-consensual intimate imagery.[47] Adhering to these recommendations in this publication is essential! Pay close attention to pages 5 to 27 to understand data tracking.

Knowing how to respond to questions asked by stakeholders is another important responsibility of IT and information system practitioners. These tools are assets you need in your archive of reliable research. Assessing these and following newly published documents that will be presented over time is key to staying up to date with how these publications are modified. Relying on content that supports your workplace usage of AI, no matter the scale or scope, is beneficial to supporting your role as a technology management/ manager in your workplace.

Aligning Domestic and International Technology Management Public Policy in the Workplace

To support your need to define effective and clearly written policies for information systems, information technology, cloud computing, artificial intelligence, and machine learning, having a reliable policy template is essential. Thus, the template provided below is a dynamic supporting document to enable you to create and define or modify your current policies to meet the needs of your workplace. These supporting documents utilized to create this policy align with policies discussed throughout this chapter and previous chapters. This methodology enables you to effectively recommend guidelines to executive leaders who need to have a clear understanding of what is needed to effectively manage all technology across the entity. Executive leaders need to understand the NIST recommendations implemented to support the integration of technology management usage, aligning with domestic and international public policies for the workplace.

However, NIST policies are not the only public policies to align with. Some additional public policies include international public policies such as the European Commission General Data Protection Regulation, a framework outlining data privacy and protection. The OECD Guideline for Protection of Privacy and Transborder Flows of Personal Data is another that focuses on cross-border data flow and privacy principles. ISO/IEC 27001& 27017 focus on information security management and cloud security. The United Nations Roadmap for Digital Cooperation outlines global digital governance policy. Cloud Computing Standards help establish architecture definitions correlating with enterprise cloud policies. In fact, the EU Cloud Code of

Conduct is crucial in understanding how to align cloud service compliance with GDPR. Furthermore, the APEC Cross-border Privacy Rules help you understand Asia–Pacific cross-border data privacy, as do the International Labor Organization Guidelines on Telework, which relate to digital remote workers. Additional public policies include the Digital Economy Partnership Agreement, which includes requirements in Chile, New Zealand, and Singapore. This framework embodies regulations on e-commerce, cloud services, and digital trade.

The policy template outlined below provides a visual display of a useful, well-organized information technology, information security policy. Reviewing this template and mirroring this approach will help you develop a clear, written legal workplace policy that ensures your usage of technology is configured effectively and correctly, and protected from external cyber attackers and internal human error incidents. This policy template will enable you to customize the technology tools and applications utilized, as well as include the workplace name. No copyright is affixed, so this template can be used without permission.

Policy Template

[workplace name] Information Security and Technology Management Policy

[Date, month, year]

[Policy designer name]

Purpose and scope

This information security and technology management policy is developed to ensure [workplace name] aligns with the CIA triad, that is, confidentiality, integrity, and availability. The CIA triad code of ethics was enacted under the influence of the US Department of Defense, which published the Orange Book in 1983 to protect its DoD Trusted Computer System Evaluation Criteria.[1] The purpose of this policy is to integrate a compliance application to protect the data and information assets developed, stored, transmitted, and secured in the computer network information system, information technology, cloud computing architecture, artificial intelligence, and machine learning technology tools and software relied on by [workplace name].

The scope of this policy includes all network applications, computer devices, Wi-Fi, peripherals, software, and technology tools used for business operations and communication. With the integration of this workplace policy, all personnel are required to adhere to and support, as well as align daily business operations and communication with the outlined policy framework regulating the security of [workplace name] for the lifecycle of this workplace's existence.

Key components

Data security and storage are a primary focus to ensure confidentiality, integrity, and availability, and are enforced to safeguard [workplace name] executive leaders, personnel, and customers' personal information from unauthorized users. Under The Privacy Act of 1974, the E-government Act of 2002, the United States Fair Credit Reporting Act, the EU GDPR, ISO/IEC 27001 & 27017, United Nations' Roadmap for Digital Cooperation, APEC Cross-border Privacy Rules, and the Digital Economy Partnership Agreement, [workplace name] is accountable for securing all digitized private and personal information stored in our information system, information technology, cloud computing architecture, artificial intelligence, and machine learning tools and technology.

Roles and responsibilities bestowed to executive leaders include working in partnership with human resource management and information technology managers, and information system managers to define [workplace name] usage requirements for technology and discuss how this technology is beneficial to the daily operation of this workplace.

It is further required that executive leaders take the initiative to design the assessment requirements under NIST SP 800-53 Rev.5 relating to *Security and Privacy of Controls for Federal Information Systems and Organizations* and NIST SP 800- 171 Rev. 3 *Protecting Controlled Unclassified Information in Nonfederal Systems and Organizations*. This is vital because it holds [workplace name] accountable to ensure security and privacy controls are implemented to access data and information assets. This also implements requirements for incident response, assessing and reporting, and system and communications protection.

In addition, the responsibility of executive leaders must align with NIST SP 800-37 Rev. 2 for *Risk Management Framework for Information Systems and Organizations*. This is required because it supports the system life cycle of [workplace name], correlating with [workplace name] security and privacy on data and information assets. This will ensure [workplace name] enforces a consistency of integrating security and privacy activities during the system life cycle, as well as help manage all risks aligning with [workplace name] information system.

Furthermore, under NIST SP 800-92 the *Guide to Computer Security Log Management*, executive leaders must enforce all human resource managers and teams, personnel and staff, as well as information technology and information system managers to maintain written logs relating to the security of data and information assets, which is done to emphasize the value of log management in detecting and assessing any [workplace name] security incident.

Personnel are responsible for ensuring alignment of all daily business operations and communication aligning with [workplace name] information technology data and information security policy, implemented to ensure confidentiality, integrity, and availability aligning with the CIA triad. This must be upheld and respected throughout the system lifecycle of this workplace. Personnel are required to ensure they meet the quarterly training assessment requirements enacted by executive leaders, human resource management, and information technology and information system management. In doing so, personnel will align their responsibilities to help [workplace name] secure all data and information assets stored, shared, and transmitted in the information system, information technology, cloud computing, artificial intelligence, and machine learning applications and hardware [workplace name] relies on for business operations and communications.

Executive leaders, human resource management, personnel and staff, as well as information technology and information system managers who transmit data or information belonging to [workplace name] across the internet, domestically or internationally, are held accountable under the Electronic Communications Privacy Act (ECPA) under Title II (The Stored Communications Act). Under the ECPA, [workplace name] executive leaders, human resource managers, personnel and staff, information technology and information system managers must balance the individual privacy rights of all consumers [workplace name] conducts business with.

[workplace name] information technology practitioners, information system analysts, consultants, developers, designers, administrators, analysts, and cybersecurity practitioners are responsible for ensuring the confidentiality, integrity, and availability of [workplace name], ensuring the alignment of such with all federal laws and public policy, domestic and international. Doing so invokes a consistency of compliance and helps reduce risk factors that often are ignored and overlooked. Under the US Stored Communications Act, the consent of private communication shared between executive leaders, human resource managers, personnel, staff, and consumers must be concealed and protected from unauthorized end-users both externally and internally.

Risk management

[workplace name] will efficiently assess all data and information assets for security vulnerabilities using an artificial office automation system and knowledge management system. The Office Automation System will help [workplace name] configure the installation of a cloud infrastructure automation that enables this workplace to scale its usage of data storage and control spending costs, because this system enables [workplace name] to control access and regulate the configuration for the specific needs of [workplace name]. Usage of cloud infrastructure will benefit the storage of secured data and information at rest. This will also increase the number of security layers through multi-factor authentication. [workplace name] will be able to control vulnerabilities that could be gateways for external cyber attackers to penetrate the surface layer of accessibility and distort, modify, or confiscate sensitive and highly monetizable information assets.

Usage of a cloud infrastructure system enables [workplace name] to configure settings in the software to collect analytics for data storage and help assess risk factors that can be catastrophic to [workplace name] security controls if the system is penetrated effectively. The deployment of electronic communication across this workplace must align with NIST 800-122 *Guide to Protecting Personally Identifiable Information*. This guideline recommends characteristics of Personal Identifiable Information, as well as conveys NIST recommendations to agencies that ensure the protection of personal information, and ensures the security, development, documentation, and implementation of information security training to align with the Federal Information Security Management Act of 2022.[2]

Usage of NIST 800 137 *Assessing Information Security Continuous Monitoring (ISCM) Programs: Developing an ISCM Program Assessment* will support [workplace name] to develop an information security continuous monitoring program. This will enable improved assessment of security vulnerabilities for each component of technology relied on for [workplace name], including information technology, information systems, cloud computing, artificial intelligence, and machine learning.

[workplace name] will strive to adhere to domestic and international laws and policies that must be evaluated to determine if [workplace name] is held accountable. The *United Nations Guidelines for Consumer Protection in E-commerce and Data Security* outline security recommendations because [workplace name] is integrating cloud infrastructure applications to secure consumer data and information. This includes business and consumer interaction and ensures secure and ethical IT practices.

[workplace name] will also align usage of cloud infrastructure automation with ISO/IEC 27017 for cloud security controls; ISO/IEC 27018 for the protection of personal data in the cloud. Doing so enhances the layer of security used for cloud infrastructure.

Office management, communication, document management, digital image processing, and software as a service (SaaS) management. Process automation, billing tools, API access management, project management, and CRM (Customer Relationship Management) are all crucial components of the information system relied on by [workplace name]. Therefore, all executive leaders, personnel, and staff will conduct daily business operation activities in alignment with the policy requirements imposed by domestic and international laws, policy, and regulations that ensure effective implementation and management of [workplace name] information system and technology management infrastructure.

The knowledge management information system will enable [workplace name] to identify, organize, store, and disseminate information securely across [workplace name]'s internal communication network. Companies with a knowledge management strategy achieve business outcomes more quickly as increased organizational learning and collaboration among team members facilitate faster decision-making across the business.[3] [workplace name] will assess explicit knowledge to enable [workplace name] to collect various document styles, including manuals, reports, guides, and enable [workplace name] to easily disseminate knowledge across teams.[4]

Data classification

[workplace name] has designated value to information and data assets to determine the scope of security required to manage and secure these assets from unauthorized personnel and executive leadership. In alignment with the World Trade Organization E-commerce and IT Services Agreement, [workplace name] will always support open access to global cloud services and IT markets. Doing so will ensure [workplace name] aligns business communication and service or product delivery with cross-border IT service integration.

The scale of security value on data and information assets at [workplace name] will remain standard under the World Economic Forum – Data Valuation Framework. This multi-dimensional valuation framework supports [workplace name] to effectively assess value using financial returns, the impact of goods for public consumers, the internal efficiency of services or products delivered, as well as the strategic competitive influence of [workplace name]. [workplace name] will also adhere to the recommendation in ISO/IEC 8000 to determine data quality as a part of data value. Furthermore, aligning with ISO 30414 [workplace name] can ensure valuation is assessed by the intangible asset for enterprise usage.

Access control

[workplace name] will continue to monitor all login processing by utilizing a multi-factor authentication credential system. [workplace name] authentication activities will align with NIST SP 800-63 *Digital Identity Guidelines*. NIST 800-63A *Identity Proofing*. NIST 800-63B *Authentication and Lifecycle Management*, including MFA, password standards, and biometrics.

[workplace name] authentication will align with the *Federal Information Security Modernization Act*, as well as HIPAA, if related to healthcare information security. [workplace name] will also align with the *Gramm–Leach–Bliley Act*, which mandates effective security control to protect customer information with secure authentication.

[workplace name] will also align authentication with guidelines enacted by the US Cybersecurity and Infrastructure Security Agency, which mandates policies for user access control to databases, secure authentication, and identity management.

In alignment with international law and policy relating to authentication, [workplace name] will align its authentication processing with recommended guidelines provided in ISO/IEC 27002 regulating authentication controls. [workplace name] will also align authentication practice with the

General Data Protection Regulation (GDPR), which values the effective security of personal data and the use of access control to secure information and data.

[workplace name] will align its authentication of secure data and information assets with the electronic identification, authentication and trust services enacted by the European Union. This supports [workplace name] in regulating electronic identification for secure transactions deployed throughout the EU, if applicable.

[workplace name] will ensure that all data and information assets collected, stored, or transmitted across the border of Asia–Pacific economies align with the Asia–Pacific Economic Cooperation Cross-border Privacy Rule, which promotes secure management of personal data transmitted via the internet from domestic to international borders of Asia–Pacific. This information security policy will integrate information security management as recommended by Dr. Michael E. Whitman and Dr. Herbert J. Mattord.

Only personnel rendered with clearance to specific databases will be granted permission to access such databases. Authorization is given to executive leaders only if access to databases and information security networks aligns with the job role and responsibility. Personnel will only be granted authorization to access controlled databases and information networks if their role and responsibilities with [workplace name] require them to have access. Access to databases is limited to role and responsibilities. Passwords will be required. All identity passwords must be approved by meeting the standard 12-character coding requirements for a secure password.

Accountability

[workplace name] issues this information security warning to all executive leaders, personnel, and staff who work with [workplace name] either contracted, full-time, part-time, or hybrid. Each executive leader, personnel, and staff member is held accountable for this information security and technology management policy. Violators will be reprimanded. Penalties include loss of vacation days, time-off without pay, temporary suspension, or termination. The severity of information security and technology management within [workplace name] is vital to the lifecycle of information security and technology management implemented within this company.

[workplace name] operates with a zero-trust access control system and will not tolerate violators of this information security and technology management policy.

As an employee of [workplace name], I [employee name] understand that I am held accountable for my role and responsibilities to this [corporation, business, non-profit] for my contracted timeline. I understand that until my termination from [workplace name], I'm responsible for securing all data and information assets owned by [workplace name]. I understand that if found in violation of this policy, I will be reprimanded and may lose vacation days, be suspended without pay, or terminated, without exception. I also understand that I must engage in ongoing information security and technology management training offered by [workplace name] to ensure my compliance with this information security and technology management policy.

Date policy issued

Chief Information Security Office name & signature (if applicable)
Chief Technology Officer name & signature (if applicable)
Chief Information Officer name & signature (if applicable)
Human Resource Manager name & signature
Chief Executive Officer name & signature

Personnel member name & signature
Date signed

Reference

[1] Hashemi-Pour, C. (2023, December 21). What is the CIA triad (confidentiality, integrity and availability)? https://www.techtarget.com/whatis/definition/Confidentiality-integrity-and-availability-CIA#:~:text=The%20history%20of%20the%20CIA%20triad&text=The%20term%20confidentiality%20may%20have,right%20one%20for%20your%20organization.

[2] Radack, S. (2010, April 28). Guide to Protecting Personally Identifiable Information. https://www.nist.gov/publications/guide-protecting-personally-identifiable-information

[3] IBM, (n.d). What is Knowledge Management? https://www.ibm.com/think/topics/knowledge-management
[4] Ibid

Global Standards of Cybersecurity, Information Security, and Technology Management for Workplace Partnerships

Having clarity on the global standards of cybersecurity, information security, and technology management for workplace partnerships is crucial to ensure all data and information assets are secured and inaccessible to unauthorized individuals. Previously mentioned global standards enabled you to grasp the validity of these regulations to support controlling access to sensitive data and information. When corporations, businesses, non-profits, government, and academia collect consumer data or information that aligns with business transactions, it is imperative to know global regulations to avoid penalties that can be costly. One example of recent disagreements across borders involves the United States, China, and Canadian tariffs, which play a significant role in how trade of products and services falls under these policies, and demonstrate the severity of the violation. When working in partnership with third-party service or product providers, it is crucial to understand the Service Level Agreements (SLAs). As mentioned in Chapter 4, SLAs are valued contractual agreements between service owners and end users. Neglecting to understand these documents can impact the quality of services rendered and impact on the ability to control rates of usage. Thus, investing in understanding global standards for how your workplace deploys cybersecurity, information security, and technology management is valuable to the reputation of your workplace.

A few of the laws and policies discussed in this chapter and previous chapters outline what regulations are essential in helping your workplace remain compliant and avoid increased costs for violating any of these regulations. As an information technology and information security or information system practitioner, it is crucial for you to take the liberty and review and comprehend these regulations. Neglecting to do so will impact your workplace's ability to remain trusted in partnerships, controlling access to sensitive data and information assets. One of the best alternative methods to understand and access global cybersecurity, information security, and technology management resources is searching openai.com. Making sure you are up to date with these global requirements will provide your workplace with the leverage it needs to compete with competitors.

Conclusion

Technology management and information security public policy play a role in supporting the usage of technology in a business, government, non-profit, or academic sector. Knowing how these policies play a role is the responsibility of technology managers. Domestic policies developed in the United States are backed by federal laws, as well as state laws. In many instances, these laws are integrated into how public policies come to exist and take precedent in controlling the enforcement of these regulations, which are developed as subsidiaries to many laws. Staying knowledgeable of the policies published under the National Institute of Standards and Technology (NIST) special publications is crucial to knowing how to effectively modify your workplace information security, information system, information technology, cloud computing, artificial intelligence, and machine learning policies.

International public policies are important to understand because businesses, government, and academic institutions partnering across borders must acknowledge these regulations and implement processes and procedures that align with them to enable their workplace to remain compliant and avoid penalties for noncompliance. Much like domestic public policies, international public policies take precedent. The EU GDPR is one of the most widely recognized regulations that must be adhered to, or violators will face penalties.

Having an archive of public policies on file in the workplace will help you stay current. Keep in mind that public policies are revised often; in some countries, revisions are made every two or three years. Staying current provides leverage in controlling risk factors that could be potentially catastrophic to the long-term success of your workplace and its business decision support. When relying on technology as a tool for communication or to store and transmit sensitive data or information belonging to consumers, it is important to align how data and information are secured. Usage of encryption and cipher text are key methods for protecting sensitive assets.

Thus, it is recommended that you continue researching. Being unique in how you develop your approach to staying current with research on domestic and international public policies that align with your usage of information systems, information technology, cloud computing, artificial intelligence, and machine learning is what will give your workplace the competitive edge over competitors. These are common technology tools, hardware, and software components integrated in today's workplace. Neglecting to stay current with policies and laws will impact your ability to effectively support your workplace from being targeted and easily victimized.

The case study provided below is an example of a scenario that has huge complications when faced in a real-world experience. If you omit the name of this corporation and replace it with your workplace name, imagine the consequences you would face. Furthermore, the chapter review questions are additional learning tools to reiterate what you have read. The answers to these review questions are located after the list of references.

Case Study

Background: Johnnie's Tech Hub LLC is a mid-sized limited liability company operating its headquarters in Canton, Michigan. Services provided include data and information storage, archiving, back-up in the cloud, and migration from on-premises to a cloud infrastructure, using Amazon Web Services as the third-party service provider. Clients of Johnnie's Tech Hub LLC reside in North America, Canada, Australia, London, Vancouver, Mexico, and Southern Asia.

Since the enactment of the EU General Data Protection Regulation (GDPR) and the Asia Pacific Cross-border Data Protection Regulation, aligning with the 2012 Protection Act in the Asian Pacific, many businesses have experienced an increase in articles published regarding the number of violators being penalized for non-compliance with regulations and policies imposed in various countries abroad. However, these regulations are not always required to be adhered to by all businesses. So, the CISO and CTO of Johnnie's Tech Hub LLC failed to consider the role they play in making sure their corporation adheres to these regulations and others alike.

Public policy focuses on standardized quality controls that alarm the public of their responsibilities to ensure the security and privacy of individuals is not violated. Johnnie's Tech Hub LLC is responsible for securing private and personal information of their clients, and if targeted successfully, it will result in loss of client trust, reputational damage, and fines. Under the EU GDPR, fines for violations are 2% of an entity's worldwide revenue earnings.[48] Or, for more severe non-compliance risk factors, fines can reach 4% of an entity's worldwide annual revenue acquired from the proceeding financial year.

Under this regulation, the usage of third-party service providers for email or cloud storage can still result in a violation. But Johnnie's Tech Hub LLC does not always comply because its information technology team and managers are not as knowledgeable about staying current with how the business aligns with these public policies. How can Johnnie's Tech Hub LLC stay current? What should the executive leadership of Johnnie's Tech Hub LLC do to ensure the corporation does not incur fines? Who should be held accountable? How will executive leaders control this risk factor?

Chapter 5 Review Questions

1. China enacted the Private Information Protection Law. [True or False].
2. Egypt considered Law 151 in 2020. [True or False].
3. When did India pass the Personal Data Protection Bill?
4. How many countries have defined public policy and laws to reduce the violation of privacy for the sensitive data and information assets owned by their citizens?
5. In what year did Australia pass the Online Safety Act?
6. What country enacted the Roadmap?
7. Under what special publication is the Artificial Intelligence Risk Management Framework classified as?
8. When was the Generative Artificial Intelligence Profile released?
9. What is the NIST 800-218A publication about?
10. What does the ISO/IEC 27001 & 27017 focus on?
11. What does NIST 800-122 outline?
12. Which state in the United States enacted the Artificial Intelligence Video Interview Act?
13. What country enacted the National Artificial Intelligence Strategy?
14. What country enacted the Personal Data Protection Law?

References

[1] Government of Canada, (2022). Canada's Digital Charter. https://ised-isde.canada.ca/site/innovation-better-canada/en/canadas-digital-charter-trust-digital-world

[2] Ibid
[3] Ibid
[4] Bernardo-Apacible, A. & Bushey, K. (2025, January 28). Data protection and privacy laws now in effect in 144 countries. https://iapp.org/news/a/data-protection-and-privacy-laws-now-in-effect-in-144-countries
[5] Baig, A. & Hasa, A. (2024, March 2). An Overview of Emerging Global AI Regulations. https://securiti.ai/ai-regulations-around-the-world/#:~:text=Global%20AI%20Regulation%20Landscape:%20Various%20countries%2C%20including,and%20legislation%20to%20govern%20AI%20use%20responsibly.
[6] Ibid
[7] Australia Human Rights Commission, (2021, March 1). Final Report: Human Rights and Technology. https://humanrights.gov.au/our-work/technology-and-human-rights/publications/final-report-human-rights-and-technology
[8] Pacheco, R. (2023). Legislative Activity: Bill 2338/2023. https://www25.senado.leg.br/web/atividade/materias/-/materia/157233
[9] Ibid
[10] Government of Canada, (n/d). The Artificial Intelligence and Data Act (AIDA) Companion document. https://ised-isde.canada.ca/site/innovation-better-canada/en/artificial-intelligence-and-data-act-aida-companion-document
[11] Office of Central Cyberspace Affairs Commission, (2022, December 11). Regulations on the management of in-depth synthesis of internet information services. https://www.cac.gov.cn/2022-12/11/c_1672221949354811.htm
[12] Ibid
[13] Ibid
[14] Ibid
[15] Ma, X. (2025, February 27). Deep Synthesis Not Deepfake: How AI Compliance Works in China. https://www.chinalawvision.com/2025/02/digital-economy-ai/deep-synthesis-not-deepfake-how-ai-compliance-works-in-china/
[16] Ibid
[17] Baig, A. & Hasan, A. (2023, September 26). Understanding the Shanghai AI Regulations. https://securiti.ai/shanghai-ai-regulation/
[18] Baig, A. & Sattar, F. M. (2025, March 13). Overview of Personal Information Protection Law of the People's Republic of China. https://securiti.ai/china-personal-information-protection-law-overview/

[19] Ibid
[20] Creemers, R., Shi, M., Dudley, L. & Webster, G. (2020, October 21). China's Draft 'Personal Information Protection Law' (Full Translation). https://www.newamerica.org/cybersecurity-initiative/digichina/blog/chinas-draft-personal-information-protection-law-full-translation/
[21] Baig, A. & Sattar, F. M. (2025, March 13). Overview of Personal Information Protection Law of the People's Republic of China. https://securiti.ai/china-personal-information-protection-law-overview/
[22] Office of the Central Cyberspace Affairs Commission, (2024, March 22). National Internet Information Office Order. https://www.cac.gov.cn/2024-03/22/c_1712776611775634.htm
[23] Ibid
[24] Malik, I.O. (2024, January 8). Understanding Cross Borders Data Transfers Under GDPR and PIPL. https://securiti.ai/blog/cross-borders-data-transfers-pipl/
[25] European Union, (2024, February 27). High-level summary of the AI Act. https://artificialintelligenceact.eu/high-level-summary/
[26] Ibid
[27] Confederation of European Data Protection, (2023, June 16). AI and Personal Data A Guide for DPOs "Frequently Asked Questions". https://cedpo.eu/wp-content/uploads/CEDPO-AI-and-Data-FAQ-12-June-2023.pdf
[28] Ibid
[29] Baig, A. & Hasan, A. (2024, March 2). An Overview of Emerging Global AI Regulations. https://securiti.ai/ai-regulations-around-the-world/#:~:text=Global%20AI%20Regulation%20Landscape:%20Various%20countries%2C%20including,and%20legislation%20to%20govern%20AI%20use%20responsibly
[30] Ministry of Innovation, Science & Technology, (2023). Israel's Policy on Artificial Intelligence: Regulations and Ethics 2023. https://www.gov.il/BlobFolder/policy/ai_2023/en/Israels%20AI%20Policy%202023.pdf
[31] Ibid
[32] e-Gov Law Search (2020, April 1). Act on Improving the Transparency and Fairness of Specified Digital Platforms. https://laws.e-gov.go.jp/law/502AC0000000038
[33] Ibid
[34] Te Mana Māori Data Sovereignty Network, (2018, October). Principles of Maori Data Sovereignty. Brief #1. https://cdn.auckland.ac.nz/assets/psych/about/our-research/documents/TMR+M%C4%81ori+Data+Sovereignty+Principles+Oct+2018.pdf

[35] Baig, A. & Hasan, A. (2024, March 2). An Overview of Emerging Global AI Regulations. https://securiti.ai/ai-regulations-around-the-world/#:~:text=Global%20AI%20Regulation%20Landscape:%20Various%20countries%2C%20including,and%20legislation%20to%20govern%20AI%20use%20responsibly
[36] Saudi Data & AI Authority, (2021, September 16). Personal Data Protection Law. https://sdaia.gov.sa/en/SDAIA/about/Documents/Personal%20Data%20English%20V2-23April2023-%20Reviewed-.pdf
[37] Republic of Singapore, (2018, March 16). Republic of Singapore, Government Gazette Acts Supplement: Cybersecurity Act 2018. https://sso.agc.gov.sg/Acts-Supp/9-2018/#:~:text=An%20Act%20to%20require%20or,or%20related%20amendments%20to%20certain
[38] UK Parliament, (2024, September 23). Data Protection and Digital Information Bill. https://bills.parliament.uk/bills/3430
[39] Government of UK, (2020, September 16). Data Ethics Framework. https://www.gov.uk/government/publications/data-ethics-framework
[40] National Cyber Security Centre, (2019, April 18). Intelligent Security Tools: assessing intelligent tools for cyber security. https://www.ncsc.gov.uk/collection/intelligent-security-tools
[41] Government of UK, (2023, June 14). Software and AI as a Medical Device Change Programme roadmap. https://www.gov.uk/government/publications/software-and-ai-as-a-medical-device-change-programme/software-and-ai-as-a-medical-device-change-programme-roadmap
[42] Ibid
[43] Malik, I.O. (2025, March 10). Connecticut Data Privacy Act (CTDPA): All You Need to Know. https://securiti.ai/privacy-laws/us/connecticut/
[44] Ibid
[45] Raimondo, M.G. (2024, July). Artificial Intelligence Risk Management Framework: Generative Artificial Intelligence Profile. https://nvlpubs.nist.gov/nistpubs/ai/NIST.AI.600-1.pdf
[46] Booth, H., Souppaya, M., Vassilev, A., Ogata, M., Stanley, M. & Scarfone, K. (2024, July). Secure Software Development Practices for Generative AI and Dual-Use Foundation Models. https://nvlpubs.nist.gov/nistpubs/SpecialPublications/NIST.SP.800-218A.pdf
[47] Raimondo, M.G. (2024, November). Reducing Risks Posed by Synthetic Content: An Overview of Technical Approaches to Digital Content Transparency. https://nvlpubs.nist.gov/nistpubs/ai/NIST.AI.100-4.pdf
[48] Wolford, B. (n.d.). What are the GDPR Fines? https://gdpr.eu/fines/

Chapter Review Question Answers

1. False.
2. True.
3. 2019.
4. 120.
5. 2021.
6. The United Kingdom.
7. NIST AI 600-1.
8. July 2024.
9. Secure software development practices for generative AI and dual-use foundation models.
10. Information security management and cloud security.
11. Guide to Protecting Personally Identifiable Information.
12. Illinois.
13. Singapore.
14. Saudia Arabia.

6

Risk Factor Security Controls

Learning objectives

- Determine the risk in your workplace reliance on technology tools and applications.
- Understand how to mitigate risk using NIST recommendations and US DoD recommendations.
- Understand how to improve security control and assess technology tools and applications for business communication, data and information storage, transmission, and security.

Chapter 5 provided clarity on the recommendations and guidelines outlined in several National Institute of Standards and Technology special publications relating to artificial intelligence and technology management. The plethora of information collected and shared from those special publications is a useful tool to include in your daily and ongoing business life cycle in correlation with the integration of technology in your workplace. Chapter 6 will increase your awareness of additional NIST special publications, particularly those relating to risk factors aligning with technology security controls. This information is crucial because many business enterprises lack knowledge regarding the significance of NIST special publications and their role in helping the private sector reduce risk factors in technology usage. Furthermore, this chapter is composed to help you determine the level of risk related to the technology integrated in your workplace. In fact, this chapter strives to help you better understand how to mitigate risk associated with technology in your workplace by adhering to the US Department of Defense mitigation recommendations. Most importantly, this chapter helps you improve security control and assess technology tools and applications for business communication, data and information storage, transmission, and security.

DOI: 10.1201/9788743809715-6

In conclusion, you are provided with 15 chapter review questions to reiterate your knowledge of this chapter.

When you consider risk factors aligning with technology usage in the workplace, it is challenging to determine the broad scope of risk there really is. In Chapter 3, Table 3.2, you were provided with details regarding threat and vulnerability mitigation resolutions. This table design helped you better understand how to assess risk levels correlating with operating systems, telecommunication systems, and peripherals. But what about the technology software applications commonly used? How can you determine the most reliable defense to secure those applications? As mentioned previously, the National Institute of Standards and Technology special publication series has been instrumental in supporting the private sector control risk factors integrated in technology commonly integrated in the workplace. Unfortunately, research reports that many companies and corporations continue to ignore the value of partnering with NIST recommendations and guidelines on risk factors and controlling the privacy of data and information assets.[1]

Thus, as leaders of information technology and information systems, cloud computing, artificial intelligence, and machine learning, it is crucial to implement effective strategies to control risk related to technology relied on in the workplace. This is now more invaluable due to the growing number of civil liability suits filed against corporations and businesses over the last 3 years.[2] To help you control risk, it is important to know what type of risk you need to control in alignment with the type of technology tools and applications integrated in the workplace.

Common technology tools in the workplace include laptops and desktop computers, mobile phones or iPhones, Wi-Fi, internet, servers, printers, fax machines, web cameras, computer microphones, postage stamp machines, payment processing systems, video conferencing, customer relationship management software, enterprise resource planning software, human resource management software, and document filing system software. The specific type of technology used in your workplace technology system differs greatly depending on the scope of business delivery and transactions. However, the technology mentioned is commonly relied on. How you determine what type of risk is developed in each technological application and tool used should be your biggest concern.

One way to assess risk in the technology you use is to do some serious research. It is recommended to rely on Openai.com to help you understand risks integrated in any technology used in business communication and operation. Doing so will help save you a lot of stress. Depending on the brand of laptop or desktop computer used in the office impacts the scope of clarity you acquire regarding integrated risk factors with such technology. If you conduct research on the brand of laptop you are using, you should be able to acquire enough knowledge to understand what risks are already found in that laptop or desktop computer brand.

Take, for instance, in the office, there are three Mac laptop computers, two Dell desktop computers, and two Lenovo desktop computers. To determine the risk of each requires knowing details such as the model and model number. For the Mac laptop, we use Air and Pro. When deploying research to understand the risk factors integrated in either device, research reports that the MacBook Air device embodies hardware-related risk, including non-upgradable components.[3] It is further noted that once purchased, there is no way to upgrade this component. As a result, research reports that the system will slow down, as well as decrease response and performance over time. And this will impact the ability to store sensitive data.

When researching the Dell laptop models, this office uses the Dell Precision 5690 Workstation. Openai.com shared details, conveying that risk factors include driver and hardware instability.[4] Additionally, this risk factor causes web camera malfunction, audio issues, and frequent blue screens. Risk also includes issues relating to the design of the device casing, as well as connectivity limitations and firewall and boot issues.[5] The list of risks also includes thermal management challenges.

Now, imagine investing in purchasing these brands of laptops for your business office. Risk relating to the device itself leads to additional risk factors. In fact, research reports that many risk factors exist when purchasing laptops, such as pre-installed applets that tend to be outdated with the manufacturer's recommended updates. Then there is concern regarding hard-drive failure, battery degradation, and overheating.[6]

So, as you can understand, it is your responsibility to enhance your risk assessment to ensure your workplace is not easily victimized. How do you proceed, you might be wondering? First, let us examine NIST 800-12 rev. 1, which was published in June 2017. This special publication was initially written to support computer security. But with the updating of information, this publication is now titled *An Introduction to Information Security*.[7] Relying on this publication is crucial because it helps you define effective strategies to prevent victimization. Adhering to the recommendations and guidelines in this publication will enable you to improve how you outline the role and responsibilities of Senior Management, the CEO, the CIO, and the officials elected to control privacy across the workplace. If this is your role and responsibility, it is recommended that you review each role and begin integrating the responsibilities of these roles into your daily business actions and communication with senior leadership.

This publication will also support your knowledge development relating to threats such as malicious hackers and malicious code. More importantly, this publication will help you outline a program policy. You were provided with a policy template in Chapter 5 for information security and technology management. Enhancing that template with the recommended guidelines offered in this publication will be a dynamic way to uniquely determine the scope of policy design needed for your business.

However, there are more benefits to relying on this publication. For instance, this publication will support your need to apply information assurance, which includes security engineering and operational assurance. This publication will also help you understand the severity of software support and configuration management, as well as cryptography. The enclosed list of control families is also useful because this helps you improve how you will assess each phase of assessing, planning, developing, implementing, and securing your workplace and its reliance on laptops and desktop computers.

Another vital special publication to consider adding to your list of NIST SPs is 800-124 Rev. 2 *Guidelines for Managing the Security of Mobile Devices in the Enterprise*. Published in May 2023, this publication outlines the type of threats to be aware of, such as the installation of unauthorized certificates, credential theft, wireless eavesdropping, mobile malware, and the type of threats to the device management system.[8] This publication also outlines mobile security mechanisms and provides recommendations for mitigating known risks. When you lack the overall knowledge of risk woven into this technology, utilizing artificial intelligence to gain clarity of additional risk factors is required to stay ahead of nefarious pranksters who engage in childish pranks that cost your workplace big money to rebuild from when successfully victimized.

It is just as imperative to have risk control over the accessibility of your workplace Wi-Fi. The NIST special publications to rely on for this support include NIST 800-97 *Establishing Wireless Robust Security Networks*; A Guide to IEEE 802.11i, which will support your ability to implement security frameworks to secure your workplace network. Security support includes port-based access control and key generation and distribution.[9] You also need to consider the recommendations and guidelines provided in NIST 800-153 *Guidelines for Securing Wireless Local Area Networks* (WLANS). This publication is important because it enables you to implement attack monitoring using basic security strategies.[10]

You also need to be knowledgeable of the US Department of Homeland Security Cybersecurity Engineering recommendations and guidelines, which you can gain access to in the March 15, 2017, version 1.0 eBook titled *A Guide to Securing Networks for Wi-Fi* (IEEE 802.11 *Family*). This guide will support your ability to effectively assess threat types, as well as understand recommended threat remediation.[11] As a bonus, you will also learn how to effectively budget for Wi-Fi security, as well as gain Bluetooth security insight.

When concerned with the security and risk associated with servers, it is suggested that you review NIST 800-123 *Guide to General Server Security*. While this publication was published in 2008, it embodies knowledge that can be useful today. This publication is beneficial because it helps you understand the risks associated with servers, including vulnerabilities and threats. This publication also enables you to understand security categorization for information systems. Using this publication will support your need to understand the role of the Chief Information Officer, Information Systems Security Program Manager, Information Systems Security Officer, and the Server, network, and security administrators.[12]

Risk factors are key components that you, as a practitioner, must have clarity on and know how to control risks that can lead to catastrophic incidents that will cost your workplace full recovery. Staying ahead of the competition is your goal. To achieve that, you need to understand how to reduce risk in printers, fax machines, web cameras, and computer microphones as well. How do you do this? What is your best method of controlling risk associated with these technology tools? What about the integration of technology within these tools? This is the Internet of Things. The National Institute of Standards and Technology has published the NIST SP 800-213 series, which focuses on federal agencies that adopt IoT devices for their system of operation. However, while this publication is designed to support federal systems, private sector entities can benefit from collecting this information and having it as a pathway to understanding IoT and the ability to integrate cybersecurity effectively.

Since the enactment of the IoT Cybersecurity Improvement Act 2020, it is recognized that any agency, public or private, that partners with the federal government is held accountable to these recommendations and guidelines, if he/she is the Chief Information Officer of any federal agency and oversee contracts relating to the use of technology reliant on the Internet of Things.[13] If your workplace is partnered with the US federal government, it is imperative to have knowledge of this law and how it impacts your workplace responsibilities to act in accordance with this law when considering implementing technology infused with IoT.

But the Internet of Things (IoT) is a challenging subject to master because IoT is integrated into printers and fax machines. In fact, it is suggested you align the usage of IoT devices with NIST 800-213A *IoT Device Cybersecurity Guidance for the Federal Government*: *IoT Device Cybersecurity Requirements.* This publication is useful because it supports your ability to implement additional layers of security using cryptology methodologies, as well as authentication and identity management practices. You will also gain the ability to improve essential strategies for securing IoT devices.[14]

The configuration settings for devices embedded with Internet of Things software can be challenging to assess risk if you are not aware of the presence of such applications. Thus, you must be diligent in determining the scale of software embedded in every technology tool you use in the workplace. Neglecting to do so will be a regret that will cost your workplace tremendously!

To ensure you are knowledgeable of how to mitigate risk, reliance on NIST special publication recommendations and the US Department of Defense open-source database known as Common Vulnerabilities and Exposure, or CVE Mitre, will be your partner for your lifecycle with your workplace and your role as an IT/IS practitioner. As pointed out previously, understanding what known vulnerabilities are embedded in your workplace technology tools and applications is crucial to controlling risk that leads to cyber incidents. In fact, when comparing the risk of a Mac Air laptop, the CVE.mitre.org website reports that in 2025, there are three reported known vulnerabilities, including CVE 2025-24085 (CoreMedia Privilege Escalation), which could enable attackers to gain high-level access to a rogue app pre-installed on the device.[15]

Keep in mind, research is vital to your role as an information technology/information systems practitioner. Neglecting to deploy effective research will haunt you. Another known vulnerability found with Apple Mac in 2025 is CVE 2025-24201 (WebKit Sandbox Escape), which enables attackers to deploy unauthorized actions or code in the system.[16]

Using Perplexity.ai enables you to gain a full scope of knowledge relating to vulnerabilities embedded in any technology tool you use in your workplace. However, word to the wise, be sure to "always double check" information provided with other open AI sources to ensure accuracy of data or information. The above vulnerability listing was compiled using Perplexity.ai. The full report for this CVE was compiled using the following keywords: what are the known CVE vulnerabilities found in an Apple Mac Air laptop 2025. Good luck!

When assessing security control for technology tools and applications for business communication, data and information storage, transmission, and security, be sure to apply recommended guidelines offered by the National Institute of Standards and Technology, as pointed out time and again throughout this chapter. However, if your business or workplace is conducting business globally and providing services or products, it is just as imperative to ensure you assess security controls for technology tools and applications for business communication, data and information storage, transmission, and security as it is required to do so in those countries your business or workplace is targeting. Avoiding liabilities and costly penalty fees is smart. Staying steps ahead of the competitor who neglects to do so is superior.

Take, for instance, research helped me understand the significance of security control for business communication in 2025. Effective January 2025 is the Digital Operational Resilience Act. Under this law, businesses must integrate cybersecurity and incident reporting that alarms and alerts consumers about the potential risk of personal information sharing because of a cybersecurity breach. This law requires financial institutions to increase security layers that deter successful cyberattacks.[17] This law covers basic principles for risk management, monitoring of third-party service provider relationships, advanced security control testing, reporting of major information and data breach attacks to authorities once discovered, and a consistency of information exchange that helps others learn from the incidents incurred by other business entities.[18]

Another regulation to learn, research, and adhere to is the EU AI Act. This was enacted to enforce security control over personally identifiable information collected or shared by businesses. Research reports that banning AI unacceptable use in the EU, when EU consumers are involved, includes:

- Cognitive behavioral manipulation of technology to invoke or incite dangerous activities or behavior in human consumers.
- Categorizing people based on demographic identities, socioeconomic status, or characteristics.
- Biometric categorizing people.[19]

By the closing of 2025, many states in the United States will have enacted laws that control the security of personal information in alignment with consumer rights, opt-out consent, and data breach notification. In Chapter 4, you reviewed many of these newly enacted laws across the United States. Staying up to date with new laws enacted throughout 2025 and those ushering in 2026 is crucial to staying ahead of competitors and avoiding penalties against your workplace.

Traditional methods of security control still work. This includes conducting system audits to ensure all data stored in files is secured, and when possible, is layered with private key encryption. It is also important to ensure that data in transit remains encrypted. Using an encryption key and ensuring such keys are only accessible to the proposed end-users is critical to ensuring data and information remain secure. Research collected from IBM reports that with public-key cryptography, the public key is not secret, but the messages it encrypts can be decrypted only by using its associated private key. The private key must be securely stored in a file that is called a keystore. Public-key algorithms alone do not ensure secure communication; you also need to verify the identity of whoever is communicating with you.[20]

Conclusion

This chapter helped you understand the significance of the risks associated with all technology tools and applications relied on in the workplace. You also gained knowledge regarding how to mitigate risk using NIST recommendations and US DoD recommendations. Staying current with these recommendations and guidelines is crucial to winning the war against cybercriminals. Most importantly, you gained an understanding of how to improve security control and assess technology tools and applications for business communication, data and information storage, transmission, and security.

Newly enacted laws and policies are helping the government control risk associated with technology storage and transmission of data and information assets. Neglecting to stay knowledgeable of these updates and how they impact your workplace, and its business operations and communication, will be a haunting experience if ever found that you have neglected to keep your workplace up to date and secure within the required perimeters of information and data security control. As recommended, the usage of Perplexity.ai, OpenAI, or other open-source artificial intelligence information databases is the best fit when relying on research to improve your control of risk factors with technology.

Most importantly, building a network of subject matter experts will enable you to stay current and gain leverage in how you tackle security issues correlating with the technology applications and tools you integrate in your workplace. You can certainly contact Dr. Bradley Fowler, Ph.D., for expertise and consulting @ bfowler@technologist.com. In the meantime, chapter review questions are provided below to support your comprehension of what you have learned in this chapter.

Chapter 6 Review Questions

1. When considering risk factors aligning with technology usage in the workplace, what is challenging?
2. Why was NIST 800-12 rev.1 initially written?
3. Why was NIST SP 800-124 Rev.2 published?
4. Why was NIST SP 800-97 established?
5. What NIST SP supports the ability to implement additional layers of security using cryptology?
6. What benefit does CoreMedia Privilege Escalation support?
7. What law requires businesses to integrate cybersecurity and incident reporting that alarms and alerts consumers about the risk of personal information and cybersecurity breaches?
8. What NIST special publication is useful for supporting increased layers of security using cryptology methodologies?
9. As a leader of information technology and information systems, it is crucial to implement strategies to control what?
10. Why is IoT a challenging subject to master?

References

[1] National Institute of Standards and Technology, (2025, April 21). NIST Updates Privacy Framework, Tying It to Recent Cybersecurity Guidelines. https://www.nist.gov/news-events/news/2025/04/nist-updates-privacy-framework-tying-it-recent-cybersecurity-guidelines

[2] DLA Piper, (2025). Data Protection Laws in the United States. https://www.dlapiperdataprotection.com/index.html?t=law&c=US

[3] EveryMac.com, (2025, April 3). Apple Silicon Mac Book Air Q & A. https://everymac.com/systems/apple/macbook-air/macbook-air-silicon-faq/macbook-air-silicon-processor-ram-ssd-storage-upgrades.html?utm_source=chatgpt.com

[4] Reddit.com, (2025, March). Precision 5690 is a PoS. https://www.reddit.com/r/Dell/comments/1ix399v/precision_5690_is_a_pos/?utm_source=chatgpt.com

[5] Reddit.com, (2024). Looking for reviews of the new Precision 5690. https://www.reddit.com/r/Dell/comments/1bfjf1r/looking_for_reviews_of_the_new_precision_5690/?utm_source=chatgpt.com
[6] AtulHost, (2024, July 15). What Factors Contribute to Laptop Failures? https://www.atulhost.com/what-factors-contribute-to-laptop-failures?utm_source=chatgpt.com
[7] Nieles, M., Dempsey, K., & Pillitteri, Y.V. (2017, June). An Introduction to Information Security. https://nvlpubs.nist.gov/nistpubs/SpecialPublications/NIST.SP.800-12r1.pdf
[8] Howell, G., Franklin, M.J., Sritapan,V., Souppaya, M., and Scarfone, K. (2023, May). Guidelines for Managing the Security of Mobile Devices in the Enterprise. https://nvlpubs.nist.gov/nistpubs/SpecialPublications/NIST.SP.800-124r2.pdf
[9] Frankel, S., Eydt, B., Owens, L. & Scarfone, K. (2007, February). EstablishingWirelessRobustSecurityNetworks;AGuidetoIEEE802.11i. https://nvlpubs.nist.gov/nistpubs/legacy/sp/nistspecialpublication800-97.pdf
[10] Souppaya, M. & Scarfone, K. (2012, February). Guidelines for Securing Wireless Local Area Networks (WLANS). https://nvlpubs.nist.gov/nistpubs/Legacy/SP/nistspecialpublication800-153.pdf
[11] U.S. Department of Homeland Security Cybersecurity Engineering, (2017, March 15). A Guide for Securing Networks for Wi-Fi (IEEE 802.11Family). https://www.cisa.gov/sites/default/files/publications/A_Guide_to_Securing_Networks_for_Wi-Fi.pdf
[12] Scarfone, K., Jansen, W. & Tracy, M. (2008, July). Guide to General Server Security. https://nvlpubs.nist.gov/nistpubs/legacy/sp/nistspecialpublication800-123.pdf
[13] Congress.gov, (2020, December 4). H.R. 1668-IoT Cybersecurity Improvement Act of 2020. https://www.congress.gov/bill/116th-congress/house-bill/1668/text
[14] Fagen, M., Megas, N.K., Brady, G.K., Cuthill, B.B., Herold, R., Lemire, D. & Hoehn, B. (2021, November). IoT Device Cybersecurity Guidance for the Federal Government; IoT Device Cybersecurity Requirement Catalog. https://nvlpubs.nist.gov/nistpubs/SpecialPublications/NIST.SP.800-213A.pdf
[15] Lakshmanan, R. (2025, January 28). Apple Patches Actively Exploited Zero-Day Affecting iPhones, Macs, and More. https://thehackernews.com/2025/01/apple-patches-actively-exploited-zero.html
[16] Telychko, V. (2025, March 12). CVE 2025-24201 Exploitation: Apple Fixes the WebKit Zero-Day Vulnerability Used in Sophisticated

Attacks. https://socprime.com/blog/cve-2025-24201-webkit-zeroday-vulnerability/
[17] European Insurance and Occupational Pensions Authority, (2025). Digital Operational Resilience Act. https://www.eiopa.europa.eu/digital-operational-resilience-act-dora_en
[18] Ibid
[19] European Artificial Intelligence Act, (2025, February 19). EU AI Act: first regulation on artificial intelligence. https://www.europarl.europa.eu/topics/en/article/20230601STO93804/eu-ai-act-first-regulation-on-artificial-intelligence
[20] IBM, (2025, January 17). Encryption of data in transit. https://www.ibm.com/docs/en/db2/11.5.x?topic=encryption-data-in-transit

Chapter 6 Review Question Answers

1. To determine the broad scope of risk, there really is.
2. To support computer security.
3. This publication outlines mobile security mechanisms and recommendations for mitigating known risks.
4. To implement security frameworks to secure workplace networks.
5. NIST 800-213A IoT Device Cybersecurity Guidance for the Federal Government: *IoT Device Cybersecurity Requirements.*
6. To enable attackers to gain high-level access to a rogue app pre-installed on the device.
7. Digital Operational Resilience Act.
8. NIST 800-213A.
9. Risk related to technology used in the workplace.
10. Because IoT is integrated into printers and fax machines.

7

Incident Response Planning

Learning objectives

- Understand why NIST SP 800-61 Rev.3 is vital to assessing and mitigating incident response.
- Understand how to incorporate cybersecurity incident response in alignment with the NIST Cybersecurity Framework.
- Understand how to prepare for incident response and improve response detection.

Incident response planning is crucial to supporting the needs of technology managers in controlling vulnerabilities and threats programmed in the technology tools and software utilized. When a security incident occurs, it impacts the ability to pinpoint when the event may have happened and understand how it happened. Furthermore, it can be challenging to determine how quickly you can recover after a security incident occurs. As outlined in the previous chapters, relying on recommendations in the special publications published by the National Institute of Standards and Technology is the best fit method for being resilient and preventing security incidents from recurring. One of the most important recommended guidelines supporting incident response planning is NIST SP 800-61 Rev. 3. This publication was published in April 2025 to support organizations' cybersecurity incident response in their risk management activities.[1] This chapter provides knowledge about incident response planning in alignment with this new US public policy. This chapter provides you with an understanding of how to incorporate cybersecurity incident response in alignment with the NIST Cybersecurity Framework. Additionally, you will understand how to prepare for incident response and improve response detection. To support your learning experience throughout this chapter, there are 10 chapter review questions provided after the conclusion to reiterate what you need to know.

DOI: 10.1201/9788743809715-7

Incident response planning is not a simple task to complete. No two organizations will ever have the same identical technology devices and software integrated in their office. So, the approach to planning for an incident is different. The only similarity in incident response planning is the process. Therefore, it is important to review NIST SP 800-61 Rev.3, pages 4–6. Doing so will enable you to understand why this publication is your “go-to” for guidance.

Looking at page 3, you find a graphic depiction of the previously recommended incident response lifecycle model. However, due to the suggested updates, this model has been modified. Examining the model on page 5, you see the incident response lifecycle model based on CSF 2.0 functions.[2] This model will be a guide for you to mirror as you deploy your own methodologies as you begin to outline the incident response planning process and procedures for your workplace.

Under the previously published edition of NIST 800-61, Rev.2, it was recommended that an incident response plan should include a mission statement, strategies and goals, senior management approval, organizational approach to incident response, and explain how the incident response team will communicate across the workplace, as well as with other external organizations.[3] In addition, it recommends including metrics for measuring the proposed incident response plan and its effectiveness and outlines the value of creating a map for maturing your workplace incident response capabilities.[4] It also helps you understand how this plan is nestled into the entire organization.

This previously published special publication also outlines recommendations about handling an incident. The recommendations suggest that you access tools and collect resources that can be invaluable to you as you manage the incident. This should include contacting executive leaders and department managers to inform them of the discovery of an incident and to reinforce their compliance with workplace policy regarding an incident discovery. If you do not have one developed yet, it is recommended that you create one and keep it with the policies you have created. You can always update this document as needed, but you need to have such in place.

In addition, it was recommended to implement methods to deter an incident from happening. This includes ensuring all networks, systems, and applications are secure with encryption and multiple layers of firewalls that can deter a successful attack. It is further recommended to identify precursors and indicators derived from alarms you have preconfigured in the intrusion detection and intrusion prevention system installation. This publication is specific about ensuring that all security software relied on is configured correctly and supports the security needs of the office.

Furthermore, it was suggested to build relationships with external partners, who you will be reporting incidents to once discovered. This is crucial because, depending on the geographical region of business operations, your workplace may be held accountable to international laws regarding reporting incidents within a specific time frame from discovery. For instance, China requires reporting of an incident discovery within 8 hours.[5] In Australia, you have 30 days, and in Europe, under the General Data Protection Regulation, you have 72 hours after the incident has been discovered to report it to the authorities and the public.[6]

This document also recommends creating a baseline scale to follow logging and auditing across all systems, and to establish a baseline scale for each critical system there is in the workplace. It was recommended to identify networks and systems and deploy research to improve your knowledge about normal behavior activities correlating with the type of networks, systems, and applications integrated. And it recommends establishing a log retention policy, which is instrumental because this demonstrates the timeline regarding how long data and information should be kept and helps outline reconnaissance activities or issues relating to any previous successful attack.[7]

Next, it is invaluable to understand how to incorporate cybersecurity incident response in alignment with the NIST Cybersecurity Framework (CSF) 2.0, published in February 2024, to support high-level cybersecurity in all organizations, despite size or sector.[8] This publication supports IT practitioners responsible for integrating cybersecurity in the workplace by helping them better assess, prioritize, and communicate with executive leaders. What this publication does not do is suggest how IT practitioners responsible for cybersecurity should perceive outcomes based on the suggestions this publication provides.

The cybersecurity functions recommended in this publication outline a tier of governance ranking from governing, identifying, protecting, detecting, responding, and recovering. These tiers of governance are standard, but will be your primary scale for identifying steps that should be taken to manage cybersecurity across the workplace. When applied effectively, you can easily adopt each of these standards to meet the demands of your organization and determine how to improve each tier. Incorporating this model is beneficial to supporting your need to effectively define a strategy to reduce cyber risk factors. If you examine page 10 of this booklet, you will discover how to improve cybersecurity risk communication and integration, as well as improve risk management communication. Having knowledge, you can present to executive leadership is essential to ensuring executives that you are knowledgeable and capable of effectively and efficiently managing the cybersecurity model of the workplace, and that you are adhering to recommendations given by the US Department of Commerce and the National Institute of Standards and Technology.

This also provides you with the ability to communicate with confidence what is expected for each executive leader to support the need for cybersecurity risk management in the workplace. Adhering to the suggestions in this booklet is key to your role as manager and shows that you are current with trends in cybersecurity for workplace environments. Neglecting to consider integrating the recommendations in this publication will haunt you in the long run. In fact, research reports that benefits aligning with this publication include improving your workplace cybersecurity posture, decreasing risk of victimization, improving personnel compliance, enhancing the communication between executive leaders and department managers, as well as helping reduce costs.[9]

Once you outline your cybersecurity risk strategy, it is imperative to present that strategy to executive leaders. Using the governance model is best. On page 3 of this publication, you will discover the structure outline of governance tiers. While these are recommendations, it is important to always consider the uniqueness of your workplace and decide how this approach can be applied throughout your workplace efficiently. Lacking this clarity will impact the success and outcome of using this model. Governance across your organization should include roles, responsibilities, policies, compliance regulations, and non-compliance penalties. Knowing how to impose penalties is crucial to ensuring everyone is held accountable and is aware that they will be punished for neglecting to uphold their responsibilities in protecting the organization from victimization. Thus, you must take authority and enforce compliance!

Identifying weaknesses in your office is crucial to controlling human error. This subject was mentioned in previous chapters. Personnel are high-risk factors because they use technology to conduct office business and to communicate. Personnel oversee development, transmission and sharing, and storage of data and information. Therefore, it is your responsibility to ensure each personnel member is knowledgeable about their role and responsibilities as they align with all the technology they use and/or encounter daily. When issues arise, you, as an IT manager and leader, are responsible for discovering the cause of the technology vulnerability issue and implementing an effective method to resolve the issue. You are also required to ensure executive leaders have knowledge. Moreover, you must ensure you are aware of all known vulnerabilities integrated in every component of hardware, software, and storage database utilized. Identifying weaknesses is important; this cannot be stressed enough.

When it comes to protecting, you are required to develop clearly conveyed training material that will support your ability to educate your workplace executive leaders, department managers, and personnel. One resource to help you stay current with such training material is the US Cybersecurity & Infrastructure Security Agency and its open-source training tools offered under the America's Cyber Defense Agency. This agency provides on-site and virtual training, as well as customizable training tools. Knowing how to access these assets is important to stay current. You can learn more about these resources here: https://www.cisa.gov/resources-tools/training [10]

These are some of the steps you must consider relying on and implementing across your workplace. This is a part of incident response planning. In fact, Dr. Michael E. Whitman and Dr. Herbert J. Mattord convey that having a written plan of how to respond before an attack, after an attack, and during an attack is essential to an effective approach to planning for a security incident.[11] Furthermore, they report that aligning the incident response plan with the outline of the NIST Cybersecurity Framework should be a consistency in controlling any incident discovery. Implementing the governance model and mirroring this model will be beneficial and help you overcome insufficiencies.

Table 7.1 provides a detailed process for action in alignment with a successful incident response plan. Using this as a guide will be beneficial for large or small incident planning actions. You can easily update this as needed to meet the demands of your workplace.

How do you improve response detection? Knowing how to prepare for incident response is your responsibility as an IT practitioner. No one else in the office has this knowledge. What do you do to ensure you are accurate in your own authority to control how response detection is assessed and managed? This is your top priority. Having a plan to recover is just as important. As mentioned, you need to deploy research that will enable you to develop an improved response detection that is above your competitors' and support the needs of your organization. Being absent from resources is not consciously acceptable. You must have a zero-tolerance attitude and encourage others to possess the same attitude. When you take authority and impose response detection methods, be sure to follow up by implementing improved training and deploying safety drills.

Table 7.1 Incident response action plan.

Detection and analysis	Containment, eradication, and recovery	Post-incident activity
Evaluate the existence of an incident.	Collect, secure, and write down all resources discovered during the discovery of data and information collection.	Develop a follow-up method and be sure to clearly convey your methods in writing to ensure executive leaders have implemented all expectations to contain the issue(s).
What are the indicators of an incident?	Secure all the information relating to the incident.	Be sure to implement training that confirms the issue has been contained and ensure everyone that methods are in place to prevent and deter future successful incidents.
Correlating factors?	Extinguish the incident once it has been discovered.	
Deploy research to locate mitigation recommendations for the technology utilized (e.g., perplexityai.com).	Recognize and mitigate any technology that was exploited.	
Document all activities and collect evidence, including taking images and labeling them effectively.	Isolate malware, ransomware, viruses, Trojans, worms, and all other threats discovered.	
Protect all data collected and secure it. If necessary, contact the authorities to report theft of data assets.	For each discovered incident, repeat each step taken in the initial incident discovered.	
Inform executive leaders and department managers as necessary.	Implement modifications to restore the information system, networks, databases, and storage files to their original settings.	
Ensure that everyone in the office knows that you have taken control of the problem and implemented methods to resolve the issue.	Recover.	

Maintaining back-ups and archiving data assets and information assets is a daily action that cannot be ignored. Doing so will impact your ability to stay ahead of criminals and cyberattack agents. Remember, no one is as knowledgeable about what should be done except you. Therefore, remain in control and always use research as your support tool to reduce threats and to discover additional information you may not be aware of. Building a forum of IT practitioners, you can rely on and share information in a secure and trusted group is another valuable way to stay knowledgeable.

Conclusion

Ineffective incident response planning will hinder your ability to recover quickly from a security breach or cyberattack. Knowing how to prepare for the incident prior to it occurring determines how long it will take for you to restore your information system and technology assets. Having knowledge of the resources needed to support your development of an effective incident response plan is crucial to understanding the role the National Institute of Standards and Technology special publications play, and how crucial this information can be in supporting your ability to bounce back. Having resilience enables you to sustain and manage the lifecycle of technology management integration in your workplace.

Outlining your threats and weaknesses and knowing how to mitigate those threats and weaknesses is essential. When you lack the know-how, you are limiting the ability of your workplace to succeed. Thus, this chapter provides additional knowledge you can build upon and include in your database of archived information assets. Staying knowledgeable is important to support the outcome of incidents. Keeping clearly written records of all daily business operations that support management of incident response planning is vital to controlling the ability to recover once you encounter a severe incident.

As mentioned previously, the NIST 800-61 Rev. 3 special publication is your "go-to" guide to enable your workplace to retain leverage in controlling potential setbacks when faced with adversarial attacks. Adopting the recommendations and guidelines delivered in this publication is essential to protecting the longevity of your workplace. Moreover, it is beneficial to continue deploying research that enables you to keep ahead of the risk factors integrated in the technology you rely on. When you have knowledge of the threats and vulnerabilities in technology used in the workplace, you decrease the chances of external attack agents gaining access and destroying what you thrive to secure. To support your learning experience, below are 10 chapter review questions. The answers to these review questions can be discovered after the chapter reference section.

Chapter 7 Review Questions

1. When was NIST SP 800-62 Rev. 3 published?
2. Why was NIST SP 800-62 Rev. 3 published?
3. What page in the NIST SP 800-61 Rev. 3 publication can you find a graphic depiction of the incident response lifecycle model?
4. What special publication recommended that an incident response plan should include a mission statement?
5. Why was the NIST Cybersecurity Framework published?
6. How can you control human error in your office?
7. What is the first benefit of aligning with the NIST Cybersecurity Framework?
8. What agency in the United States offers open-source training tools under the America's Cyber Defense Agency?
9. According to the Post-incident Activity in Table 7.1, what is your initial step?
10. How do you improve response detection?

References

[1] Nelson, A., Rekhi, S., Souppaya, M. & Scarfone, K. (2025, April). Incident Response Recommendations and Considerations for Cybersecurity Management. https://nvlpubs.nist.gov/nistpubs/SpecialPublications/NIST.SP.800-61r3.pdf
[2] Ibid, p. 5
[3] Whitman, E. M. & Mattord, J.H. (2017). Management of Information Security, 5th ed. Cengage Learning, Boston, MA.
[4] Ibid, p. 415
[5] Goel, I. (2024, February 20). Data Breach Notification Rules Around the World. https://www.gira.group/post/data-breach-notification-rules-around-the-world

[6] Ibid
[7] Whitman, E. M. &Mattord, J.H. (2017). Management of Information Security, 5th ed. Cengage Learning, Boston, MA.
[8] The National Institute of Standards and Technology, (2024, February 26). The NIST Cybersecurity Framework (CSF) 2.0. https://nvlpubs.nist.gov/nistpubs/CSWP/NIST.CSWP.29.pdf
[9] Rock It Fuel Technology, (2024, April 4). A Simple Guide to the Updated NIST 2.0 Cybersecurity Framework. https://rockitfueltech.ca/a-simple-guide-to-the-updated-nist-2-0-cybersecurity-framework/
[10] Cybersecurity Infrastructure and Security Agency, (n.d.). Training. https://www.cisa.gov/resources-tools/training
[11] Whitman, E. M. &Mattord, J.H. (2017). Management of Information Security, 5th ed. Cengage Learning, Boston, MA.

Chapter 7 Review Question Answers

1. April 2025.
2. To support organizations' cybersecurity incident response in their risk management activities.
3. Page 3.
4. NIST 800-61, Rev.2.
5. To support high-level cybersecurity in all organizations, despite size or sector.
6. By identifying weaknesses.
7. Improving your workplace cybersecurity posture.
8. Cybersecurity & Infrastructure Security Agency.
9. Develop a follow-up method and be sure to clearly convey your methods in writing to ensure executive leaders have implemented all expectations to contain the issue.
10. Knowing how to prepare for incident response is your responsibility as an IT practitioner.

8

Disaster Recovery for Technology Management

Learning objectives

- Understand how to prepare and recover from technology usage disasters.
- Understand how to develop a disaster recovery outline with NIST SP 800-34, Rev.1
- Understand how to assess the weaknesses and strengths of a disaster recovery plan.
- Understand how to outline mitigation strategies that improve your disaster recovery methods.

With the consistency of technology integration in today's workplace, both public and private sectors, and throughout the lifecycle of workplace existence, ineffective technology management leads to disasters. In many instances, disasters can have a long-term impact on the ability of the organization to regain control over the issue and fully recover. When information technology, information systems, cloud computing, artificial intelligence, and machine learning orchestration are effectively and efficiently managed, the tidal wave of catastrophic events that follow can be recovered much faster. As a result, disaster recovery has become a crucial component in the overall orchestration of technology integration. Understanding how to prepare and recover from technology usage disasters is not about knowing what steps to take after an incident occurs. The value is in knowing how to predict an event before it happens and having a plan to support your ability to bounce back and restore your information technology and information systems with minimum loss of data and limited costly liabilities. To achieve a concise plan of recovery requires understanding how to develop a disaster recovery outline in alignment with recommendations outlined in the National Institute of

DOI: 10.1201/9788743809715-8

Standards and Technology (NIST) special publication (SP) 800-34, Rev.1. Furthermore, it is imperative to understand how to assess the weaknesses and strengths of your disaster recovery plan to ensure the proposed plan works. Most importantly, it is vital to understand how to outline mitigation strategies that improve your disaster recovery methods. Otherwise, as the leader and manager of your workplace technology applications and tools, you will be a complete hazard with minimal preparation for recovery. As a result, this chapter aligns with the previous chapter as a medium of guidance to support your need for clarity on how to be strategic in developing a recovery plan, which you can rely on and revise as needed throughout the lifecycle of your workplace's reliance on technology. Thus, this chapter conveys each learning objective and reiterates your learning experience with end-of-chapter review questions to enhance your comprehension of what is required of you as the technology manager.

One of the most important steps in technology management, next to having an incident response plan, is knowing how to prepare and recover from technology usage disasters. The increased number of recorded human error incidents in the workplace proves a consistency of mismanagement with training development, implementation, and assessment of employees and personnel across public and private sectors. So much research explains that 95% of security breaches in 2024 resulted from human error.[1] Research also conveys that many security breaches contributed to a small number of employees' inability to adhere to workplace security policy. Phishing attacks via email were the primary gateways that enabled these attacks to occur.[2]

Thus, to improve strategies to deter future successful security breaches, defining a plan to prepare for disaster is important. One of the most helpful tools published and available in the United States is provided by the National Institute of Standards and Technology, which consistently offers an outline of a clear path of defining a disaster recovery plan, you can align your workplace usage of technology tools and applications with. Relying on the readily available NIST 800-34 Rev. 1 *Contingency Planning Guide for Federal Information Systems* is a unique tool you can use as a starting point to outline your disaster recovery plan. Under this plan, you can understand the value of effective planning for disasters that correlate with the management of technology systems, including applications. Depending on the technology systems, applications, and tools your workplace use will determine the scope of your disaster recovery plan. Table 8.1 provides a well-outlined disaster recovery plan that can be adopted and integrated into your workplace. Using this as an outline is your decision, but knowing how to upgrade this template is beneficial to having a long-term disaster plan you can easily modify as needed.

Table 8.1 Disaster recovery plan template.

Type of technology	Purpose of technology	Configuration requirements	Date of last system update	Results of last system update	Restoration method after incident
Hardware	Utilized in desktops, laptops, networks, information systems, mobile devices, printers, telecommunications, Wi-Fi, internet, and intranet.	Desktop configurations include maintaining operating system updates as recommended by manufacturers, and scheduling system updates to automation and scheduling system back-ups to automation. Laptops should be assessed for vulnerabilities. The operating system should be updated as needed and backed up as recommended by manufacturers.	01/04/2025 Conducted by Bradley Fowler, Ph.D. 01/24/2025 Conducted by Janice Fowler 02/04/2025 Conducted by Tracy Greene 02/24/2024 conducted by Bradley Fowler, Ph.D. This should be a consistent method of recording system updates.	Laptops were due for updates because the listed updates were posted. The automation setting was not configured to allow updates to be implemented automatically. Desktops were outdated, so I had to update the Microsoft OS to Windows 11, ensure all staff desktops were updated, and each staff member was aware of the update and knew what they needed to know to stay aligned with the updates.	Laptops were assessed for vulnerabilities, including updating the operating systems. Automation configuration was set to ensure the updated downloads were set and reports would be stored correctly. All document files were stored on external hard drives prior to the incident, making it easy to restore data and information assets.

(Continued)

Table 8.1 *Continued.*

Type of technology	Purpose of technology	Configuration requirements	Date of last system update	Results of last system update	Restoration method after incident
		System updates must be scheduled in alignment with the service and product provider. Multi-factor authentication should be updated to ensure an applied layer of security is applied using two layers, that is, username/password. **Following this structure consistently will help you outline the vital components of hardware your workplace relies on, providing the consistency of effective technology*		**Your approach to defining this section can mirror this approach. Be sure to maintain a written outline of all results so you have clarity going forward on what issues were discovered and how those issues were handled.*	Desktops were updated with the current Windows OS. Microsoft has issued a press release confirming the limited support Windows 10 will incur after October 2025. **Going through each of the hardware components utilized and reporting the outcome of assessments and having these reports will keep you up to date, reduce redundancy, and ensure security is applied effectively.*

		management infrastructure and management needed for the distinguished hardware used.			This will enable you to bounce back more easily if a successful disaster occurs.
Software	Intrusion detection/ intrusion prevention, document files, ERP, CRM, SAP auditing, Windows 11, Antivirus, VPN, Slack, Teams, Zoom, Excel, PowerPoint, Dropbox, Browsers, etc.	Each one of these software applications has its own need for configuration. Knowing how to manage these configurations is crucial to ensure these software applications are used correctly and can perform as needed when needed. Neglecting to keep these systems up to date can create vulnerabilities. Knowing how	Intrusion detection software was updated on 01/04/2025 as recommended by the manufacturer. A baseline was established, and a test was done to ensure compliance. Maintaining this infrastructure consistently is important to have a readable outline of what is required throughout the lifecycle of this disaster recovery plan.	The previous system update encountered a misconfiguration that resulted in the system producing false alarms. This was corrected, and a series of tests was implemented to ensure this issue was resolved. A report was developed and is being kept on file and updated as needed.	Bradley contacted the service/ product provider to request clarity on the false alarm settings. He was given a thorough consultation that resulted in him being able to reset the alarms by resetting the baseline. This has helped manage the risk of potential threats.

(*Continued*)

Table 8.1 *Continued.*

Type of technology	Purpose of technology	Configuration requirements	Date of last system update	Results of last system update	Restoration method after incident
		these software applications must be updated, secured, and backed up is just as important. One of your most supportive databases to help you stay current with the configuration of each software application is the manufacturer. Researching the software to learn of potential risks, known vulnerabilities, and how to mitigate such is important.	Adopting this approach requires due diligence to stay current with trends in software used and relied on.	This consistency is important when determining the previous dates system updates were implemented. This also conveys what was done, who did it, and why. Having this type of outlined system helps you stay organized.	

Cloud	Cloud is used for file storage and the web interface of end-users visiting the website to complete forms and request services/products. This is also used for the security of data and information assets. We also use this for backup and archiving, and our email application. Services are provided by Amazon Web Services. Our Service Level Agreement ensures AWS provides 24-hour Tech support as needed.	Usage of virtual servers requires consistent monitoring and updating. When configured for automation management, it reduces the need to be hands-on because the automation provides that support and delivers analytic reports that enable you to understand the vulnerabilities, threats, and update needs. Thus, depending on the service/product provider will determine what scale of configuration is needed.	01/04/2025 Bradley Fowler, Ph.D., assessed the system and implemented automation with Cloud Watch Monitoring. When applying this method, be sure to always include the date, who did what, and what was done.	The configuration of automation was deployed. Since we are utilizing AWS EC2 Instances, it is recommended to be sure to configure instance permissions for System Manager.[2]	Depending on the incident, it determines the recovery process. If the EC2 Instance was terminated without manual processing, it requires restoring the backup and assessing the cause of the action. The same applies to each issue relating to the downtime of an Instance or virtual server. Again, it depends on the type of issue or problem that caused the need for restoration. When I experience a restoration issue, I rush to research

(Continued)

Table 8.1 *Continued.*

Type of technology	Purpose of technology	Configuration requirements	Date of last system update	Results of last system update	Restoration method after incident
	**Having a detailed outline of the purpose of your cloud services/ products and understanding the Service Level Agreements (SLA) is crucial to managing your usage of these applications and controlling the risk factors that encompass the usage of these applications.*	If working with Google Cloud, Azure, Oracle, or AWS EC2 Instances, it will determine the scope of support you have and how each application needs to be managed and configured.			the various methods to restore and understand what could have been the cause, and try to ensure that such an issue or problem does not recur. This is why it is important to always be knowledgeable of every component and how it works, why it is working on behalf of the organization, and how it needs to be restored as quickly and effectively as possible. Downtime can impact security and productivity.

Artificial intelligence	This application supports our need for automation and rendering quality analytic reports that help us understand what is occurring and how to improve our management of the system.	The configuration settings of AWS automation applications are various, that is, inference, training, storage, security, and networking. So, if you utilize an additional service/product provider, you will need to research thoroughly to understand the scope of how AI needs to be configured correctly for the purpose of usage.	The installation of AI for security and storage was applied during the initial installation. Bradley Fowler, Ph.D. assessed the installation on 1/04/2025 and again on 1/24/2025. Operating in alignment with AWS requirements is what he is depending on. However, we are reliant on the tech support of AWS because our usage of the PaaS renders AWS support throughout the lifecycle of our premium contract.	Ensuring that each system application is aligned with AWS AI/ML will ensure consistency of usage and applied security. You can rely on various reports for details correlating with recent updates. For instance, you can retrieve data protection and privacy reports. You can also retrieve model evaluation and bias reports, and you can collect vulnerability and misconfiguration reports.	Consult with the service provider to ensure a realignment of services is effective. A backup plan was implemented to restore data files that were lost. A written report was generated, and log reports were compiled and filed. **Having a well-written restoration report helps provide clarity and enables the organization to maintain effective written records of problems with any technology tool or assets.*

(Continued)

Table 8.1 *Continued.*

Type of technology	Purpose of technology	Configuration requirements	Date of last system update	Results of last system update	Restoration method after incident
		**Again, reading the Service Level Agreement provides the clarity you need to understand how to effectively configure your application to your system.*	**If you are using a Basic contract for PaaS, this will not be applied the same.*		

Many of the technological tools and applications integrated in your workplace will differ from those listed in Table 8.1. However, having this general guidance on what is necessary during the recovery process is crucial to staying ahead of cybercriminals and issues relating to internal human error.

Developing a disaster recovery plan that mirrors the recommendations of NIST SP 800-34, Rev. 1, should become a second nature in thought and practice. Take, for instance, this special publication aligns with contingency planning. This can also apply to disaster recovery. Utilizing the outline of steps delivered in this publication, such as creating a policy that should be adhered to and respected, will enforce compliance that can help decrease the immediate use of a disaster plan. Prolonging an actual incident is key. Being prepared is required. Furthermore, you should also deploy a workplace analysis to determine what weaknesses exist and acknowledge the scope of prevention in place, and to assess if additional protective procedures should be implemented. This can be essential if you have never developed this before. However, using Perpelixtyai.com will help you create a template that can be modified to meet the needs of your unique workplace.

In addition, you must assess current prevention controls that are in place. What processes and procedures have you installed to help you govern risk factors that align with each and every technological tool and application installed throughout the organization? Knowing these answers helps reduce your stress but also requires you to maintain the update of these processes and procedures to prevent downtime and prevent long-term ability to bounce back from an incident. In fact, research reports that it is taking 25% longer for many organizations to gain control after an incident has occurred.[3] Too often, the discovery of an incident impacts organizations almost 7 months after an incident. You cannot allow your workplace to be victimized and stagnate in bouncing back after a cyber incident. This is why you need to have clarity on what is necessary for you to take control and maintain that control for the lifecycle of reliance on technology.

The NIST SP 800-34, Rev.1, is a tool that can enable you to organize your plans. If you examine Chapter 3 regarding the Information Security Contingency Planning Process, you can gain a clear outline of what is expected and how to align your workplace issues with these recommendations. As you will read, training is key. When employees and executive leaders are knowledgeable about the technology they use daily, understand how to ask for support when needed, and are given the professional training required. This can decrease human error. It can also reduce the need for noncompliance training. Policy plays a role in managing this issue. However, when assessed correctly, this is not an issue. You can control issues before they surface. Staying knowledgeable about what is necessary is vital to protecting your technology assets and tools.

Also, keep in mind that contingency planning details that mirror those outlined in NIST SP 800-34, Rev.1 will help you tremendously! On page 13 of this special publication, you can see Figure 3-1 for the Contingency Planning Process. Copy this. Make this a part of your disaster recovery planning process. Additionally, you will need to develop a disaster recovery plan policy statement. Having clarity on what is encompassed in this statement is important. As recommended in the NIST SP 800-34, Rev.1 document, the key components include roles and responsibilities, the scope of each technological tool or application, and how these tools and applications are used and relied on across the organization. You can utilize Table 8.1 for this.

Additionally, you should have a list of resources you will need and rely on. Having these assets is helpful and can reduce those moments of inadequacy, where you may lose track of thought or ideas. Furthermore, you need to have well-outlined and well-designed training material. Working with a learning management system (LMS) such as Canvas or Blackboard can be instrumental in supporting your need to deliver training virtually. Some useful tools for virtual training can be discovered on the US Cybersecurity and Infrastructure Security Agency (CISA) website. There, you can acquire virtual training tools for your workplace regarding standard technology applications and cyberattack methods. For instance, training is offered to non-federal professionals, public incident response training, workforce training, critical infrastructure operators, including continuous diagnostics and mitigation, industrial control systems, and access to cybersecurity exercises.[4]

Most importantly, it has a process for ensuring back-ups are done as often as necessary. This cannot be stressed enough. Making sure the proper procedures are implemented to provide effective back-ups is crucial to being able to bounce back after a disaster occurs. This is why it is imperative to know how to assess the weaknesses and strengths of your disaster recovery plan. Having this knowledge enables you to overcome many technical concerns and stay ahead of competitors. Research reports that an effective methodology to assess the weaknesses and strengths of a disaster recovery plan should include the following:

- Conducting regular simulations and testing of all processes and procedures to ensure compliance with policy and that all technology relied on operates as expected.
- Thoroughly analyzing the outcome of these simulations and tests to ensure consistency. This includes ensuring executive stakeholders have

knowledge and are aware of the problems and how these problems are managed. This provides assurance that you have effective management skills and know-how.

- Solicit feedback from stakeholders. This will give everyone a voice and you the ability to gain ideas that may be beneficial.
- Implement a SWOT analysis. Doing so will enable you to gain clarity of the strengths, weaknesses, opportunities, and threats you may not be completely aware of.
- Always compare your issues with those suffered by competitors. Learn from their mistakes and implement strategies to deter your workplace from experiencing these problems.
- Perform risk assessment and business impacts.
- Implement third-party audits.[5]

When you have a strong hold on what is required of you, there is no limit to what you can do. Disaster recovery planning is essential. Implementing tests and penetration testing on technology, using software that helps you control risk, as well as setting baselines for intrusion detection and prevention, are just some of the steps needed to ensure alignment with effective strategies to control external threats. Knowing your vulnerabilities gives you the leverage to control those vulnerabilities and decrease risk factors that can lead to serious consequences. Neglecting to take these key steps and stay ahead of issues before they occur will cost you and your workplace tremendously. In fact, research reports that direct costs of a cyberattack can range from $10,000 to $1,000,000, depending on the size of the organization.[6]

Meanwhile, it is important that you understand how to outline mitigation strategies that improve your disaster recovery methods. Having the contingency plan is certainly good, but not enough. With the growing trend of cyberattacks and incidents growing at an alarming rate globally, it is imperative that you have all of your ducks in a row. After all, mitigation strategies need to align with the scope of technology relied on daily for business operations and communication.

Research suggests that the mitigation risk control strategy is beneficial when you need to effectively concentrate on preparation and reducing damage that has been done once you have discovered the incident or disaster has occurred.[7] Thus, one of the highly recommended strategies to incorporate with your mitigation risk control strategy is preparing an acceptance risk control strategy. Dr. Michael Whitman and Dr. Herbert Mattord provide a detailed outline of what should be included in the mitigation plans. Much like Table 8.1, their recommended strategy includes a table that has five columns, each column is named specifically (e.g., plan, description, example, when deployed, and time frame). These details co-exist with each row that is named as follows: Incident Response Plan, Disaster Recovery Plan, and Business Continuity Plan.

To achieve the outcome sought, it can be useful to consider the recommended strategies offered by experts who have invested time in learning how to prepare for and mitigate against disasters and incidents. But providing an example of the table offered by these experts as a way of showing you the outline of such and what you should include in your own table, certainly would be a great way to demonstrate what they suggest is important for you to consider relying on. Thus, Table 8.2 outlines the details you need to integrate into your mitigation strategy plans.

This approach can be useful when applied effectively. Being more in-depth with details about each section is crucial to having that mitigation plan in place. Having a reliable and supportive backup to enable you to restore services and use of technology is crucial. Since you are the leader of IT/IS, as well as the manager of the integration of technology and all its components. Everyone is looking at you for their next instructions on what to do. When you do not have a clear path to achieve the best outcome, it can and will impact the success of your ability to recover from a disaster. Having clarity on the scale of risk you are willing to take is important to determining what methods of risk management will be useful and what will not.

Conclusion

Having a well-outlined disaster recovery plan is important to both the short-term and long-term success of your workplace's ability to leverage technology and control the risk associated with using technology. When you align your daily business operations and communication with the recommended guidelines offered in the special publications published under the National Institute of Standards and Technology (NIST) series, you have a greater chance of successfully managing technology and reducing the threat of disasters from impacting your ability to recover. Neglecting to align with the recommendations and guidelines will impede your restoration, both in time and cost. Thus, it is important to take action and reduce the threat of a disaster prior to having a disaster impact your workplace. Knowing what to do and how to do it is vital to preventing your organization from becoming liable for monetary cost under domestic and international laws governing how information and

Table 8.2 Mitigation strategy plans.

Plan	Description	Example	When deployed	Time frame
Incident Response Plan (IRP)	Steps you will take once you discover an incident has occurred.	Have a detailed list of steps to take during an incident. Ensure you collect all visible information about the incident. Conduct a thorough information analysis to gain clarity of the information you have compiled.	What happened as the incident occurred? Who saw what? Who acted? Who made notes and wrote an incident report?	How fast was the action taken? Be sure to write down the date, time, and name of everyone involved during data collection.
Disaster Recovery Plan (DRP)	What procedures do you have in place if a disaster occurs? What plans do you have to deter and thwart a disaster from occurring? What are the step-by-step processes that should be followed?	How will lost data and information be recovered? What steps will be deployed to reinstall the technology that was impacted?	How quickly will steps be taken to gain control of a disaster?	The recovery phase should be fast. What steps should be implemented to make sure this happens?

(*Continued*)

Table 8.2 *Continued.*

Plan	Description	Example	When deployed	Time frame
		What are the steps to take to turn off the system to prevent additional problems from occurring?		
Business Continuity Plan (BCP)	What steps should be taken to overcome a disaster once an incident has been discovered?	What are the specific methods to activate an off-site campus or back-up archive? How many alternative locations are hosting physical technology and storing data and information that can be relied on to increase restoration?	Once the disaster has been discovered, what processes and procedures will be implemented to support the continuation of the business's daily operations and communication?	What range of stability is expected, that is, short or long-term?

data are secured in networks and cloud environments. One way to achieve consistency in managing disaster recovery is to have a reliable plan and to modify that plan as needed. Doing so will give you the leverage needed to protect your organization from an unauthorized intrusion that seeks to take whatever is valued and destroy the reputation of your organization. To help you retain knowledge shared in this chapter, there are chapter review questions for you to complete. You can find the answers to these chapter review questions listed after the references.

Chapter 8 Review Questions

1. What is the most important step in technology management next to having an incident response plan?
2. Many small numbers of employees' inability to adhere to workplace security policy contributes to what?
3. What must be done to improve strategies to deter future successful security breaches?
4. What is a unique tool you can use as a starting point to outline your disaster recovery plan?
5. When employees and executive leaders are knowledgeable about the technology, they use it daily to do what?
6. Why is it important to make sure the proper procedures are implemented to provide effective back-ups?
7. What should an effective methodology to assess the weaknesses and strengths of a disaster recovery plan include?
8. What does knowing your vulnerabilities give you the leverage to control?
9. What is one way to achieve consistency in managing disaster recovery?
10. Why must you have a disaster recovery plan?

References

[1] Coker, J. (2024, March 11). 95% of Data Breaches Tied to Human Error in 2024. https://www.infosecurity-magazine.com/news/data-breaches-human-error/

[2] Amazon Web Services, (2025). Managing EC2 instances with Systems Manager. https://docs.aws.amazon.com/systems-manager/latest/userguide/systems-manager-setting-up-ec2.html
[3] McCann, K. (2024, November 14). Fastly: Incident Recovery Taking 25% Longer-Why it Matters. https://cybermagazine.com/articles/fastly-incident-recovery-takes-25-longer-why-it-matters
[4] Cybersecurity & Infrastructure Security Agency, (2025). Cybersecurity Training and Exercises. https://www.cisa.gov/cybersecurity-training-exercises
[5] Perplexityai.com, (2025). How to assess the weaknesses and strengths of a disaster recovery plan? https://www.perplexity.ai/search/how-to-assess-the-weaknesses-a-gVSGm0p_Qg2YgrHMHfjDaQ
[6] Aligned Insurance, (2025). The True Cost of Cyberattacks on Small Businesses: What Every Business Owner Needs to Know. https://alignedinsuranceagency.com/posts-general-liability/the-true-cost-of-cyberattacks-on-small-businesses-what-every-business-owner-needs-to-know/#:~:text=According%20to%20recent%20studies%2C%20the,Customer%20Notifications%20and%20Credit%20Monitoring
[7] Whitman, E.M. & Mattord, J.H. (2017). Management of Information Security, 5th Ed. Cengage Learning. Boston, MA.

Chapter 8 Review Question Answers

1. Knowing how to prepare and recover from technology usage disasters.
2. Security breaches.
3. Define a plan to prepare for a disaster.
4. NIST 800-34 Rev. 1 Contingency Planning Guide for Federal Information Systems.
5. Decrease human error.
6. To bounce back after a disaster occurs.
7. Implement a third-party audit.
8. Vulnerabilities and decreased risk factors that can lead to serious consequences.
9. Having a reliable plan and modifying that plan as needed.
10. Because they are essential.

9

Artificial Intelligence and Machine Learning for Technology Management

Learning objectives

- Understand how to distinguish third-party support for automation of artificial intelligence and machine learning.
- Understand how artificial intelligence and machine learning provide security and analytic reporting.
- Understand methods to configure artificial intelligence and machine learning tools for enhanced security and information protection.

To cultivate an effective technology management strategy in 2025 and beyond, it is crucial to have reliable, impenetrable, effective technology applications, hardware, and software, you can rely on, without heightened concern for exploitable vulnerabilities being successfully controlled by external attack agents. While the usage of incident recovery plans (IRP) and disaster recovery plans (DRP) plays a role in providing some level of assurance, these strategies are not a complete firewall to stop your workplace from being victimized. In fact, there is no 100% impenetrable method to stop any entity from being victimized. What is 100% guaranteed is integrating multiple layers of cybersecurity leadership and risk management that can effectively deter and thwart unauthorized intrusions. But to achieve this also requires an integration of artificial intelligence (AI) and machine learning (ML). And with the growing trend of artificial intelligence and machine learning becoming a mainstream component in technology applications, for public and private entities. Having a clear understanding of the role these applications and tools play in supporting technology management is crucial to supporting the success rate of each layer of cybersecurity and risk management, you intend to integrate into your platform, infrastructure, or service of information systems. Thus, this chapter

DOI: 10.1201/9788743809715-9

provides some knowledge that can help you improve how you assess the usage of artificial intelligence and machine learning to distinguish third-party support for automation of artificial intelligence and machine learning. This chapter will also provide some details to help you understand how artificial intelligence and machine learning provide security and analytic reporting. This chapter enables you to understand how to configure artificial intelligence and machine learning tools provided by Amazon Web Services (AWS). To help reiterate this knowledge-gaining experience, at the close of this chapter are ten review chapter questions. Answers to these review questions can be found at the end of the chapter reference list.

The great truth behind the usage of artificial intelligence in the workplace continues to evolve. While one workplace may rely on AI applications such as ChatGPT for 24-hour customer service support via their e-commerce web interface, other entities are relying on AI to understand methods and strategies to enhance projects, deliver results, and control risk factors relating to information systems, information security, and information assurance. In correlation with the latter, the usage of AI for technology management has become an essential asset to the ongoing development and reliance of technology in the workplace as a means of gaining leverage over competitors. In fact, research reports that many organizations are eagerly excited about integrating AI in the workplace, but their reliance on their technology managers and leaders is not equally enthusiastic.[1] One reason this could be happening is that many technology managers and leaders do not have the full grasp of knowledge to understand how to align AI in their current workplace environment because they are absent the skills, training, and education. Or perhaps the reason could be more obvious: they do not want to integrate a system of support that could very well outthink them and replace them.

Research has continued to evolve, encompassing this very idea. After all, AI has been replacing many employee roles in the workplace for some time. Research shared by the eLearning Industry conveys that the World Economic Forum reported that 85 million jobs could be replaced by AI by 2025.[2] Furthermore, it is reported that AI is not fully taking over job roles but supporting many human tasks that reduce some of the stress and concerns that many organizations have about training employees for new roles and task responsibilities. This is a benefit to technology managers who are operating with a limited staff or team. In fact, research shared by Microsoft in June 2025 suggests that AI adoption in the workplace, as a partner with technology managers, is not solely reliant on technological advancement but on human-centered intelligence.[3]

Thus, gaining support and understanding of the role artificial intelligence plays in helping you effectively control risk, train employees, and share knowledge with executive leaders is what this chapter intends to provide you with. Subject expertise to improve clarity on what role artificial intelligence has in supporting you as technology manager, IT team leader, or information security leader, manager, or cybersecurity practitioner, manager, or leader. However, to gain a full scope of artificial intelligence and its machine learning partnership, it is imperative to understand the AI/ML third-party service provider, who is reliable and provides the most effective and secure applications that support AI/ML.

Provided in Table 9.1 are top-rated AI/ML service providers, who are considered the "go-to" providers in technology supporting systems in 2024. Reviewing this list of third-party providers is important because it will enable you to distinguish which partnership can best serve the needs of your organization. Moreover, this will help you distinguish what scope of AI/ML you can rely on and why. Most importantly, this table will help you understand the scale of risk management and the cybersecurity applications available for you. However, keep in mind that what was major in 2024 is not necessarily reliable in 2025 and beyond. Technology evolves rapidly, and unless you evolve with it, you could very well find yourself struggling to unravel a mess you did not foresee happening.

Examining this table, Amazon Web Services (AWS) is the top listed ranked AI/ML service provider, and a highly recommended third-party service provider, you should consider building an alliance with. After all, when integrating technology services and products from multiple service and product providers, you need to understand the compatibilities of such tools, services, hardware, and applications, and how those tools, services, hardware, and applications align with the current technologies you are utilizing for daily business operation and communication. When you lack that clarity on technology integration compatibility, you end up misconfiguring technology, enabling threats of misconfiguration to become exploitable.

Take, for instance, research explains that many IT managers lack the capability to be effective leaders.[12] Furthermore, it is reported that IT managers lack the skills to actually lead teams of IT workers and lack the ability to meet the expectations of the role and responsibilities. Thus, leadership that is ineffective impacts the ability to integrate technology that is compatible with current trends in artificial intelligence and machine learning. To combat this, your new companion must become artificial intelligence and machine learning. Why? Because automation will help you focus on other components that

Table 9.1 Top 5 artificial intelligence and machine learning service providers in 2024.

Provider	Key services	Cybersecurity/risk management
Amazon Web Services	Managed AI/ML services, speech recognition, chatbots, computer vision, quality control, online ecommerce fraud detection, and cloud integration.[4]	IT audit certifications, risk analysis for cloud, automated security assessment, compliance certifications, data encryption, Identity Access Management, and compliance support for auditing needs.[9]
Microsoft Azure	Natural language processing, computer vision, machine learning model training/development, and cloud-based AI platform.[5]	Compliance management, security posture assessment, auditing tools, Security Information and Event Management (SIEM), encryption and access management, IT auditing, and global and domestic compliance with statutory requirements.[10]
Google Cloud AI	AI for business analytics, pre-built ML application programming interfaces, the Vertex AI platform, and the translation of speech to text.[6]	Cloud audit logs, risk detection and assessment monitoring, cloud identity access management, and AI-enhanced threat intelligence.[11]
IBM Watson	Natural language processing, custom ML modeling, virtual agents or conversational AI agents, and AI-powered automation for enterprise.[7]	Currently, on July 27, 2025, there is no clear research available regarding IBM Watson's significant cybersecurity or risk management.
C3 AI	Industry-related ML, including energy, supply chain, inventory optimization, enterprise AI applications, generative AI, and automation tools.[8]	Currently, on July 27, 2025, there is no clear research available regarding C3 AI's significant cybersecurity or risk management.

are relevant to daily business communication and operation. However, to become executable, you need to understand why AWS artificial intelligence and machine learning are a "go-to" for your workplace.

In fact, when examining Table 9.1, you should take into consideration the risk of becoming overburdened with Service Level Agreements (SLA). As pointed out previously, the Service Level Agreement (SLA) is your companion to understanding what you are held accountable for and what the service provider is accountable for. With AWS, it is clear to understand Service Level Agreements (SLA) because these policies are available for you without needing to sign up for full-service usage.

But to help you understand this process a little more, I was able to retrieve details regarding AWS Service Level Agreement (SLA) for artificial intelligence and machine learning from Perplexityai.com. AWS SLA is applicable to all paid subscribers. Under the SLA for AI/ML, you are guaranteed 99.99% uptime or service per month. Additionally, you are provided with support and only given credit for downtime, but only when that downtime was enacted by AWS. If you are accountable for the cause of the downtime, you will not receive the credit for that time without service.[13] Be aware that AWS only provides all over security for its infrastructure package. Thus, this enables you to gain the support you need and ensures your workplace compliance with international regulatory standards such as ISO, SOC, and PCI DSS.

Under the ISO 27001/ISO 27002 regulatory, an internationally recognized standard, the usage of artificial intelligence for business operations is held to strict requirements. This compliance regulation requires the protection of consumers' personal information and managing consumer trust.[14] Additionally, this regulation requires enhanced data security, improved risk management, regulatory compliance, and enhanced trust and reputation.[15] ISO 27001 also requires risk assessments, data protection, compliance with regulations, consistent monitoring, incident response, and employee training consistently. When deployed effectively, results include effective collection of documentation regarding policy and policy compliance, procedures deployed to ensure effective compliance is adhered to and respected by IT practitioners, executive leadership, and personnel.

Much different than ISO 27001 is SOC, which is an acronym for the Security Operations Center. In alignment with the usage of AI and machine learning, SOC applies governance aligning with the General Data Protection Regulations (GDPR), Health Insurance Portability and Accountability Act (HIPAA), and PCI DSS (requiring the security of credit card information). When aligned with artificial intelligence and machine learning, SOC enforces increased threat detection, management of automated compliance reporting, and lowers the number of false positives.[16] SOC compliance is invaluable because it invokes increased automated triage and investigation, which is crucial because it helps improve an incident response investigation and reduce the manual workload of an IT practitioner.[17] Furthermore, SOC is adaptable for efficient modifications integrated throughout the lifecycle of the AI and machine learning application usage.

When applied effectively, AI and machine learning are key assets that any business needs to effectively and efficiently manage information security in information systems, information technology applications and tools, software, and hardware. AI and machine learning also align effectively and securely with the usage of cloud computing. The dynamics woven in the reliance of cloud computing, as it correlates with the usage of IT and information systems, provide the broader scope of security required to ensure you are provided with the necessary security posture needed to protect digital assets.

Today, Amazon Web Services (AWS) delivers Software as a Service (SaaS) that can be adapted to any business operation and communication needs and enhance information security that aligns with federal and state law and policy, domestically and internationally. Applications integrated with artificial intelligence and machine learning delivered by AWS are key tools you can rely on to enhance your need to integrate risk management, auditing, and collection of log data, and provide the assurance that data and information assets are secured and procedures and security align with laws and policies.

To help improve how you configure artificial intelligence and machine learning tools rendered by Amazon Web Services for your workplace information systems, and define an infrastructure to help improve how you assess, design, manage, and secure such assets. It is recommended to deploy reliance on artificial intelligence search applications. These applications are reliable tools that render clear paths to orchestrate and design clearly conveyed frameworks you will need to know and understand how to effectively develop, deploy, and implement. One recommendation is ensuring that all details and information you collect from artificial intelligence search applications are accurate. Thus, it is important that you compare the information you attain from artificial intelligence search queries.

Take, for example, one artificial intelligence search application, which I like to research with, is Perplexityai.com. You also may be familiar with openai.com. Whatever artificial intelligence tool you rely on for search inquiry, always ask the same question from one to another and vice versa. If you get different responses, you can decipher what differences in details can be retrieved and integrated with the framework you are considering developing and deploying. In fact, you can ask this search application to provide explicit details about how to. When asking, you ask as if you are talking with an expert. For example, "How can I develop an effective artificial intelligence cybersecurity framework for my workplace?" Simple. Keep in mind, do not use this content as a verbatim methodology. Because no two workplace tools, software, hardware, or AI usage requirements are identical. Thus, you must be explicit in detail when asking questions. For instance, "How much storage does my workplace need for effective cybersecurity risk management in a cloud system?"

Knowing what you need will make your quest to comprehend your required approach to defining effective supporting applications and frameworks much easier to achieve. This provides you the leverage over competitors. Competitors who are absent from this knowledge remain baffled and lack the step-up; you have gained by understanding how efficient artificial intelligence is for your workplace.

Machine learning is a supporting asset to your usage of artificial intelligence for many reasons. Research explains that machine learning can support predictive analytics regarding behavior and help control fraud and unauthorized access to cloud storage applications. Machine learning will compile information about daily activities regarding login, scalability, bandwidth usage, and file systems that enable it to understand patterns and behaviors that help set baselines to enhance protection.[18] In collaboration with artificial intelligence, machine learning will enable you to set baselines to determine abnormalities in configuration settings and alert you prior to incidents occurring, as well as help you manage the usage of software applications woven into your cloud infrastructure or platform.

Thus, to stay current with trends in managing technology effectively, not only are you required to understand artificial intelligence and machine learning, but you are also required to know how each of these applications can be used in your workplace correctly and effectively, to leverage your organization in a competitive industry of business. This means leveraging technology for short and long-term goals. Neglecting to understand this will continue to impact your ability to become a dynamic technology manager. Taking the initiative to lead your organization toward ease of technological adaptation is a crucial component as a technology manager.

Conclusion

This chapter helped you gain the knowledge to distinguish third-party support for automation of artificial intelligence and machine learning. You also gained a clearer understanding of how artificial intelligence and machine learning provide security and analytic reporting. And you gain a broader understanding of the methods needed to configure artificial intelligence and machine learning tools for enhanced security and information protection. Using Perplexityai.com and OpenAI.com as tools for research to help guide your path to understanding what is needed to control risk and adopt artificial intelligence and machine learning as tools in partnership with your role as technology manager is vital to staying current with trends of technological advancement in the workplace. When you neglect to rely on AI/ML, you risk falling behind and placing your organization in a position that could cost reputational damage. To help reiterate the knowledge shared in this chapter, below are chapter review questions. Answers to these questions can be found after the reference listing.

Chapter 9 Review Questions

1. In 2025, what is needed to cultivate an effective technology management strategy?
2. It is reported that IT managers lack the skill to actually lead teams of IT workers, as well as lack the skills to do what?
3. What internationally recognized standards require strict regulation for the usage of artificial intelligence for business operations?
4. What is the meaning of the acronym SOC?
5. What does gaining the support and understanding of the role of artificial intelligence help you with?
6. Why are entities relying on AI?
7. What can machine learning support you with understanding?
8. What is adaptable for efficient modifications integrated throughout the lifecycle of AI and machine learning application usage?

References

[1] Mayer, H., Yee, L., Chui, M. & Roberts, R. (2025, January 28). Superagency in the workplace: Empowering people to unlock AI's full potential. https://www.mckinsey.com/capabilities/mckinsey-digital/our-insights/superagency-in-the-workplace-empowering-people-to-unlock-ais-full-potential-at-work

[2] Pappas, C. (2025, July 24). Is AI Taking Over Jobs? 20 Surprising AI Job Replacement Statistics. https://elearningindustry.com/is-ai-taking-over-jobs-surprising-ai-job-replacement-statistics

[3] Bowers, T. (2025, June 30). AI-powered innovation: How leading organizations are shaping the future. https://www.microsoft.com/en-us/microsoft-cloud/blog/2025/06/30/ai-powered-innovation-how-leading-organizations-are-shaping-the-future/
[4] Perplexityai.com, (2025). Top 5 AI/ML service providers in 2024 and the services they provided? https://www.perplexity.ai/search/top-5-al-ml-service-providers-gFSOtWNiQFCgCpOF14K0Rg
[5] Ibid
[6] Ibid
[7] Ibid
[8] Ibid
[9] Ibid
[10] Ibid
[11] Ibid
[12] Pratt, K.M., (2024, October 28). 10 reasons IT managers fail to exceed your expectations. https://www.cio.com/article/3587239/10-reasons-it-managers-fail-to-exceed-your-expectations.html
[13] Perplexityai.com, (2025, July 27). What are the service level agreements for AWS artificial intelligence and machine learning. https://www.perplexity.ai/search/what-are-the-service-level-agr-LC2TDCVgSP2jBRiFUe4cFQ
[14] IT Gov Docs, (2024, June 27). Achieving ISO 27001 AI Compliance. https://www.itgov-docs.com/blogs/iso-27001/iso-27001-ai-compliance
[15] Ibid
[16] Gurucul.com, (2024, August 1). The Role of AI and Machine Learning in Modern Security Operations Center (SOC). https://gurucul.com/blog/role-machine-learning-ai-modern-security-operations-center/
[17] Ibid
[18] Brown, S. (2025, June 2). Machine learning and generative AI: What are they good for in 2025? https://mitsloan.mit.edu/ideas-made-to-matter/machine-learning-and-generative-ai-what-are-they-good-for

Chapter 9 Review Question Answers

1. Reliable, impenetrable, effective technology applications, hardware, and software.
2. The ability to meet the expectations of the role and responsibilities.
3. ISO 27001/ISO 27002.

4. Security Operations Center.
5. Effectively control risk, train employees, and share knowledge with executive leaders.
6. To understand methods and strategies to enhance the project, deliver results, and control risk factors.
7. Predictive analytics regarding behavior and help control fraud and unauthorized access to cloud storage applications.
8. SOC.

10

Industrial Organizational Psychology for Technology Management

Learning objectives

- Understand how industrial organizational psychology can improve the implementation of artificial intelligence (AI) in the workplace.
- Understand why readiness in the workplace needs to be addressed to help employees accept and adapt to workplace changes.
- Understand why motivation in the workplace is necessary to improve employee acceptance of workplace changes.

Introduction

This chapter helps you examine how industrial organizational psychology can improve the implementation of artificial intelligence (AI) in the workplace. After all, machines and new technologies are making the workplace a new frontier that requires new skills and knowledge to effectively conquer competitors and stay ahead. This chapter discusses the readiness of the workplace and the need to address concerns with changes to help workers feel comfortable and acquire a willingness to work through such changes. Motivation in the workplace is crucial to encourage individuals to improve how they cope with changes around them. Change in the workplace can be difficult with resistance; however, employees can quickly develop the skills needed to effectively change.

Changing Landscape

Artificial intelligence applications streamline workflows, tasks that are automatic, and require strategies for effective integration into workplace processes.[1] In the ever-changing landscape of technology, artificial intelligence is

DOI: 10.1201/9788743809715-10

a powerful force that can transform workplaces worldwide.[2] Machine learning is also a crucial aspect where computers improve their abilities and adaptability without explicit programming. Artificial intelligence applications are used in various sectors to optimize workflow, automate routine tasks, and improve decision-making. In the robotics industry, the emergence of chatbots enables natural interaction between humans and digital systems, highlighting the shifting dynamics of human-to-robot and robot-to-robot collaboration in the workplace.[3]

The educational sector is undergoing a shift in focus on expediting skill growth through artificial intelligence learning possibilities, which impacts teaching and learning processes. Robots and automation are transforming the operations in the workplace and creating a demand for skilled workers. The advance of artificial intelligence brings new changes in the job market, with almost all occupations being somehow impacted. Industrial organization psychology is very important for the workplace today because it can help individuals navigate workplace changes due to artificial intelligence integration. Machines, robots, and artificial intelligence are making the workplace more efficient, but the workplace has become a new frontier for many.

Assessing Organizational Readiness

Assessing organizational readiness is the process of evaluating whether an organization is prepared – culturally, operationally, and strategically – to undertake a specific change, initiative, or transformation. This can include adopting new technology, launching a strategic project, or implementing organizational changes. Some of the key areas to assess organizational readiness are visions, goals, clear procedures, organizational culture, and communication. Leaders within the workplace need to be unified in their vision and goals of what needs to be accomplished. Leaders need to clarify their leadership goals. Employees accepting AI into the workplace and the smooth rollout of AI depend on the relationship between management and employees. In the ever-evolving landscape of the workplace, artificial intelligence (AI) is a powerful force transforming workplaces worldwide.[4]

However, there is still much to be understood about the impact of AI adoption on employees' work outcomes. In this dynamic, AI-driven work environments, job crafting, the process by which employees personalize their job roles to better fit their interests, skills, and values, enhances job satisfaction and engagement – appears as a critical adaptability mechanism. Industries such as services and mining are undergoing significant shifts toward automation, improving productivity, while raising concerns about job security and skill development. Professional services companies utilize digital technology and AI for skill-based planning, stressing innovation and service quality.

Robots and automation are transforming operations in the manufacturing industry, creating a demand for skilled workers. The impact of these automation technologies on jobs is a concern in various industries and deserves careful consideration. The advance of AI is bringing new changes in the job market, with almost all occupations being somehow impacted by AI adoption. The increase in technological unemployment and changes in the skills demanded by workers emphasize the role of robots and autonomous systems in enhancing human capacity in different types of occupations.

Change Management and Technology Adoption

Industrial organizational psychologists help employees and workplaces adapt to new technology and new AI Tools. The workplace has changed over the years since the dawn of modern technology. Change in the workplace is an inevitable part of business growth and transformation, but many individuals in the workplace resist any change, and it is a situation that management must deal with. This resistance may include new technology or may consist of the introduction of a new strategy, or a shift in company culture, which can cause opposition.

Understanding why people resist change and implementing effective strategies to overcome resistance is critical for business leaders, HR professionals, and internal communicators. In today's rapidly evolving workplace, the ability to navigate change successfully can be the difference between thriving and merely surviving. Organizations that effectively manage resistance to change gain a competitive advantage, while those that struggle may find themselves falling behind more adaptable competitors.

Resistance to change in the workplace can be influenced by psychological, cultural, and organizational factors. This resistance is not always immediately apparent and can reside beneath the surface, showing up as decreased productivity, increased absenteeism, or a subtle decline in the quality of work. Recognizing resistance early allows managers to address concerns before they escalate. It is important to assess employees when you witness these indicators:

- *Decreased productivity or performance*: When employees resist change, they often become less efficient or effective in their workplace roles.
- *Increased complaints or negativity*: A sudden rise in complaints or negative comments about the organization may signal resistance.

- *Higher absenteeism*: Employees may avoid the workplace, delaying dealing with changes.
- *Reminiscing about "the old ways"*: Frequent references to how things used to be better can indicate resistance.
- *Minimal participation*: Low engagement in meetings or training related to the change initiative.
- *Compliance without commitment*: Going through the motions without embracing the change spirit.
- *Formation of resistance coalitions*: Groups of employees banding together against the proposed changes.

It is also important to understand different forms of resistance. Types of resistance:

- *Logical resistance*: Based on rational concerns such as the feasibility, cost, or impact of change. This type of resistance often comes from thoughtful analysis and legitimate questions about the change's merit.
- *Psychological resistance*: Rooted in emotions like fear of the unknown or loss of control. This form of resistance stems from how employees feel about the change rather than what they think about the actual change.
- *Sociological resistance*: Stemming from group dynamics, peer influence, or workplace culture. This resistance develops when changes threaten established social networks, status hierarchies, or cultural norms.
- *Systemic resistance*: Arising from structural or process-based barriers within the organization. This might include incompatible systems, insufficient resources, or competing priorities that make change difficult.

Individual Factors behind Resistance

1. Fear of the unknown

Humans are creatures of habit, and uncertainty about the future can cause anxiety. Employees may worry about job security, their ability to adapt, or how changes will affect their workload. When faced with ambiguity, our brains naturally perceive potential threats. This evolutionary response triggers a stress reaction, making people resistant to change even when the change may ultimately benefit them. Without clear information about what lies ahead, employees fill the void with worst-case scenarios.

2. Loss of control

Employees may feel powerless if changes are imposed without their input. A perceived lack of autonomy can foster resentment and opposition. People generally prefer having some degree of control over their work environment. When change is dictated from above without consultation, it can feel like a violation of psychological ownership over one's role or workspace.

3. Disruption of routine

Change often requires employees to learn new skills, adopt new workflows, or abandon familiar habits. The discomfort of breaking routines can lead to resistance. Routines create cognitive efficiency. When we perform familiar tasks, our brains operate in an energy-conserving mode. New processes require more mental effort and energy, leading to cognitive strain. This increased mental load can make employees resistant to change even when they understand its potential benefits.

4. Increased workload concerns

Often, change initiatives temporarily increase employees' workloads as they balance maintaining current operations while learning new systems or processes. The prospect of doing more with the same resources creates stress and resistance. Without addressing these capacity concerns, resistance becomes almost inevitable.

5. Fear of failure

Many people resist change because they worry they will not succeed in the new environment. This is particularly true when changes involve new technologies or skillsets. Employees who have mastered their current roles may suddenly feel like novices again. This threat to competence – a fundamental human need – creates anxiety and resistance. Their self-identity as capable professionals becomes vulnerable during significant transitions.

Organizational Factors behind Resistance

1. Lack of communication

Poorly communicated changes breed confusion and resistance. Employees need clarity on why the change is happening, how it benefits them, and what steps are involved in implementation. Without effective communication, the rumor mill takes over, often amplifying fears and spreading misinformation. This information vacuum creates fertile ground for resistance to grow.

2. Past negative experiences

If previous changes were poorly managed, employees may be skeptical about new efforts. Unsuccessful past transformations can create a culture of doubt and cynicism. Organizational memory runs deep. Failed change efforts leave scars that make future initiatives more difficult. Employees who have lived through multiple "flavor of the month" programs that were abandoned midway will approach new changes with well-earned skepticism.

3. Organizational culture and peer influence

Workplace culture plays a significant role in shaping employees' attitudes toward change. If peers resist change, individuals are more likely to follow suit. Culture acts as a powerful filter through which employees interpret change. In risk-averse cultures where innovation is subtly discouraged, resistance to change becomes normalized. Social proof – looking to others for cues about how to respond – means resistance can spread rapidly through peer networks.

4. Lack of trust in leadership

When employees do not trust their leaders' motives or capabilities, they are more likely to resist the changes those leaders propose. Without trust, even well-designed change initiatives face an uphill battle.

5. Misalignment with values

Employees resist changes that seem to conflict with their personal or professional values or with the stated values of the organization. Value conflicts create deep-seated resistance that is particularly difficult to overcome. When changes appear to contradict what the organization claims to stand for, employees experience cognitive dissonance and may resist maintaining their sense of integrity.

Immediate Impacts of Resistance to Change

- *Decreased productivity*: Employees spending more time resisting change rather than adapting can lead to inefficiencies.
- *Low morale*: Resistance fosters frustration and disengagement, leading to dissatisfaction. Team cohesion suffers as divisions form between change supporters and resistors.
- *Project delays and budget overruns*: Change initiatives face setbacks when resistance slows implementation, often resulting in missed deadlines and increased costs.
- *Communication breakdowns*: As resistance builds, information sharing diminishes. Employees may withhold valuable feedback that could improve the change process.

Long-term Consequences of Unaddressed Resistance

- *Higher turnover*: Employees who strongly oppose changes may seek employment elsewhere. This brain drain represents a significant loss of institutional knowledge and talent.
- *Damaged customer relationships*: Internal turmoil eventually affects external relationships. Clients and customers may experience inconsistent service or products during transition periods.
- *Innovation stagnation*: A culture where resistance to change is the norm discourages new ideas and creative thinking. Employees become reluctant to suggest improvements.
- *Stalled growth*: Companies unable to implement necessary changes risk falling behind competitors. In today's fast-paced business environment, adaptability is not just an advantage – it is a requirement for survival.
- *Diminished change capacity*: Each poorly managed change initiative decreases the organization's overall capacity for future changes, creating a downward spiral of increasing resistance.

Organizations that proactively manage change resistance can mitigate these risks and foster a culture of adaptability. By addressing resistance systematically, companies can transform potential obstacles into opportunities for growth and improvement.

How to Overcome Resistance to Change

Successfully managing resistance to change requires a comprehensive approach that addresses both the emotional and rational aspects of transition. Organizations must recognize that overcoming resistance to change is not about forcing compliance but about creating conditions where employees willingly embrace new directions.

Strategic Planning for Change Management

1. Assess change readiness before launching any change initiative

Before initiating change, organizations must understand where they stand. Readiness assessments help identify strengths, risks, and barriers to successful adoption.

- *Analyze past change successes and failures*: Identify patterns that reveal what works – and what does not – so you can be more effective than before.
- *Identify potential resistance hotspots*: Pinpoint departments or teams likely to push back so that you can plan accordingly, proactively anticipate, and get ahead of potential challenges.
- *Gauge leadership alignment and commitment*: Ensure top leaders are unified in vision and messaging. If misalignment exists, take time to build consensus before launching the change.
- *Determine resource availability for supporting the transition*: Confirm the tools, budget, and capacity exist to support the transition, and where you need outside support from an agency partner.

2. Create a compelling change vision

- *Develop a clear, concise explanation of the change purpose*: Articulate the purpose of the change in simple, jargon-free terms so employees understand it and know what it means for them and why it is happening.

- *Connect the change to organizational mission and values*: Demonstrate how the change advances the organization's purpose and helps employees see their role in driving it forward.
- *Articulate specific benefits for different stakeholder groups*: Show how the change supports each group's goals, addresses their pain points, and contributes to their success.

3. Develop a comprehensive communication strategy

One of the most effective ways to manage resistance to change is through clear, transparent communication. Leaders should:

- *Communicate early and often*: *Use multiple channels*: Different employees absorb information differently. Utilize town halls, team meetings, one-on-ones, intranet updates, and visual aids.
- *Explain why*: Clearly articulate why the change is necessary and how it aligns with organizational goals and values.
- *Outline benefits*: Highlight what is in it for both employees and the company, addressing personal concerns directly.
- *Be transparent about challenges*: Acknowledge potential difficulties rather than glossing over them, which builds credibility.
- *Create feedback loops*: Establish mechanisms for employees to ask questions and voice concerns.
- *Tailor messages*: Customize communications for different departments or roles based on how the change will specifically affect them.

4. Involve employees in the change process

When employees feel they have a voice in decision-making, they are more likely to support the change. Ways to involve employees include:

- *Create co-creation opportunities*: Involve employees in designing implementation details, giving them ownership in the process.
- *Establish feedback mechanisms*: Regular surveys, focus groups, and suggestion systems provide valuable insights and give employees a voice.

- *Empower managers as change leaders*: Equip middle managers with information and resources to support their teams through transition.
- *Delegate implementation decisions*: Where possible, allow teams to determine how to implement changes within given parameters.

5. Provide comprehensive support

Resistance often comes from concerns about handling new processes or uncertainty about available resources during transition.

- *Deliver targeted training*: Offer skills development opportunities tailored to different learning styles and specific needs.
- *Create mentorship programs*: Pair change-hesitant employees with early adopters who can provide peer support.
- *Allocate sufficient resources*: Ensure teams have the time, tools, and budget needed to implement changes effectively.
- *Provide psychological safety*: Create environments where employees can practice new skills without fear of punishment for mistakes.
- *Offer well-being support*: Recognize the emotional toll of change and provide resources for managing stress and anxiety.

Leadership Approaches to Overcome Resistance

Resistance to change is one of the most common – and misunderstood – challenges organizations face. Whether it stems from fear, confusion, or past experiences, resistance can derail even the best-planned initiatives if left unaddressed. Yet with the right leadership approaches, it is possible not just to overcome resistance, but to turn it into momentum. Here are five strategies for leading teams through change with empathy, clarity, and confidence.

1. Lead by example

Employees look to leadership for cues on how to respond to change. Leaders should:

- *Demonstrate enthusiasm*: Show genuine commitment to the change through words and actions.
- *Practice what you preach*: Adopt new behaviors or processes visibly, showing personal investment.

- *Share personal challenges*: Being vulnerable to your own adaptation difficulties builds trust and *authenticity*.
- *Maintain consistency*: Ensure your behavior aligns with the change message to avoid sending mixed signals.
- *Stay visible and accessible*: Increase your presence during changing periods, making yourself available for questions and concerns.

2. Address emotional resistance with empathy

Recognizing employees' emotions and validating their concerns can make them feel heard and valued.

- *Acknowledge feelings*: Legitimize emotions rather than dismissing them as irrational.
- *Listen actively*: Create safe spaces for employees to express concerns without judgment.
- *Show compassion*: Demonstrate understanding of the challenges employees face during transition.
- *Personal approaches*: Recognize that different people's processes change differently and adapt your support and communications accordingly.
- *Provide emotional resources*: Conduct well-being check-ins with your team and offer coaching, counseling, or other mental health support during significant changes when applicable.

3. Focus on early wins and recognition

Building momentum through visible successes helps overcome persistent resistance.

- *Identify quick wins*: Plan for early, achievable successes that demonstrate progress.
- *Celebrate success*: *Recognize* both team and individual accomplishments throughout the change journey.
- *Share success stories*: Highlight examples of positive adoption and resulting benefits.
- *Reward change adopters*: Acknowledge those who embrace change and contribute to successful implementation.

- *Document progress*: Track and communicate improvements to reinforce the value of the change.

4. Implement change in phases

Rolling out changes gradually allows employees time to adjust. A phased approach reduces resistance by providing opportunities to test and refine new processes before full-scale implementation.

- *Start with pilots*: Test changes with smaller groups before organization-wide rollout.
- *Create transition periods*: Allow overlaps between old and new systems when possible.
- *Establish clear timelines*: Provide a roadmap of implementation stages with specific milestones.
- *Build in reflection points*: Schedule regular reviews to assess progress and make necessary adjustments.
- *Adjust pace as needed*: Be willing to slow down or accelerate based on adoption rates and feedback.

5. Address specific resistance types strategically

Different forms of resistance require tailored approaches:

- *For logical resistance*: Provide data, research, and evidence supporting the change rationale.
- *For psychological resistance*: Focus on emotional support, reassurance, and addressing fears directly.
- *For sociological resistance*: Work with informal leaders and intact teams to shift group norms toward acceptance.
- *For systemic resistance*: Remove structural barriers and align systems to support the desired changes.

By implementing these comprehensive strategies, organizations can effectively overcome resistance to change and create environments where transformation is embraced rather than feared. The key lies in recognizing that resistance is a natural human response that requires thoughtful, empathetic management rather than forceful opposition.

Key Takeaways for Sustainable Change Management

- *Anticipate resistance*: Expect and plan for resistance rather than being surprised by it.
- *Communicate purposefully*: Strategic communication before, during, and after change initiatives is essential for overcoming resistance.
- *Involve employees meaningfully*: Give people a voice and choice in the change process to transform resistance into engagement.
- *Support comprehensively*: Provide the resources, training, and emotional support needed to navigate transitions successfully.
- *Lead authentically*: Demonstrate genuine commitment to change through consistent words and actions.
- *Learn continuously*: Use each change initiative as an opportunity to strengthen organizational change capabilities.

Internal communicators and business leaders play a crucial role in shaping how change is perceived, making strategic communication, employee involvement, and leadership support essential components of successful change management. By managing resistance to change effectively, organizations can foster resilience, innovation, and long-term growth. When employees feel heard, supported, and informed, change becomes less of a challenge and more of an opportunity for progress in today's dynamic business environment.

Motivation and Performance

The positive psychology field is about valued personal experiences: well-being, contentment, satisfaction, hope, flow, and happiness. In individual experience, it is about positive individual traits, the capacity to love, interpersonal skills, and forgiveness.[4] On the group level, it is about civic virtues and the institution, better citizenship, tolerance, and work ethic.[5] Positive psychology can deal with human strength to change the outlook of situations with the theory of gratitude in the workplace.

In the study in the article titled *Increasing worker motivation using a reward scheme with probabilistic element*, the authors studied lottery tickets and motivation. The study awarded lottery tickets for workers' performances and compared that to offering the employee more tickets and comparing the motivation of the worker. The authors discovered that lottery tickets increased motivation and performance, which the authors believed increased motivation in the worker.[6] In this study, the authors concluded that offering an incentive to workers increased job satisfaction and productivity, but when offering the employee multiple lotteries, workers' performance increased and motivation increased further in anticipation of more tickets. The authors compared the study to individuals who purchase coffee with a punch card reward for a free cup when completed. The individuals bought more coffee frequently to get the free cup. The study leads to the understanding that employees' motivation may increase with certain incentives, but motivation is not built on incentives alone.

Understanding employee motivation is important to the success of the organization because the degree of worker motivation is part of the quantity and quality of work that affects the organization. [7] The study also showed that some employees only felt motivated when receiving more tickets and with the anticipation of more lottery tickets. Assuming this study is accurate, can gratitude be effective in motivating employees? Some employees may consider the incentive important and require that ticket on a weekly or monthly basis.

Furthermore, a study was done with health care workers using gratitude journaling and the well-being of health care workers. The study was done by the authors due to the COVID-19 crisis and the effect it had on the mental well-being of healthcare workers and their motivation on the job. A similar study was conducted in Australia with 20 community workers and found that participation in a mindfulness-based intervention program decreased their emotional distress on the job and off the job. The current study in the article titled *Pilot Study on the Impact of Gratitude Journaling or Cognitive Strategies on Health Care Workers,* included participants over 18 years of age employed by a medical center who worked 20 hours or more per week. The participants were enrolled in either a gratitude journaling intervention or a cognitive intervention program. Those individuals involved in the journaling intervention were instructed to write three things down at the beginning of each day and at night, three things that went well for 14 days. Cognitive interventions were given exercises and different exercises to expand on their negative feelings. In both groups, anxiety and depression scores were reduced, but not by a significant margin, and the subjects reported high acceptability.[8]

The study looked at each intervention and the effect it had on depression, anxiety, and psychological well-being. Both interventions reduced depression and increased the well-being of the participants; the results were compatible, and both interventions reduced depression and anxiety in the participants on the job and in their personal lives. The study suggests that these self-paced independent coping strategies may help organizations maintain their sense of meaning and purpose.[9] This study supports the concept that gratitude and cognitive intervention can increase motivation in employees, which can also enrich the personal life of that individual. Burnout in employees is also an issue that reduces motivation in employees; gratitude intervention can also be used to reduce burnout and increase motivation.

Burnout occurs when aggressors persist over a certain time and have been noted to consist of two scopes, disengagement and exhaustion.[10] Burnout has been found to have negative consequences for organizations and workers, which can result in absenteeism, decreased performance, and high turnover.[11] Gratitude is known as a positive emotion, which is also known as a social emotion that can reduce stressful experiences.[12] Workplace gratitude can be used by companies and individuals to reduce burnout and change individuals' attitudes about the workplace. Previous studies have explored the function of gratitude in how it nurtures bonds and stimulating helping behavior in individuals and how gratitude can stimulate old relationships and bind them together in individuals.[13]

Furthermore, in the study done in the article *Paying gratitude forward at work*, how work-specific gratitude can affect burnout through interpersonal behavior during a 5-week period, 353 participants were chosen through a survey and offered a gift card after completing the survey. Gratitude was measured using the Gratitude Questionnaire – Six Item Form. Emotional exhaustion and interpersonal helping behavior were also measured using different surveys to measure the results. The study was to measure the relationship between workplace gratitude exhaustion and disengagement. The results of the study showed a negative relationship between work-specific gratitude and exhaustion, and disengagement. The study suggests that work-specific gratitude may help the individual regain a positive state and reduce the disengagement and exhaustion the individual was experiencing. Employees helping each other and employees being rewarded verbally increased motivation and reduced burnout. The study may be used to help understand the benefits of work-specific gratitude can be used to motivate the individual and reduce exhaustion and other factors that affect the individual in the workplace. Absenteeism is shown to be high in workers who are unhappy and feeling depressed; a study using gratitude showed similar results of improvement in the individual.

Many companies deal with employee absenteeism and employee presenteeism, which is low motivation or preexisting health concerns. Employees' presenteeism can be caused by overwork, no communication between workers and management, and low pay to the employees. A study done by the authors Chen, C., Okubo, R., Hagiwara, K., Mizumoto, T., Nakagawa, S., and Tabuchi, T. (2024) looked at absenteeism in workers. Negative emotions, such as depression and anxiety disorders, are the leading cause of global diseases and cause economic burdens, such as sick days.[14] Employee burnout can also cause low productivity from employees due to existing health concerns and low motivation.

Positive psychology emphasizes the importance of positive emotions for building and creating a positive workplace. The study looked at the association between positive emotions, such as gratitude and happiness, and the effect on absenteeism. Happiness was assessed using the question presented to workers: "Do you think you are happy?" Gratitude was measured with the Gratitude Questionnaire, and it was measured using a scale of 5 to 35 on the 5-item survey. The individuals were asked about their absenteeism and work motivation in a separate evaluation. The results of the study showed that happiness was associated with lower odds of absenteeism, and gratitude was associated with lower odds of presenteeism.

In a further study from the article titled A critical examination of the effectiveness of gratitude intervention on Well-being Outcomes, gratitude to another individual has been defined as a feeling of thankfulness when receiving something that can help individuals complete their task or intervention, and can be someone giving encouraging words to another individual.[15] This current study looks at the effectiveness of gratitude intervention on multiple daily well-being including negative outcomes, stress, depressive states, and life satisfaction. A total of 163 participants for the study, where gratitude was measured by the Gratitude Questionnaire-6, which was used daily after each gratitude intervention. Each individual participant was asked about stress, anxiety, life satisfaction, and social support. If they experienced any of these items, they were given a separate survey to complete.

The study showed that the gratitude intervention had a significant effect on the individual and increased their gratitude level. The intervention also lowered that individual's depression, loneliness, and anxiety level, and increased their life satisfaction level. The study did not show any increase in life satisfaction levels or any increase in positive influence when individuals were told to practice gratitude to others. The study does not show any real evidence that gratitude had any lasting effect on the individuals tested. A larger group needs to be studied to get better results for this study.

Furthermore, another study was conducted between two interventions, the first gratitude and the second a mix of appreciation and increasing social connectedness. The article titled *An examination of two positive organizational interventions: For whom these interventions work* recruited 92 employees to evaluate the effectiveness of the two interventions in improving employee motivation. They use the sustainable happiness model, which is an everyday positive cognitive activity. The participants were assigned one or two interventions, which they were to complete two times a week during a 4-week period, and they were to complete a survey before the study began and complete the surveys again after the study was completed. This study aims to show that gratitude intervention on daily well-being outcomes, which include positive effects, negative outcomes, stress, anxiety, and life satisfaction. The results of the study showed an increase in happiness and well-being satisfaction, but the results were evenly split between the two interventions. The study showed some individuals may not the affected by gratitude interventions with distrust and lower agreeableness.[16]

The importance of employee well-being in work and non-work-related activities so scholars have begun to broaden the research on workplace well-being interventions by using positive psychology.[17] Studies have stressed the importance of well-being in stating various desirable outcomes, in health and longevity.[18] The studies listed in this paper show that gratitude can be used to increase happiness in individuals. The concept of journaling is to increase the happiness of the workers and to increase their level of gratitude, and reduce their level of anxiety and depression. The methods of research show that gratitude intervention, happiness intervention, and positive emotions have all been shown to increase employee motivation, which can also increase productivity.

A study done by Hartanto, Kaur, Kasturiratna, Quek, and Majeed used a gratitude journal and a survey response daily for ten days to complete their study. The study showed that the gratitude intervention had a daily positive effect on the well-being of the participants, which included daily negative, stress, and anxiety reduction.[19] This study gave evidence that gratitude interventions reduced negative indicators in the participants. The findings were significant and are evidence for this study being proposed.

Happiness is beneficial and can lead to numerous successful outcomes, longevity, physical and mental health, work success, and family and social life. Happy individuals enjoy what they do and express that through work productivity. Depressed individuals and individuals who have anxiety are more often to have burnout at work and high absenteeism.[20] The study on burnout by Kersten, van Woerkom, Kooij, and Bauwens (2022) looked at the benefits of gratitude interventions, such as journaling, to improve the outlook of the workers. Workers with burnout, according to the study, can have high absenteeism and depression that can cause the individual to have issues with their productivity and motivation. The study showed that journaling created motivation in the employees and a happiness level.

Using positive emotional intervention to motivate individuals to reduce their work stress was successful; workers who are motivated and happy have less absenteeism and work anxiety. Companies in some of the studies used gift cards and other physical items to motivate the workforce, which created grateful employees and motivated those employees to be helpful to other employees, which created more gratitude on the job. The study methods used by the authors Camilleri, Dakoda, Ortiz, and Neelim (2023) used a reward scheme. The positive or happiness interventions to be used for comparison to journaling are giving small tokens daily as prizes at the end of the study to initiate gratitude in the individual.

Conclusion

AI is being integrated into the workplace today and changing the face of the workplace worldwide. Machine learning is a component of computers utilized to improve workplace capabilities and adaptability, with limited programming required for effective usage. This chapter has shown you that AI can improve workflow, automate routine tasks, and improve decision-making. This chapter has shown that educational sectors are changing their focus, and AI is changing the learning process.

Workplaces need to be ready to implement AI and help employees adapt to the changes AI is helping implement. Industrial organizational psychology can help organizations and their team of managers understand the changes AI brings and ensure a smooth transition successfully. Changes in the usage of AI in the workplace will help organizations become successful while impacting the overall ability to achieve goals and reducing threats in daily business operations. This chapter also conveyed that resisting change can affect profits, performance, absenteeism, and low employee motivation. Workplace motivation has been shown to increase productivity and lower absenteeism, as shown in this chapter. With the implementation of AI, making sure the workforce is motivated and ready to accept this innovative change is crucial to AI being effectively implemented.

Chapter 10 Review Questions

1. Employee resistance to change in the workplace: Can you identify four ways in which they resist change?
2. What are some of the organizational factors behind resistance?

3. What are some of the different forms of resistance?
4. What are some of the ways to lead by example?
5. What are the long-term consequences of unaddressed resistance?

References

[1] Babashahi, L., Barbosa, C. E., Lima, Y., Lyra, A., Salazar, H., Argôlo, M., Almeida, M. A. d., & Souza, J. M. d. (2024). AI in the Workplace: A Systematic Review of Skill Transformation in the Industry. Administrative Sciences, 14(6), 127. https://doi.org/10.3390/admsci14060127

[2] Ibid

[3] Anagnoste, Sorin, Isabelle Biclesanu, Fabrizio D'Ascenzo, and Marco Savastano. 2021. The role of chatbots in end-to-end intelligent automation and future employment dynamics. In Business Revolution in a Digital Era: 14th International Conference on Business Excellence, ICBE 2020, Bucharest, Romania. Berlin/Heidelberg: Springer, pp. 287–302.

[4] Seligman, M. E. P., & Csikszentmihalyi, M. (2000). Positive psychology: An introduction. American Psychologist, 55(1), 5–14. https://doi.org/10.1037/0003-066X.55.1.5

[5] Ibid

[6] Camilleri, A. R., Dankova, K., Ortiz, J. M., & Neelim, A. (2023). Increasing worker motivation using a reward scheme with probabilistic elements. Organizational Behavior and Human Decision Processes, 177. https://doi-org.ezproxy.snhu.edu/10.1016/j.obhdp.2023.104256

[7] Ibid

[8] Roche, K., Mulchan, S., Ayr-Volta, L., Elias, M., Brimacombe, M., Morello, C., & Hinderer, K. A. (2023). Pilot Study on the Impact of Gratitude Journaling or Cognitive Strategies on Health Care Workers. Journal of Pediatric Health Care, 37(4), 414–424. https://doi-org.ezproxy.snhu.edu/10.1016/j.pedhc.2023.02.002

[9] Ibid

[10] Kersten, A., van Woerkom, M., Kooij, D. T. A. M., & Bauwens, R. (2022). Paying gratitude forward at work: How work-specific gratitude can affect burnout through interpersonal helping behavior. *Journal of Personnel Psychology*, *21*(3), 137–148. https://doi-org.ezproxy.snhu.edu/10.1027/1866-5888/a000296

[11] Ibid

[12] Ibid
[13] Ibid
[14] Chen, C., Okubo, R., Hagiwara, K., Mizumoto, T., Nakagawa, S., & Tabuchi, T. (2024). The association of positive emotions with absenteeism and presenteeism in Japanese workers. *Journal of Affective Disorders*, *344*, 319–324. https://doi-org.ezproxy.snhu.edu/10.1016/j.jad.2023.10.091
[15] Hartanto, A., Kaur, M., Kasturiratna, K. T. A. S., Quek, F. Y. X., & Majeed, N. M. (2023). A critical examination of the effectiveness of gratitude intervention on well-Being Outcomes: A within-person experimental daily diary approach. *The Journal of Positive Psychology*, *18*(6), 942–957. https://doi-org.ezproxy.snhu.edu/10.1080/17439760.2022.2154704
[16] Winslow, C. J., Kaplan, S. A., Bradley-Geist, J. C., Lindsey, A. P., Ahmad, A. S., & Hargrove, A. K. (2017). An examination of two positive organizational interventions: For whom do these interventions work? Journal of Occupational Health Psychology, 22(2), 129–137. https://doi-org.ezproxy.snhu.edu/10.1037/ocp0000035
[17] Ibid
[18] Ibid
[19] Hartanto, A., Kaur, M., Kasturiratna, K. T. A. S., Quek, F. Y. X., & Majeed, N. M. (2023). A critical examination of the effectiveness of gratitude intervention on well-Being Outcomes: A within-person experimental daily diary approach. *The Journal of Positive Psychology*, *18*(6), 942–957. https://doi-org.ezproxy.snhu.edu/10.1080/17439760.2022.2154704
[20] Kersten, A., van Woerkom, M., Kooij, D. T. A. M., & Bauwens, R. (2022). Paying gratitude forward at work: How work-specific gratitude can affect burnout through interpersonal helping behavior. *Journal of Personnel Psychology*, *21*(3), 137–148. https://doi-org.ezproxy.snhu.edu/10.1027/1866-5888/a000296

Chapter 10 Review Question Answers

1. Decreased productivity or performance, increased complaints, high absenteeism, minimal participation in meetings, and forming groups of employees to fight against change.

2. Lack of communication, organizational culture, past negative experiences, lack of trust in leadership, and misalignment with values.

3. Logical resistance, psychological resistance, systematic resistance, and sociological resistance.
4. Develop a clear, concise explanation for change, connect the change to organizational mission and values, articulate specific benefits for different stakeholder groups, communicate early and often during the change process, and be transparent.
5. Higher turnover, damage to customer relations, innovation stagnation, stalled growth, diminished capacity change.

Glossary

Bluebugging: Involves a similar activity correlating with Bluesnarfing. This enables an attacker to gain control of an insecure device via Bluetooth without the device owner's knowledge. This is commonly deployed to enable attackers to install malware to retrieve data that is commonly stored on a mobile device, including messages, phone call data, and personal data.

Bluejacking: Involves a hacker sending unsolicited messages to an open Bluetooth within 30 feet to steal data from a mobile device. This requires end-users to ensure their Bluetooth is disconnected and ensure no one can gain access at all.

Blue snarfing: Involves confiscating digital asset data from an unsuspecting end-user via insecure Bluetooth. This method requires conducting research to discover open access that is vulnerable through Bluetooth.

Burnout: Occurs when aggressors persist over a certain time and have been noted to consist of two scopes, disengagement and exhaustion.

Drive-by attacks: Involve an attacker driving through a community, public or private sector, and connecting to any open network link that is available to obtain access to the network and spy on all electronic communication.

Evil twin attacks: Involve hackers establishing a fake Wi-Fi network to capture unsuspecting end-users trying to connect to an open network. This enables the attacker to eavesdrop on activities end-users are deploying while utilizing the assumed insecure network.

Gratitude: A positive emotion, which is also known as a social emotion, that can reduce stressful experiences.

Gratitude to another individual: A feeling of thankfulness when receiving something that can help individuals complete their task or intervention, and when someone gives encouraging words to another individual.

Incident response planning: Is crucial to supporting the needs of technology managers in controlling vulnerabilities and threats programmed in the technology tools and software utilized.

Information assurance: Is a significant component in effective management of information assets that aligns with the CIA triad-confidentiality, integrity, and availability; information assurance clarifies the value of information assets.

Information Usage Profile Table: Includes a description of the information assets, scale of sensitivity correlating with each scale of information, as well as reports how the information asset is relied on and processed.

Organizational readiness: Is the process of evaluating whether an organization is prepared – culturally, operationally, and strategically – to undertake a specific change, initiative, or transformation. This can include adopting new technology, launching a strategic project, or implementing organizational changes.

Parking lot attacks: Involve an attacker parking in a nearby business parking lot and manipulating access to the network and hacking into vulnerable, insecure networks listed to deploy malicious actions.

Positive psychology: Deals with human strength to change the outlook of situations with the theory of gratitude in the workplace.

Repudiation: Requires reassessing all previously deployed steps to ensure effective deployment of security and technology management is applied and that nothing is overlooked or ignored in protecting information assets from email tampering.

Risk factors: Key components that you, as a practitioner, must have clarity on and know how to control risks that can lead to catastrophic incidents that will cost your workplace for full recovery.

Rootkits: Malicious software installed without easily being identified. Rootkits enable attackers to remotely access the device and control it.

Spoofing: Occurs when an external intruder gains information about an executive leader or personnel member and successfully exploits that information to gain entrance into the network, information system, and technology tools to unleash malicious activities.

Spyware: Is deployed through software downloaded on a computer or network without evidence of its presence.

Tampering: Involves extracting data files as they are transmitted across the Internet, internally and externally.

Threat modeler: Is a one-click approach to deploying effective threat modeling that can be relied on to ensure compliant applications are integrated within your information system.

Warchalking: Involves locating open access to free networks for wireless Internet connectivity.

Wardriving: Involves utilizing a free open-source software application that can be downloaded offline. Wardriving can involve attackers downloading software onto a victim's computer, such as a Botnet, to gain control and possibly acquire keystrokes for passwords and other sensitive data.

Index

About the Authors

Dr. Bradley Fowler Ph.D. is instrumental in supporting information technology, information systems, cybersecurity, cloud computing, and cyberpsychology practitioners at the graduate level as adjunct professor at Capitol Technology University and Avila University. Dr. Fowler's teaching philosophy is encouraging students to always conduct research to stay current with trends and to rely on scholarly peer-reviewed research to validate their facts. Dr. Fowler has conducted extensive research on cybersecurity public policy enacted across 43 countries, and research encompassing cybersecurity leadership for healthcare organizations and institutions of higher education. His research is published in the World Journal of Advanced Engineering Technology and Sciences and the Global Journal of Engineering and Technology Advances. Dr. Fowler has published textbooks such as Cybersecurity Public Policy SWOT Analysis for 43 Countries, AWS for Public and Private Sector Cloud Computing Architecture for Government and Business, and others. Dr. Fowler is currently Chief Technology Officer of DOC Technology Systems, LLC., and a peer review journal article reviewer for River Publishing in the Journal of Cybersecurity and Mobility.

Dr. Fowler's has earned a Bachelor of Arts in eMarketing and Master of Arts in Teaching and Learning with Technology from University of Arizona Global Campus, Master of Science in Cybersecurity from Bellevue University, Master of Public Policy in Cybersecurity Policy from American Public University System, Master of Science in Management Information Systems from Bellevue University, Master of Science in Cloud Computing Architecture from University of Maryland Global Campus, Master of Research in Cyberpsychology and Doctor of Philosophy in Cybersecurity Leadership from Capitol Technology University. In 2026, Dr. Fowler will be conferred with a Doctor of Education in Administration from California Coast University and Doctor of Management in Information Systems and Technology from University of Phoenix. Master of Science in Technology Management from University of Arizona Global Campus. Dr. Fowler is a lifetime member of Golden Key International Honour Society and National Society of Leadership and Success.

Bruce Chaundy earned a Bachelor of Arts in Psychology from University of Arizona Global Campus, a Master of Science in Industrial Organizational Psychology from Southern New Hampshire University. Mr. Chaundy is co-author of Cyberpsychology Can Help Us Understand Cybercrime and Cybersecurity Leadership for Healthcare Organizations and Institutions of Higher Education. He has 45 years of managerial experience in industrial and occupational commercial corporations and is a member of Phi Beta Kappa Honour Society and a certified Personal Fitness Trainer and Nutritional Specialist.

For Product Safety Concerns and Information please contact our EU representative GPSR@taylorandfrancis.com Taylor & Francis Verlag GmbH, Kaufingerstraße 24, 80331 München, Germany